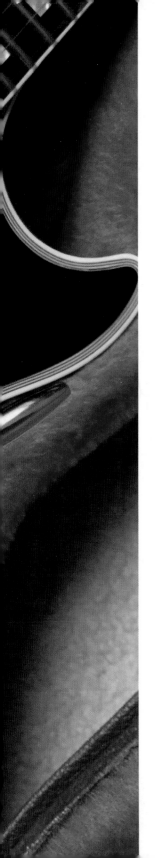

W9-BBT-590

A Little More Les

A Little More Les

by
Steve King and Johnnie Putman

Copyright © 2015 Steve & Johnnie Media, LLC
All rights reserved.

No part of this publication may be reproduced, stored in a retrieval system or transmitted in any form or by any means without the prior written permission of the publisher.

Correspondence to the publisher should be by email: bantrybaypublishing@gmail.com, or by telephone: (312) 208-4296

Contact the authors via email: emailus@steveandjohnnie.com

Printed in the United States of America at Lake Book Manufacturing, Melrose Park, Illinois

ISBN 978-0-9850673-7-3

Library of Congress Cataloging — Publication Data has been applied for.

Photos and images are the property of Steve & Johnnie Media, LLC, unless otherwise indicated.

The Les Paul Foundation generously opened its Les Paul Archives to share several of Les's historic photos.

Chris Lentz, longtime Les Paul photographer and friend, provided the cover photo and photos throughout the book as noted.

Chasing Sound, the consummate Les Paul biopic, was produced, directed and written by John Paulson. John generously allowed the use of multiple screen grabs that are prominently featured on pages 5, 25, 39, 105, 129, 263, 289 and 342.

The Les Paul Gold Top image used as background on chapter beginning pages is ©Sarawut Polsamart, via 123rf.com. Robot photo on page 227, courtesy of Lionel Chetwynd.

Les Paul guitars are often used by artists both as the subject for photos, and as a canvas for painting. Throughout the book, you'll see some of our favorites.

Les Paul quotes highlighted at the end of some chapters are from his conversations with Steve and Johnnie, and courtesy of the Les Paul Foundation.

A Little

> ## Verba volant, scripta manent
>
> A Latin proverb whose translation is:
> "Spoken words fly away, written words remain."

In memory of our parents, Roy, Mary & Joyce.

More Les

To the WGN Radio listeners who, for over a quarter of a century, welcomed us into their bedrooms, coffee shops, 18-wheelers and any place else we could be found hanging out inside a speaker. You went out of your way to let us know how much you enjoyed our conversations with Les Paul. The book you said we "had to write" is now in your hands.

To Lee, for sharing _The New Sound!_ with Steve and asking, "How does he do that?"

To all those married couples who, like us, are fortunate enough to work together … and enjoy it!

A Little More Les

Conversations, photos and memories from a treasured friendship with the legendary Les Paul

by

WGN Radio Legends

Steve King

and

Johnnie Putman

BANTRY BAY PUBLISHING

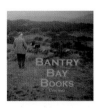

Contents

A little more Les ...

" *I think the most important thing about playing is to walk out with confidence, look the people right in the eye and say, 'Here I am,' and go and do your thing. As soon as they know you're confident, they're confident. As long as you adjust to them, you're not in trouble. You should eyeball them, find out what they want, and give it to them. They didn't pay to come out and look at the tapestries. — Les Paul*

Les visited Steve and Johnnie in the WGN Radio studio on December 3, 1996.

Paula Cooper

Will Crockett

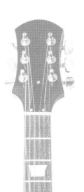

Hello!

*T*hank you for picking up this book! We're very glad you did. And since you did, we assume you already know that Les Paul was a pretty incredible real person and not just a name on a guitar. But, on the off chance that you might not know just how incredible he was, even a quick read of his resume would show you his pioneering of

- the electric guitar
- multi-track recording
- reverb
- delay
- phase shifting
- close-miking

and many other electronic marvels that paved the way for today's recording industry. And we can't forget those million-selling hits like "How High The Moon" and "Vaya Con Dios" with Mary Ford, or his Grammy-winning collaboration with Chet Atkins, or scoring more Grammy metal for his first rock album ... recorded when he was 90!

Yep, Les Paul is more than a name on a guitar ... much more!

We also assume that you have a working knowledge of who the heck Steve King and Johnnie Putman are and why the pages you now are perusing were an idea whose time, we thought, was overdue.

However, if you have come a little late to our part of this party, we'll just take an introductory minute or two and fill in some of our biographical blanks.

Introduction

As of this writing, we've spent a combined total of 87 years finding opportunities to hang out inside your radio speakers. Following solo careers at other radio stations, we joined WGN Radio after we got married and began a span of 27 years proudly spent behind that legendary station's microphones co-hosting what became Chicago's #1-rated overnight show. While at WGN, we had the extraordinary good fortune to meet, get to know, and, more importantly, become friends with Les Paul.

Along with some of the behind-the-scenes stories and photos we're bringing to the table, we'll be sharing many of Les's stories in his own words, transcribed from some of our late-night/early-morning conversations. One of the many lucky coincidences of our relationship with Les was his "night owl" lifestyle aligning with ours.

Several very talented and well-known mutual friends, some of whom we introduced to Les, have been kind enough to enthusiastically share memories of times they spent both behind the scenes and in the spotlight with "The Wizard of Waukesha."

In the liner notes accompanying Les Paul's seminal album *The New Sound!*, Capitol Records wrote:

> "A guitar virtuoso of many years standing, Les Paul now brings us a captivating demonstration of his theory that what is good on one guitar is eight times as good on eight guitars — and to prove it, he plays them all himself. How this can be done is Les's secret, and he steadfastly refuses to divulge it ... but we do know that the results are bright, gay and intriguing — and filled with good humor."

This book recounts some of the highlights of the 18 years we were privileged to have Les Paul in our life. You'll find many of those secrets he so "steadfastly refused to divulge" back in 1950 embedded throughout our late-night conversations. We hope you'll find the results intriguing. We know you'll find them filled with Les Paul's unfailing spirit of good humor.

You'll notice that we occasionally use ALL CAPS on a word or phrase. We're not shouting; we're just conveying, via our transcribing, the emphasis and emotion as Les and we spoke it.

After Les passed away in 2009, we incorporated a regular weekly feature into our Monday night shows around the same time Les used to call us when he got home after playing at New York's Iridium Club. The name of that feature is the name we immediately chose when this book started making the journey from idea to reality, because, although Les may not be around to play that amazing guitar, think up those incredible inventions, or tell those wonderful stories, his music and stories and history need to be heard again and shared with new generations.

And, besides that ... we still miss him. So we very happily welcome you to *A Little More Les*.

August 2015

Steve and *Johnnie*

Chris Lentz

Chris Lentz

Great friends and two of the greatest guitar players of all time, Les Paul and Duane Eddy, at the Gibson guitar factory in Nashville

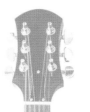

Foreword

I first heard Les Paul and Mary Ford when I was a teenager. To a young guitar player, it was magic! I couldn't believe my ears. Mary sang so beautifully, and Les played in a way we'd never heard before. At the time, I never dreamed I'd get to know Les personally.

We met in 1987 at the Hard Rock Cafe in New York City. It was an enormous birthday celebration for Les, and the place was packed. Someone introduced us, and after some polite, "It's a pleasure to meet you," etc., a man rudely inserted himself between us and told Les he was due to speak, that he had to get his cake and had to go with him "right now!" Les gave me a rueful look and I smiled my understanding, knowing he wanted to say more and get acquainted. But it was not to be on that evening. It was impossible to get close to Les again, and we certainly couldn't have had a coherent conversation.

I didn't see Les again until we worked together on the TV show *Nashville Now*. The guest host was Garrison Keillor and the show that night was all about guitar players, and to make it complete, they had invited Chet Atkins. We each played our own songs, and Chet and Les played a duet. Then the producer asked the three of us to play a song together, and since it was that time of year, we chose "White Christmas." In between performances, we sat on a couch where Garrison interviewed Les, then Chet, then me. I was sitting between them and the interview was stalling a bit, so I spoke up.

Duane Eddy

"You know, Les, my very first electric guitar was a '54 Gibson Les Paul Gold Top."

Les answered, "Oh, I didn't know that … never heard that."

"Yes, I bought it at a hardware store in Coolidge, Arizona."

Then Chet spoke up and, with a smile at Les, said, "Yeah, but Duane, tell him what you traded it in for!"

Chet knew I'd traded my Les Paul in on a Gretsch Chet Atkins 6120, in 1957, at Ziggie's Music Store in Phoenix.

They began trading good-natured insults, and this went on for several minutes until I interrupted and pointed out that I had my own signature model by then, made by Guild Guitars. The audience applauded that comment and Garrison was able to regain control of the show once again.

The next time I spoke with Les was on Steve and Johnnie's popular all-night radio show on Chicago's WGN. 50,000 watts of broadcasting power carried their show to a vast audience in America, from East to South to Midwest. Les loved Steve and Johnnie, and every New Year's Eve, he would call their show to talk with them. It was on one of those evenings that they called me and to my great surprise, Les was also on the line!

"Happy New Year, Duane," he said. He asked how I was, then immediately took off with one of his many jokes — mostly musician jokes, I might add. That night, he told about the guy who locked his accordion in his car and rushed into a store to buy something, telling the storekeeper, "I'm in a hurry! I left a valuable instrument in my car and have to get back before it gets stolen." He rushed back out and, sure enough, the back window of his car had been smashed! He looked into the back seat in a panic, and there were TWO accordions sitting there! We all laughed, and Les laughed the hardest. But that was Les, always with a joke or a story.

The next time I saw Les was in July 2000. My wife, Deed, and I flew to New York City to spend a couple of days doing a photo shoot for the magazine, *Vanity Fair*. It was putting together an issue of pop music figures of the 20th century who had influenced other artists and the music itself. The magazine wanted a picture of Les Paul and me together, to be shot by the great photographer, Annie Leibovitz.

We were driven an hour or so out of the city into the New Jersey countryside to Les's home in Mahwah, New Jersey. It was a beautiful, big home set back in the trees with a bridge over a creek that ran in front of the lawn. Crossing the bridge, we drove up the branch of the driveway that circled around to the back of the house and stopped. Les was there to greet us, and he took us through a door into his studio.

The studio was amazing! Guitars and cases everywhere, microphones and amps as well, and in some spots what looked like plain junk. We discovered later that it wasn't. It was remnants of some of Les's experiments with ideas for the electric guitar.

Annie Leibovitz showed up shortly after that with her crew and began setting up her lights and deciding how she wanted to photograph us. It certainly was a rich environment for her to choose from, with antiques, interesting-looking equipment, and unusual instruments all over the room.

Les showed Deed and me around and explained how, as a young man, he'd "borrowed" the receiver from his father's phone and placed it under some wires that he had strung up on a plank of wood, with a barn door hinge at one end and pins at the other. He was experimenting, trying to pick up sound from the wires and run it back to a radio speaker, making an electric guitar.

We also saw the famous "log," which has since been displayed in The Smithsonian Institution, The Rock and Roll Hall of Fame and Museum, and The Country Music Hall of Fame and Museum.

I stopped to look at a mic on a stand near the center of the room. It was roughly the size of a big coffee can, but was an RCA mic. I'd never seen one that big. Les appeared at my side and ex-

Deed Eddy

During a break in the Annie Leibovitz photo session at Les Paul's house, Deed Eddy took a photo of Duane and Les, with Les wearing Johnnie's present to him the previous Christmas — her WGN Radio jacket.

plained, "That was the mic that Mary sang 'Mockin' Bird Hill' into" in 1951. Seeing history of that kind was stunning, especially since I had loved that record, as had my family. How could I have ever dreamed I'd be standing next to Les Paul hearing about how the recording was made?

Another one of "those moments in life" occurred a few minutes later. Annie's crew had set up a stool for Les and a chair for me. We sat down and rested a moment. Then Les jumped up, came over to me and suggested, "Let's swap guitars and see if anyone notices!" Nobody seemed to be paying any attention to us at the time, so he took my Gretsch 6120 Duane Eddy signature model, and I took his Les Paul Gibson, and we put them on. As I said earlier, my first electric guitar was a '54 Les Paul Gold Top. Now, here I was, standing next to Les Paul, with Les Paul's Les Paul Gold Top strapped around my shoulders! And of course, it played like a dream, much better than my old one. I couldn't believe it. It was definitely a very important highlight in my life, and I've had many.

After a few minutes, one of Annie's assistants asked, "Have you guys got the right guitars on?" Les totally cracked up, laughing really hard and saying, "I wondered how long it would take!" I handed him his guitar back and he handed me mine saying, "That really has a lovely neck on it." I was happy to hear that and pleased that he had noticed, as I believe I have one of the best necks on any guitar in the business.

We were sitting there talking and relaxing while Annie was very casually pointing her camera, first at one of us and then the other, seeming to be lining up her ideas for the final photograph. We kept waiting for a warning so we could prepare ourselves. She suddenly said, "Okay. I think I've got it." Les and I looked at each other and he said, "No posing or smiling needed?"

Annie said, "No, I think I've got all I need. Thank you." When we saw the final portrait in *Vanity Fair*, I realized what she meant. She had shot a casual picture of us pausing during our conversation, and somehow the photo told the whole story. As a friend of mine observed, Les and I looked like "two old guitar-slingers who had seen it all, and done it all, their own way."

Les Paul's contributions to guitar players and recording studios in the 20th century are incalculable, and in my estimation his ideas were as important to us as Thomas Edison's original invention of the phonograph. Personally, Les was a very funny, kind and gentle man who was a great friend to everybody he knew. He was loved and admired by every musician on earth, and there will never be another quite like him.

A little more Les ...

It's not guitar-playing technique, it's what you have to say. – Les Paul

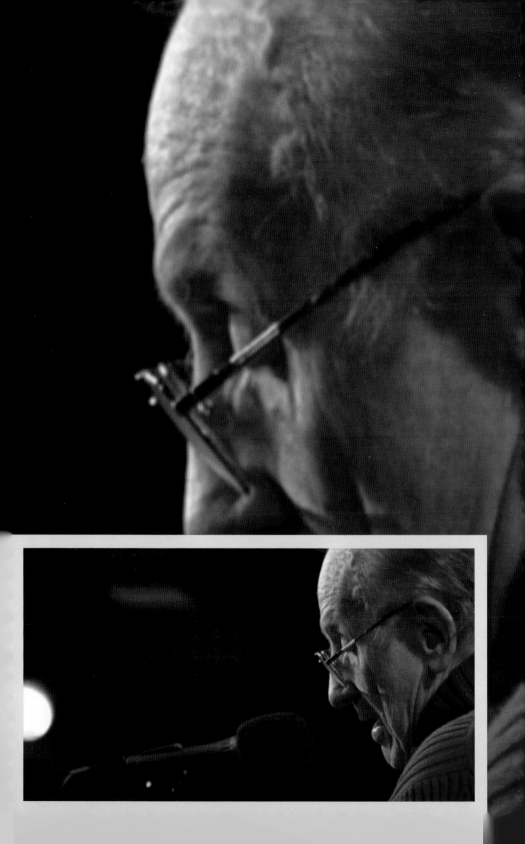

*Steve and Johnnie with Deed and Duane Eddy,
taken in Nashville, July 2004*

a little more about ...
Duane Eddy

The legendary man with the "twangy" guitar, Duane Eddy, is the most successful rock 'n' roll instrumentalist of all time, with total record sales of over 100 million and counting. The official "Titan of Twang," as honored by the city of Nashville, is a Grammy-winning member of The Rock and Roll Hall of Fame, and was the second recipient of the *Guitar Player* magazine "Legend Award."

Les Paul was the first.

Les once told us about Duane: "You know, he is cool. REALLY cool!"

You'll get no argument from us.

We are more than proud to count Duane and Deed as long-time friends. We are beyond honored that Duane readily agreed to write this book's foreword, and that Deed let us use the picture she took of Les and Duane.

Steve and *Johnnie*

Les Paul and Steve King at the WGN Radio studios in December 1996. Steve is holding his 1959 Gibson. At that time, he didn't own a Les Paul, but that would change in the most surprising of ways.

Under the Wizard's Spell

Steve King

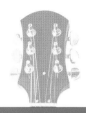

y earliest awareness of the magic of Les Paul was just what "The Wizard of Waukesha" intended — a magical experience. I must have been around seven when my brother, Lee, shared this little two-record, 45 rpm, extended-play album called *The New Sound!* with me. I remember both of us standing in front of our phonograph, looking at the album cover picture of Les with multiple guitars surrounding him as we listened and tried to figure out how this guy was playing all those guitars at once.

We were amazed. I was hooked.

A couple of years later, long before I got my first guitar and began my lifelong love affair with wood and steel, I had my first "air guitar" experience. Standing in front of that same phonograph, as I listened to Lee's newly purchased copy of "How High The Moon," something about that amazing guitar sound made me want to pretend I was the one playing it. So I did. Over and over, "How High The Moon" played as I mimed along on my invisible guitar until that ground-breaking guitar solo etched itself onto the jukebox in my mind, where it still regularly plays.

Hooked, indeed.

At the time, neither Lee nor I realized the significance of

The 45 rpm extended-play record that hooked seven-year-old Steve King on Les Paul's guitar playing

Les and Steve's brother, Lee

John Kruzan

that first introduction to *The New Sound!*, but several decades later I got to thank Lee when Les — who, by then, Johnnie and I were fortunate to count as a dear friend — was nice enough to help us surprise Lee on his birthday. Les brought Lee on stage during one of Les's Monday night shows at the Iridium, and invited him backstage after the show .

So again, thank you, Lee. And again, thank you, Les.

Fast forward to 1991.

Johnnie and I had been co-hosting the all-night show on Chicago's WGN Radio for several years. Finding it hard to recycle on our off-nights, one Saturday night we were home listening to Mike Rapchak's show on WGN. Mike was a well-known, longtime Chicago broadcaster. His Rolodex included names and numbers for many show business legends including — we found out as we listened to his live interview with Mike — Les Paul.

I was riveted.

This was a big deal. This was Les Paul! He would stay up late to do a live radio interview? Les and Mike seemed to have an easy familiarity with each other that made for a great conversation. Was there any chance he would stay up late for another interview? Would Mike mind sharing Les's number with us?

Our schedules didn't overlap that often, but we went out of our way to make sure we found an excuse to be in the studio at the same time Mike was, and after telling him how much we had enjoyed his program with Les, I hesitantly asked Mike if he would mind sharing Les's number, and if he thought Les might not mind staying up late for another interview.

Mike could not have been more gracious. He said of course we could have Les's number, and from what he knew of Les, he didn't think another late-night interview would be a problem at all.

Having a contact number for Les was one thing. Actually making that contact was another. Even though I had many years of broadcasting experience and had spoken to hundreds of celebrities, this felt, somehow, a little more personal, and I was too intimidated to make the initial call. Fortunately, it was easy enough to pass the number on to our producer to make that call.

Finally, the interview was scheduled for December 2, 1991.

A little more Les ...

> You can't go to the store and buy a good ear and rhythm. – Les Paul

"The Fretless Wonder"

THE INCOMPARABLE
LES PAUL CUSTOM GUITAR

Here is the ultimate in a solid body Gibson Electric Spanish Guitar—players rave about its extremely low, smooth frets and easy playing action, call it the "Fretless Wonder." Now with three humbucking, adjustable pickups, this new and improved "Les Paul Custom" guitar has increased power, greater sustaining and a clear, resonant, sparkling tone, with the widest range of tonal colorings. Finished in solid ebony color for rich contrast with the gold-plated metal fittings.

Solid Honduras mahogany body, graceful cutaway design with carved top; bound with alternating white and black strips • mahogany neck with exclusive Gibson Adjustable Truss Rod • bound, ebony fingerboard with deluxe pearl inlays • Three powerful, humbucking magnetic pickups • individually adjustable gold-plated polepieces • separate tone and volume controls • three-way toggle switch provides a new method of tone mixing: top position selects top pickup for rhythm; center position activates the center and lower picks simultaneously for extreme highs and special effects; lower position operates lower pickup for playing lead. Tailpiece can be moved up or down to adjust string tension • Tune-O-Matic bridge permits adjusting string action and individual string lengths for perfect intonation • gold-plated Sealfast individual machine heads with deluxe buttons • gold-plated metal end pin and strap holder. Padded leather strap included.

SPECIFICATIONS
12¾" wide, 17½" long, 1¾" thick, 24¾" scale, 22 frets

Les Paul Custom—Ebony Finish	$375.00
No. 537 Case—Faultless, gold plush lined	47.50
No. ZC-CLP Zipper Case Cover	21.50

One of the ads by Gibson Guitar Company promoting its hugely successful Les Paul line of electric guitars

Edward Butkovich

Johnnie and Les on stage at The Pabst Theater in Milwaukee, 2008

A Bittersweet Moment

Johnnie Putman

My whole life, I knew the name Les Paul, but I never imagined actually speaking to the man that I had come to know not only as a hit maker from the '50s, but as the name on perhaps the most popular guitars in the world. Being married to a Les fan, of both the music and the guitar, I knew that Steve's dream was to one day talk to Les.

Ironically, the day Les was scheduled to be on WGN Radio with Steve was a long, sad day in our lives. Steve's father, Roy, had been admitted to Chicago's Northwestern Memorial Hospital. Steve wanted to postpone the interview, but his father said that since the hospital was just a few blocks from the studios, Steve should do the show. Besides, Roy was also a big Les Paul fan, and said he wanted to hear the interview.

When we arrived at WGN, Steve was anxious about doing the interview. I was back in the office, because, at that time, I would join Steve at a halfway point in the show and stay through morning drive to do traffic reports for Bob Collins' show. I got my cup of coffee and turned up the radio. Steve did a montage of Les's hits as Les waited on the line to be introduced. When Steve came out of the music he welcomed Les to the show, and I remember staring at the radio stunned at what I was hearing. Les sounded exactly like Steve's father. Same tone, timber and lilt to his voice. I remember smiling — it was so crazy. I know our emotions were raw due to the situation just down the street at Northwestern Memorial, but I also know I wasn't imagining or projecting my father-in-law's voice into the man speaking on the radio.

We never got to speak to Steve's dad again or hear his voice, but I always smiled when we welcomed Les on the air or had a message from him on our answering machine. I felt like family was on the other end.

Johnnie Putman

A little more Les ...

> To this day, no one has come up with a set of rules for originality. There aren't any. — Les Paul

A Les Paul Guitar ad in the days before the Internet. Notice the directive to "Write Dept. 707 for more information."

Somewhere There's Music

When we first joined WGN Radio in the mid-'80s, it was not that unusual to hear music sprinkled throughout some of the programs. Music had been a part of WGN's DNA since its inception. Certainly, in the '30s, when Les Paul was first heard on WGN, music played a large part in each day's programming.

As we settled in to our run at WGN, the cost of playing music for a station like ours was increasing. Without boring you with all of the minutiae, suffice it to say that an all-music station is able to get a "blanket" license, while, on the other hand, a station like WGN featuring talk, sports and other programming usually has a "pay per play" license. That license, based on a station's annual revenue, can turn out to be pretty expensive. When you add that figure to the cost of major market personalities, sports affiliations and other promotional and fixed costs, you can wind up with a figure that has many zeros in it. So, over the years, as WGN Radio's programming became more and more talk oriented, we were encouraged to be conscious of any music we played and the hours we played it.

From day one of our time at WGN Radio, we fought the battle to keep music a part of our show. Of course, we covered the breaking hard news and pop culture news of the day, but with both of us having backgrounds at music stations, and having a love for music and the people who create it, music was a part of our DNA, too. Add to that the six-hour length of our overnight show and the opportunity to have performers who had just finished a gig stop by … well, we think you see our logic. Over time, the compromise we reached with management was, "Make sure you have a good reason for any music you play." Without a doubt, Les Paul was a good reason.

After that first interview in 1991, slowly at first and then with increasing frequency, Les Paul would be listed on our show's promo sheet. The increasing frequency of Les's visits certainly made us happy. From the calls, letters and emails we received, we could tell our listeners were happy. And, from Les's spontaneous calls, we got the feeling he was happy, too.

If anything is a constant in the world of radio, it is change. While we were fortunate enough to spend, in radio years, several lifetimes at WGN, we have lost count of the number of producers who helped us pilot our overnight adventures. Some left because they were moving on to other shows or occupations. Some left because, although they initially thought they could handle it, they found out that a lifestyle built around living on the other side of the clock was not something they, or in some cases, their families, could live with. Some left because of the pressure of being part of a comparatively small crew that had to move quickly and make snap decisions when a major story broke in the middle of the night.

The daytime norm of managers and meetings everywhere you look is not part of the third shift lexicon (actually, the all-night crew at Chicago's O'Hare International Airport calls it the first shift, but that's another story), so you really do have to think for yourself. Occasionally, a meeting with a new management type would result in questions about our middle-of-the-night decision process. Over the years, we developed our own question in response: "So from now on, you want us to call you at 3 a.m.?" Usually, following a pregnant pause and a long sip of coffee, it would be decided that, unless Rome was burning, we should continue to do what we thought was best.

Point is, with some very notable exceptions, we got used to the drill of welcoming in new producers and familiarizing them with our overnight skeleton-crew-decisions-on-the-fly mode of operation. Along with making sure they had access to all of the news contacts, knew where the "panic" button was, had a keycard to get them in to WGN's vast music library and knew how to find things quickly, there was one other thing we had to prepare them for: "When the private line rings at 2 a.m. and a wisecracking guy says, 'Hey doll, this is Les Paul,' it really IS Les Paul!" Reactions would vary, but ranged from, "You're kidding," to our favorite: "THE Les Paul?!"

Les being Les, it usually only took a couple of phone calls before a new producer would fall under his spell and during a commercial break, would come into the studio to let us know he was on the line, and share some joke or personal exchange the two of them had had.

Les was becoming a welcome fixture on our show … and in our lives. As welcome as it was, so far, this "relationship" had been a long-distance one.

But that was about to change.

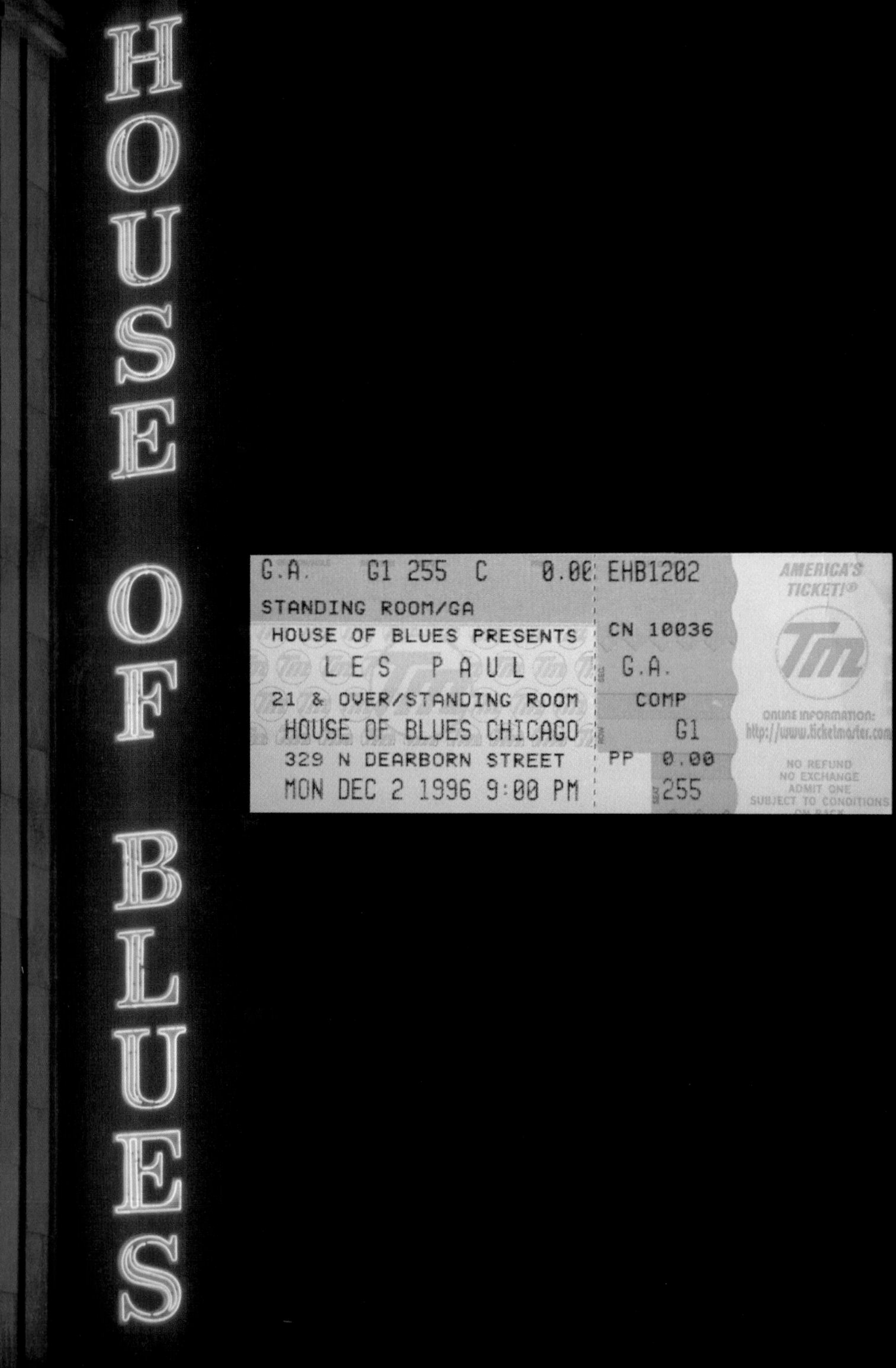

G.A.   G1 255 C   0.00 EHB1202
STANDING ROOM/GA
HOUSE OF BLUES PRESENTS   CN 10036
L E S   P A U L   G.A.
21 & OVER/STANDING ROOM   COMP
HOUSE OF BLUES CHICAGO   G1
329 N DEARBORN STREET   PP 0.00
MON DEC 2 1996 9:00 PM   255

AMERICA'S
TICKET!®

TM

ONLINE INFORMATION:
http://www.ticketmaster.com

NO REFUND
NO EXCHANGE
ADMIT ONE
SUBJECT TO CONDITIONS

Sweet Home Chicago

*L*ooking back on it now, it almost seems like there was some outside force involved in the timing of Les's appearance at Chicago's House of Blues. By then, we had moved beyond just a professional relationship with Les. We had a true friendship. His appearances on our WGN Radio show had increased in regularity, and it had become not at all out of the norm for Les to call us at our home in Chicago, or while we were driving to or from our vacation home in Florida, just to check on us. Les was becoming a member of our extended family. However, we had never had a face-to-face meeting. So, you can imagine how enthusiastic we were when, during one of our on-air conversations, Les mentioned that he had just signed an agreement with the House of Blues and it looked like he would be coming to Chicago.

We were thrilled and it was obvious that Les was, too. He was excited at the possibility of returning to his Midwestern roots and, specifically, the town that had played such a pivotal role in his professional development and was responsible for much of his early radio success. And the icing on the cake was that, after several years of getting to know each other over the phone, we would finally have the chance to meet in person. It took a little while for all the details to be worked out but, one night after one of his shows at New York's Iridium Club, Les called in to announce that a date had been set for his Chicago return.

The date? Monday, December 2, 1996. Exactly five years

from the first time Les was a guest on our show! While that timing might not be worthy of a mention in *Ripley's Believe It Or Not*, as we prepared to recount some of the highlights of our 18-year friendship with Les in book form, the "coincidence" of that date's significance to us and our relationship with Les stood out as one of many things that came together to make it a very special night.

Leading up to Les's return to Chicago, there were many on- and off-air conversations with Les, several of them with our producer at that time, Paula Cooper. As Les did with Johnnie in their many off-air conversations, Les couldn't resist flirting a little with Paula, too.

While we normally didn't go out on a "school night," there was no way we were going to miss Les's appearance at the House of Blues. We drove in to WGN's Tribune Tower studios earlier than usual and made sure any "show prep" was taken care of. Since it was snowing, we took a cab the few blocks to the House of Blues. By the time we got there, it was already standing room only. We made our way to the main floor and found a really good vantage point at the back from which to watch the show.

Les was introduced to a standing ovation. As he started playing, one of the things that stood out to us was that even in a live performance, Les's guitar sound was as distinctive as it was on recordings. Unlike many of the Gibson guitars bearing the Les Paul name, his personal guitar, the Les Paul "Recording" model, was equipped with low-impedance pickups and several other unique features Les had developed to allow him to get the sound he wanted. Another thing that stood out was how beautifully Les played, even at age 81. He may have "picked" and chosen his notes a bit more carefully than in his younger years, but he was still a very impressive player who could surprise you with a lightning fast run or lick when he wanted to. Regardless of his age or physical limitations, Les was in control.

Very quickly, it became apparent that Les, accompanied

by the exceptional players who made up his trio, had the multi-generational crowd in the palms of his hands. As familiar as we were with Les and his music, it was an education to see how he worked the crowd with one-liners as well as his playing. Spontaneous applause, laughter and frequent ovations peppered Les's performance. The Chicago House of Blues may have been a new venue for him, but Les was very much at home on this stage.

We found Paula Cooper, who was with her brother, Joe, and made our way to the second level in time to see Les introduce a special guest — Slash. The former Guns N' Roses guitarist may have come from a different musical background, but his respect for, and appreciation of, Les was evident. As formidable a player as Slash is, Les was far from intimidated, and you could almost see him thinking "been there-done that" as he enjoyed the fun of a good jam session. Since we had to get back to WGN, we were not able to stick around for the rest of the show, which included Slash and Neal Schon (probably best known for his great guitar work with Journey) joining Les for a finale jam.

Before we left, we firmed up our post-concert "game plan." Paula and Joe were going to find Les and his son, Russ. Paula would have to hurry back to WGN for the beginning of our show, so Joe would stay and drive Les and Russ to the station. While our plans were set, we weren't sure how well they would mesh with the plans Gibson or the House of Blues might have had for Les's after-show activities.

Even though our in-studio interview with Les had been heavily promoted for weeks, and Les and Russ were ready to leave, Paula and Joe found the House of Blues staff less than accommodating. In fact, at one point a House of Blues representative told them that Les "would not be doing the interview." Fortunately for us, the House of Blues didn't know they were dealing with "Colonel" Cooper.

Paula had earned the nickname "Colonel" early on during

her time as our producer when it became apparent that, when it came to getting an important interview, she would not take "no" for an answer. Our show's scooping of the morning network TV shows with an on-scene interview with a U.S. Army General after a bombing in Saudi Arabia was just one of the many feathers in "Colonel" Cooper's cap.

After navigating their way to the House of Blues backstage area, Paula and Joe finally spotted the friendly face of Russ Paul. Russ welcomed Paula with a hug, and confirmed that Les was definitely going to WGN to do the interview. Russ knew that Paula had to leave, but told Joe to stick around and meet up with Les and Russ after the show.

After the last notes were played, Joe again made his way backstage, but was told by a House of Blues employee that Les and Russ had already gone back to their hotel. Following "Colonel" Cooper's instructions, Joe hung around backstage and, sure enough, a few minutes later saw Russ, who told Joe to bring his car to the rear of the House of Blues so they could load Les's gear and head over to WGN.

Joe later told us that one of the many things he appreciated about Les was really in evidence after they had loaded Les's gear. Even though Les knew our show was starting and we and our listeners were anticipating his arrival, he didn't want to rush any of his fans who were waiting for an autograph.

Les always loved his fans ... and they always loved him back.

One of the early ones: a 1959 Les Paul Standard Sunburst

December 3, 1996

Hello, Again, for the First Time

Steve: I think that will suffice for a mini-course in appreciating the man who is just, he's the guy. When he walks into the room, all the guitar players say, "We're not worthy! We're not worthy!" We had the pleasure of seeing him at the House of Blues tonight, and he was nice enough after a long day to come on over to the studio. Les, it's a real pleasure to meet you. Thank you for being here. What a great show tonight.

Johnnie: It was!

Les: You know I was just listening to that (music montage), and if it wasn't for Mary (Ford, his late wife and music partner), I wouldn't be here. Believe me, believe me … and the interesting thing is it started here in Chicago. That's so wonderful. I'm just daydreaming here, thinking back to how wonderful it was at the New Lawrence Hotel, Mary and I. And Mary, all the way driving here, said, "What if it doesn't work?" I said, "It'll work, it'll work." It was the invention of the sound-on-sound tape machine.

(Authors' note: To avoid repetition, Les's sound-on-sound story was deleted from this section. It is told in greater detail in the "Another Les Paul Surprise" chapter beginning on page 130.)

Johnnie, Les and Steve at WGN, 1996

Steve: Do you recall what song you did the most overlays on?

Les: Yes, one that wasn't released that I made for Bing for one of his radio shows. It was called "Night and Day." It was never released, (even) yet. It's still sitting at home, 37 parts.

Steve: Why? Why was it never released?

Les: It just wasn't as good as some of the other things. (Even) "How High the Moon" sat at Capitol for a year. They didn't think it was commercial. The president (of Capitol Records) said, "Listen to it: 'Somewhere there is music, how high the moon,' does it make sense?" (*laughter*) I said, "Well, Anita O'Day sang it, it made sense." Well, they weren't listening to lyrics, what makes you think they're going to listen to lyrics now? I said, "Why don't you put it out?" It took a year and finally, they decided to put it out. Jim Conklin came to Chicago, and wired me from Chicago and said, "You've got a hit." Dave Garroway was the one that broke "Lover," broke many of the hit songs for us. Right here in Chicago.

Johnnie: But you weren't really surprised when "How High the Moon" became a hit.

Les: No, no ...

Johnnie: Well, what's the song that comes to mind when you were told, "It's a hit?" You said, "What? It is?"

Les: Oh, "Nola."

Johnnie: "Nola?"

Les: Yeah, a guy come to my backyard and he said, "Can I try my accordion?" I said, "Okay." He played, dada-da-dada-da, and I go to bed that night and I was thinking, you know, he's playing that too fast. He should go da-da-da-da so you could walk to the men's room. If you're on the dance floor, you don't have to dance, just walk to the men's room. (*laughter*) I said, "Hey, he's playing it too fast," so I got dressed, went out to the backyard, made the thing, and took it down to Capitol and gave it to them. Forgot about it. When Mary and I went to New York from the New Lawrence Hotel, the thing came out and it was a hit. Mary and I didn't have a radio. We were broke, and we were in New York making "How High the Moon" and did not know that "Nola" was number one. A hit song. It's a crazy world.

Johnnie: Yeah, it is!

Steve: What do you think when you have an experience like tonight (at the House of Blues)?

Les: I think I'm the most lucky guy in the world. To put in 81 years, and go out of the business like I went into the business, a very lucky guy. When I was here in 1929, when this was "Sam and Henry" at WGN — there are a few of us out there who probably remember that. What a great thing that is, to be here, at the beginning of jazz in Chicago. With the Art Tatums, with the Roy Eldridges and all those great, great, wonderful players. When I (first) came to Chicago, there wasn't one electric guitar player, no jazz player. So the guitar player was nothing. When I came here and had to make up an electric guitar, I went over to Bell and Howell and asked if I could get one half of the projector. I didn't want the projector, just wanted the amplifier with that long hose on it. (*laughter*) I said, "Give me that thing with the box and the handle and the speaker." When I told them what I was going to do with it, they gave it to

John Paulson, *Chasing Sound*

In the bedroom at his Mahwah, New Jersey, home, Les shows his first electric guitar, "The Log."

me. Bell and Howell here in Chicago. That's how I started.

Johnnie: Did you go back in your hotel room and start tinkering? I mean, your mind is amazing. You knew this would work. Right?

Les: I didn't know anything would work. You know why I invented these things? Cause you couldn't go over to a Guitar Center and buy one. If you can't buy it, you make it. It's survival.

Johnnie: Right.

Les: There wasn't a multi-track machine so, you invent one.

Johnnie: There wasn't an electric guitar, so you make one.

Les: When I walked to Gibson, which was in Chicago, I went to the Gibson people with this log with some strings on it. A 4" x 4" log, and said, "Here's the way it should be done."

Johnnie: You're not kidding ... it really was a log.

Les: Yeah.

Steve: You've still got that, don't you?

Les: Yeah, I've got it. I've got it. They labeled me the character with the broomstick with the pickups on it. They laughed at me for 10 years and finally called me and said, "Hey, come in here with that thing and let's do something with it." If it wasn't for Leo Fender in my backyard saying, "Les, you gonna do something with that thing?" And I said, "I'm going to wait for Gibson." He didn't. He rattled their cage. Then they called me and said, "You want to come in here and do something with your guitar?"

Johnnie: How much did that weigh?

Les: It weighs a ton. That's why my back is a problem. That's why I'm going to the Mayo Clinic. They told me to get rid of my guitar.

Johnnie: Yikes!

Les: *(laughing)* I'm kidding you!

Steve: You better be kidding!

Les: I can hear it at Gibson now ...

Johnnie: Driving off the road ...

Steve: Jumping out of windows!

Les: If you listened to the show tonight, it was wonderful. The fact you can hit one note, eat, come back and it's still playing — *(laughter)* sax players can't do that. Piano players can't do that. You gotta get a plank of wood to make it talk like that. That's what it's all about.

Steve: This is the first time I've seen you perform live. What amazed me is you still seem to be enthusiastic. (I) don't know how many times you've played "How High the Moon," yet you still throw fresh stuff in there.

Les: Yes! You don't play it the same. David Merrick asked me if I would do a show on Broadway, "Hello, Dolly!" and I said, "David, in all fairness, I don't want to do it because I'd be changing it in every show." So if you play the same, you don't improve. If you're out looking and searching, you try something different. You feel it. You don't feel the same way every time, so you create something new. Sometimes it's not as good, so you don't do that again. Right? But you do improve.

Johnnie: When you go out, do you have a particular song that helps you read the audience? Or, do you just dive in?

Les: You dive in, but if it don't stick on the wall, you change it in a hurry! So, when I go out and throw a line or play something and there's not a response to it, I say, "Well, I won't go there again." So, you're constantly feeding. Let me give you an example. In Chicago at the Blue Note, I said to Mary, "We got a problem. We're great on Mondays, pretty good on Tuesdays, Wednesdays … uh … fair, Thursdays is the maid's night out (they're coming down from Evanston)." I said, "This is no night for anybody, Friday. They start preparing to get drunk. Saturday night the guy says to the ol' lady, yeah, let's go out. He just hangs on and talks, argues, you can't control Saturdays." They're the same in Terre Haute, Rock Island, Chicago, New York at the Paramount. You have to read your audience.

Johnnie: Talking about reading our audience, you have 20-somethings and seniors plugged into you. No generation gap.

Les: (*agreeing*) For example, Perry Como didn't have that. I was very fortunate I invented the guitar, the solid body, electric guitar. Engineers, those in the control room say, "I know Les Paul cause he does this, this and this." The echo, the delay. These things are something a person like Perry Como doesn't have. They don't have the things to lean on to bridge the gap. The kid today that's 15 years old knows Les Paul. He thinks I'm a guitar. There isn't a Perry Como guitar. He only reaches his audience. I go back to a nine-year-old who says he's got to get a Les Paul guitar. I go the bank and the gal, the clerk, says, "Oh you're not a guitar, you're a person." (*laughter*) They're surprised! I say, "Yeah, I guess so." She says, "My boyfriend keeps raving about Les Paul. I thought you were a guitar."

Johnnie: Like you were named after the guitar!

Les: Exactly.

Steve: Well, I've got to ask you a question for all the guitar players. What's your favorite guitar?

Les: You play guitar … the whole world is one guitar now. Don't you know that? (*laughter*) When I was a little kid and started to play the piano, my mother said, "I don't think so." I said, "Why not, Mom?" She said, "You've got your back turned to the people." I said, "Well, I'll play the saxophone." She said, "No you've got something in your mouth, you can't sing or talk." So, the harmonica went out and I said, "I'll get a drum." She said, "Not in this house! You won't bring a drum!" So, finally I went to a guitar. She said, "Now you're talking, now you got it." From Sears I got the guitar. As I opened it and got it out of the carton, one string caught in the cardboard and went "ding." Mother said, "You're great already." (*laughter*) I was on my way! Mother said, "No matter what you do, you sound great when you play the guitar." The guitar has that magic.

Steve: But, do you have a favorite out of all of your Les Paul guitars?

Les: No. The one I play happens to be the one I like. I play it now, but tomorrow I may pick up another one and in 10 minutes, I love it.

Steve: You have a gift that is a rare thing among instrumentalists. When we watched you on stage tonight you have a wonderful sense of humor. We knew that from our conversations, but you're able to make your sense of humor come through your guitar.

Les: That's right. You've got to say it with your hands.

Johnnie: When that guitar laughs, everybody laughs.

Les: And you make it cry, too. When a person is in your audience and you see tears in their eyes, you know you're saying the right thing. It's terribly important what you can say with your head and your hands, and the more you play the guitar, and the more you use your head instead of your hands, you only need to say one thing, one note. Louis Armstrong proved it, Count Basie proved it, the Tommy Dorseys proved it. All you have to do is hit one note, and if it's the right note … But how many notes can you pick to put there that are wrong? It's terribly important to play the right note. When you play the blues you don't play a million notes. One note and it's the right note. That's the important part about playing.

Steve: Who makes you cry?

Les: Two things. Probably like working with Al Jolson, which I did. Working with Judy Garland, which I did. The thing that really gets you is when they put you up, then bring you down. When Al Jolson did his thing and dropped to one knee and did "Sonny Boy," boy, I'll tell you, it tears your heart out. Judy Garland did it with "Somewhere Over the Rainbow." It's hard to do that with a thousand people like at the House of Blues. That's why I chose, after my heart surgery, what do I want to do? I took a piece a paper and drew a line down the center and put plus and minus. I wrote the things I didn't particularly like in my life, and the things I really, really love to do. I was surprised to find I want to play in a little club. Intimate, with a few people. Don't go to the dressing room, but go with the people and listen to them. Make new friends and keep your old friends. In a small club I can look 'em right in the eye. A big club, like the House of Blues, you're lost. So Jimmy Page or Eric Clapton, when they're playing to 50,000 people, they never know what their audience is thinking, what they're saying. They're whisked away, like Sinatra in a car, they never see their audience. But, when you're in a little club, like in New York where we're at, and Tony Bennett or Slash stop in, they love it. Chet Atkins was there a month ago and said, "I'm going to do what you're doing Les! I'm going to get a little club down in Nashville and do the same thing." Just a little club, so you can get with your friends.

Johnnie: So it's like therapy. It's not work.

Les: Johnnie, you got it. Therapy, that's the secret to getting old and staying with it. That's therapy. No longer is it a job. But I never thought in my life that I was working. I did everything and it was fun.

Johnnie: Really? Even when you were struggling?

Les: I'll tell you a short story. I was working in the Wrigley Building making a thousand dollars a week in 1931.

Johnnie: GASP!

Steve: That was big money.

Les: Tremendous money. I didn't know what it was to be poor, starving. When I didn't want to do country music, I wanted to do jazz, I went to the North Side and went to work at Sun Dodgers Rendevous playing along with a phonograph record and my guitar for five dollars a week. I worked with Jackie Gleason at the 5100 Club and made 35 dollars a week and deliberately starved. To play jazz! And I found out if you want to starve to death, play jazz. (*laughter*) I learned two things. The Atlass Brothers said come on back, and I went back as Les Paul, and Rhubarb Red. Rhubarb Red made the money and Les Paul enjoyed playing with Art Tatum and all the great jazz players. When jazz, country and blues all hit big, you'd still starve playing jazz. Country, you'll make a fortune, and blues you'll make a living. (*laughter*)

Steve: What was the last time you worked at WGN Radio?

Les: Ah, probably 1931. The studios have changed so much. You had enormous studios then.

Johnnie: This is considered big by today's standards.

Les: It is? No 95-piece band could fit in here! When I worked at the Wrigley Building, I would walk across the street with my guitar. It would be snowing out, and I didn't even put it in a case. Walk from the Wrigley Building back over here to do a show and never put it in a case. Those days I cherish.

Johnnie: You were busy, too. You would go back and forth to other stations, too.

Les: Oh, WJJD, WIND, WCFL. That's when Rudolph, Pratt and Sherman were big, and Don McNeil was doing The Breakfast Club, and my singer was Fran Allison of Kukla, Fran and Ollie. She was a lovely lady.

Steve: It sounds like that was a very creative time.

Les: It was. There were only a few of us, and we were pioneering.

Steve: Do you have tapes of those shows?

Les: Sure.

Johnnie: You're a bit of a pack rat, aren't you?

Les: I can't tell you how much stuff I have for the museum ... including ME! It's a trip. My mother did the same thing. She kept all my wigs, comedy things, my harmonicas.

Steve: Les, I've taken a black and white picture off the wall. I'm curious, do you recognize any of these performers in the picture?

Les: Hmmm ... no. Who are they?

Johnnie: We don't know either, other than they worked at this station! We were hoping you would know them.

Les: I recognize the microphone! That's a double-button carbon mic. I don't know the fellow or the girl, either.

Steve: It says that's Jane Carpenter, pianist at the Drake Hotel, and Clyde McCoy.

Les: Clyde McCoy? Hmmm, makes me think of a story ... it isn't about Clyde McCoy, but Louie Panico. He was playing over at the Wrigley Building, and I'd go hang out with him. One time, Louie told me, "All the horn players are copying me with their wah-wah on the trumpet." I asked him, "How can you prove it?" He said, "I will prove it!" He took his trumpet and poked a hole in it (the derby). A few weeks later we went around town to all the different clubs and sure enough every trumpet player we saw had poked a hole in his derby. Louie proved to me they were copying him. He was the leader. He said, "See, I poked a hole for no reason just to prove they were copying me." He was right. (*laughter*)

Steve: Our engineer, Aubrey Mumpower just brought in another old picture. Thankfully, these pictures are on display because the station really has a sense of its history.

Johnnie: Now, this is a group of guys performing. It's interesting, so many of these pictures are of guys. Where are the ladies?

Les: Oh, there were ladies. I used to come across here to the "Laughing Lady" show on WGN. She was on Sunday mornings and she'd do her thing then laugh. She'd laugh and laugh till she broke everybody up.

Johnnie: I could do that! Now, here's a picture of what you would have seen when you were coming across from the Wrigley Building to the Tribune Tower.

Les: Yes.

Steve: Actually I think that picture is of the little building next door. The old Chicago American Building.

Johnnie: Oh, I see. I know Les has been around for a while but, maybe not as long as the Tribune Tower.

Les: Well when did the networks start? Was it about 1926 for NBC?

Steve: There were the Red and Blue networks.

Les: That was over at the Merchandise Mart. We made all our "race records" — blues records were made at the Furniture Mart. In 1935, I was making records for Montgomery Ward.

Johnnie: They were called "race" records?

Les: Yeah, when you found them, they'd come out on Maxwell Street and sell on Sundays for a nickel.

Johnnie: Did you record those under your name?

Les: I'd be playing for the artists on "race records." They weren't called rhythm and blues or just blues; they were "race records."

Steve: Did you ever record with Django Reinhardt?

Les: Yes. No! I performed with him, but never recorded with him. It was a wonderful experience. I was at the Paramount Theatre. Fella comes up to my dressing room and says, "There's a guy downstairs who wants to meet you. He says he's Django Reinhardt." So, I made a couple of comments because I think this is a joke and I said, "Bring him up and bring a case of beer back when you come back." For those who don't know, Django was probably one of the most creative, dynamic guitar players of all time. When he walked into my dressing room we shook hands, and he started looking around for a guitar. I had a pair of them on the bed. I always had two in case I broke a string. So I'm at the Paramount with the Andrews Sisters, Django comes in and he's playing guitar, and I'm finishing up shaving. Right then and there I should have cut my throat! Boy, oh boy, he was good! That's the first time I met him. The last time I saw Django in the States, he was here in Chicago, he was playing

Les Paul Archives

Mary Ford, Django Reinhardt and Les Paul

with Duke Ellington at the time.

Steve: Really?

Les: Yes, we were on tour and for some reason landed at the same town. For example, Duke would be in Cincinnati and me and the Andrews Sisters would be in town at another theater, and Django would come over to say hey. Finally, he said, "I'm lonesome for home, I want to go back." When he went back, he was very discouraged because he wasn't accepted over here.

Steve: He was a genius.

Les: Yes, he was.

Steve: There's a wonderful picture in the box set, Les Paul: The Legend and the Legacy — run out and get it if you don't have it — there's a wonderful picture in there of you, Mary and Django.

Les: Yeah. Mary took a picture then handed the camera to someone else to get the three of us. That was the last picture we got together. In 1953, Mary and I had just flown home and they called me and said Django had died. He'd had a stroke and died. We turned right around and went back to Paris and buried him. Someone that great … you just wonder, how did it all happen? You wonder how someone who isn't truly gifted in music and makes it and someone is gifted with talent, with rhythm and doesn't. You don't go down to a Guitar Center and get rhythm. You don't buy an ear. You can't buy a sense of humor.

Steve: You talk about going to a Guitar Center to buy various things. Do your own inventions ever bother you? By that I mean, you took the time to work. You invented the echo and all the recording techniques we use. Today the average kid can go in and get a lot of this stuff and …

Les: Abuse it.

Steve: Yes, abuse it and not really know how to play. Does that ever bother you?

Les: No. No, not any more than when Slash breaks one of my guitars! They say, "What do you think about that?" I say, "Great! I'll sell him another one!" (*laughter*) We can't lose, can we? No, I think it's great that the youngster today can do better than I did when I sent away for a guitar from Sears and Roebuck. He can buy a fine guitar today. He can learn from the others out there how to play and play correctly. He can learn fast. When I was a kid they didn't have guitar picks. So, I broke the last key off the piano.

Johnnie: No!

Les: That's what I filed down for my pick because I didn't have one.

Steve: Just the ivory from the key.

Les: Yes, just the ivory from the last key.

Johnnie: Wow! We'll add that to the list of things you've invented. We'd overlooked that!

Les: Yep.

Johnnie: Your mind was always working, wasn't it? It went in places other kids' minds obviously don't go.

Les: Yes, my brother would say, "Ma, the nut's at it again!" He'd say, "Now he's taken the telephone apart!" Mother would say, "He'll put it back together again."

Johnnie: She was a cool mom, wasn't she?

Les: Oh, she was cool. I was telling folks tonight at dinner that I can look back and recall when Mother played the piano, and she played the blues. So it was in the family.

Steve: Did your dad play?

Les: My dad would go out on a drunk and gambling thing and come home with say, a trombone. He'd open the window and try to play it, and the slide would go out the window, and he'd throw the whole thing into the snowbank. Throw out the whole horn, then turn and go to bed! He'd say things like, "Son, I'd have been a great violinist, but my fingers are too small." You know, things

like that. (*laughter*)

Steve: Was there ever any idea, anything you wanted to invent that you couldn't invent?

Les: Yes, the electric guitar! I still haven't gotten it the way I'd like to have it.

Johnnie: No!

Les: Yep.

Steve: What don't you like about it?

Les: Well, as soon as you put a pickup under the string, you're limited to where you place the pickup, and that string is vibrating and you're only picking up part of it. OK, you want to talk the whole pie and take what you want from the whole pie. But, if you don't have the whole pie to begin with and you're taking something from it, you're taking something that is not complete yet. If I had my wishes, my wannas, I'd want to have something that was the whole pie. Everything that's happening on that string and then take out what I don't want. Equalize it to the sound I want. In other words, distort the sound in a good way. Distortion doesn't mean bad. EQ on this microphone isn't necessarily bad — it makes it sound better.

Steve: Why do I get the feeling you're going to invent a laser pickup?

Les: Ah … I went through that already!

Johnnie: Oh, never mind!

Les: I went through that so heavy. In fact, I gave a lecture back in the '50s for the Audio Engineering Society. My belief at that time was they were on the wrong track with tape machines and disc recorders and what they should have is something they put in their pocket and nothing moves. Well, it's here. It just took a while. It's digital. Now, as you know, you can get a Casio player and play "Mary Had a Little Lamb" and push the button and play it back. Nothing moves. We have to keep working on these ideas. Nothing moves. When I made the very first disc player here in Chicago, I had a big flywheel from a car. It was barbaric, but it worked!

Steve: It was an old Cadillac flywheel, right?

Les: Yes, my dad was in the garage business. I went to him and said, "Dad, I've got to make a turntable." He said, "What's that?" (*laughter*) I said, "I want to play records on it." I told him, "It has to be dynamically balanced." He said, "Nibs, go out in the alley and do a hysterectomy on one of those old cars and take the flywheel out. That'll do it." That's what I did, that's where the idea came from.

Steve: What's a favorite invention you didn't invent?

Les: Oh! I would say everything Thomas Edison did. I had the pleasure to go to his museum many times, and I actually recorded on one of his original machines. A cylinder machine, and I used an electric guitar! That's a no-no!

Johnnie: Do you think he was rolling over in his grave? (*laughter*)

Les: Oh he was! Think about the things he did. Here's a man who gave us the electric light, the motion picture, the phonograph … When you think of these things and many more, this man did it.

Johnnie: Yes, and Les, you are in his company. You're in the Inventors Hall of Fame with Edison.

Les: Believe me, many people out there are saying, "So that's the guy putting out this angry music! That darn guitar is driving me nuts."

Johnnie: But that was a real kick of a lifetime, to be recognized in the same category as Edison. That was the ultimate, wasn't it?

Les: Yes, but, I really don't think of myself in his league. I'm uncomfortable being in his class.

Johnnie: Well, you'll get used to it. Especially when we get a Les Paul stamp!

Les: Oh, now you're dreaming!

Johnnie: Well, it is the middle of the night. You know we're very fortunate that we get to work together.

Les: Yes, you are.

Johnnie: I know we've talked about this in the past. Being married and working together like you and Mary did. People ask us, and I'm sure they asked you two, "How can you be together all the time?"

Les: I remember when Jack Paar asked, "How do you two stand being together 24 hours a day?" In some ways, you will burn out if you work, work, work. That's one of the difficult things you have to be careful of when you hit it big. When you've got a line in Chicago that goes on for blocks to get into The Chicago Theatre, you're breaking attendance records, your records are #1, you're on every day for Listerine, guests on the *Ed Sullivan Show* you ... you can burn out.

Johnnie: You've said it before, success will change you.

Les: Oh, yes, and money will change you.

Johnnie: So Steve, we're safe ... no money, no fame. *(laughter)*

Steve: You said in the book in your box set that is really what stopped you from having more hit records. There were too many things happening at once.

Les: Yes, if you're inventing and they call you to do the Sullivan show and you say you can't, something is wrong. Bing would call and say, "Les, I keep asking you to do the show, why won't you?" I'd say, "I'm in the garage inventing a New Sound." I remember him saying, "What in the world is a New Sound?" Let me, as quick as I can, tell you how the "New Sound" came about. My mother came down from Waukesha. I was at the Oriental Theatre with the Andrews Sisters; it was 1946. Mother said, "Lester, I heard you last night on the radio. You played great." I said, "Mom, I wasn't on the air, I was with the Andrews Sisters on stage at the Oriental." She said, "You mean that was someone else? You better do something about that." I said, "What can I do if someone plays like me?" She said, "If I can't tell you from the other guy, you're in trouble." I thought about it and said to the Andrews Sisters, "I'm going to do the thing for Bugsy Siegel at the Flamingo, and then I'm going to jump ship." I did, and I went home and locked myself in the garage and said, "I'm not coming out of here until I have a sound my mother can tell from everybody else." Bing would call and say, "Are you ever coming out of that garage?" I'd say, "Not until I get the New Sound." I went to Capitol Records and they asked, "What're we going to call it?" I said, "Call it the New Sound." That's how that came about.

Johnnie: Interesting, you really had motivation.

Les: Yes, I sure did. I was turned down by Decca Records. Decca said, "It's a novelty, one time around the block." Ha! You know, speaking of novelty, did you know I named the Chipmunks and made that first record for David Seville?

Johnnie: What?!

Les: Yeah, "The Chipmunks" came from me. I went to buy some property at Sunset and La Brea in Hollywood. You won't believe this, but I went to my friend Howie and said, "Howie, wait till you see what I just bought." I took him to the half-block I'd bought at Sunset and La Brea, and it was obvious he wasn't impressed very much.

A short time later, my friend Vern came over and said, "What are you doing hanging out with Howard Hughes?" I said, "WHAT ... Howard Hughes?" Vern said, "Yeah, that's your friend Howie. Howard Hughes." Now I knew why he wasn't impressed when I'd taken him to see my property! Shortly after I found out who he was, he asked me what was happening with my property. I told him I was losing sleep worrying about the property I'd bought. I was going crazy. I'd never had anything like that. Well, one afternoon we're having a hamburger and I said, "What's that red light down the street?" He said, "I don't know, let's go find out." We walked down from Sunset and there's a light outside a studio,

Liberty Records. We climbed the fire escape and I knocked. A guy comes over and says, "What do you want?" I said, "I'm Les Paul." He said, "The Les Paul?" I said, "Yes, if it will get us in!" We went in, and there's David Seville working on a recording. At some point, I said, "Why don't you speed it up and I'll go get my guitar and fill in." I went and got my guitar, got back and they recorded the first Chipmunk record. The name was obvious after they speeded up the song. I gave him the idea, and David was forever grateful.

Johnnie: That is wild.

Les: It was an accident … an accident.

Steve: What a story.

Johnnie: I just realized it was five years ago this month that we first talked to Les Paul. I remember that well because your father had just moved up from Florida, and he said to you, "Son, you've been in the business 25 years. You've made it, you're going to talk to Les Paul."

Steve: Yes. And to be fair, we have to thank Mike Rapchak. He gave us your phone number and put us in touch with you.

Les: I have his number in my book.

Johnnie: Steve was beside himself because he had so much he wanted to talk to you, Les, about. The beauty of a Les Paul interview is you ask him a question and he goes!

Les: Yep, forget about it!

Johnnie: How do you feel — I was looking at a book of vintage guitars, I looked through page after page of the Les Paul guitars. $30,000 Sunburst guitar, $24,000 — I mean, does that make your head swim to think one of your guitars is worth what some guy makes in a year?

Les: They asked that question at the Guitar Center today. What makes that guitar worth $30,000 and you get a new one today for a thousand dollars? He said, "Is the other one better?" I said,

"No." The fellow at Guitar Center said, "That is very interesting." (*laughter*) That is very interesting. What makes one guitar so valuable that it's worth a fortune? Okay. It's in the eyes of the beholder … the ears of the beholder.

Steve: Does anything have to do with the technology? We have the debate now between analog and digital. Tube amps and solid state amps and things like that.

Les: Basically, there is no change in the electric guitar from the time it was first created and now. No difference at all. It's the same thing. No change at all. Maybe a better magnet. Not any better wire. When I listen to this station, I was thinking. I sat on an Indian mound in Waukesha and I said (to my friend), "Harry, what are you doing?" We were supplementing the newspaper — you had to put in the middle section, the sports section, then you'd roll 'em up and sling 'em at the door. Harry said, "I'm making a crystal set." I said, "What's that?" He told me what it was. So, I take this toilet roll and I start winding that wire on the thing and put a slider from a beer can on there, and I put a crystal in there. Cat's wire. I picked up WGN and WBBM out of Chicago. The only two stations I could get. That's how I listened to your station back in the 1920s; '25, '26.

Johnnie: Wow!

Les: Way back at the beginning of time … it hasn't changed a bit.

Johnnie: That's before you were the pride of Waukesha.

Les: The Wizard! They labeled me that after I got a job at a barbecue stand halfway between Waukesha and Milwaukee. There was a critic, some guy who sat in the rumble seat of a car and said to the carhop, "Tell that red-headed kid up there I can hear his singing fine, but not the guitar." I was singing through the telephone into my mother's radio. They could hear me singing, talking and playing harmonica but, as the guy said, the guitar wasn't loud enough. So I went home and thought about it and said, "You know, he's right.

You have to listen to your public." I figured, "What can I do? I'll get my dad's radio!" Figured I'd put that on the other side and get two battery chargers. So this thing was bubbling and smoking. I got the big squeezer ball to check the batteries!

That's where the Wizard of Waukesha came from. They said, there he is out there with all those weird things, batteries, two radios — Mom's and Dad's radios and I'm singing into the telephone, the mouthpiece. Eventually, the other half, the ear piece — like we're listening here — that was a magnet and a coil. I pushed it under the guitar string and, lo and behold, I heard the guitar. I heard the string. I ran to my mother and said, "I got it, I got it!" She said, "What've you got?" (Just) like Mary. Before I had Mary it was my mom. I was then known as the Wizard of Waukesha with all those batteries and things.

Johnnie: Was your brother older or younger than you?

Les: My brother (Ralph) was seven years older than me.

Johnnie: Ah, that's why he called you the nut.

Les: Yeah, I was a nut! He'd say, "Ma, he's at it again!"

Steve: Older brothers are like that!

Les: My brother was handsome. He passed away a long time ago (in 1971). I miss him. My brother loved to dance, he loved to live, he loved to eat. We had a wonderful time, but I was curious and he wasn't. He would say, "What do you worry about? Throw the switch and the light goes on." I would say, "But why?" I had to know why. Why did the light go on? So I would take it apart and find out. When I had my first radio in the car, I couldn't pick up any stations, so I drove out to the transmitter and parked underneath it. Then I could hear the radio. We'd sit there. My girl would say, "Aren't we ever going to do anything besides listen to the radio?" (*laughter*)

Steve: I've got one for you. Talking about being near a transmitter ... I was having a shoulder problem and seeing a doctor in Schaumburg. I was having a therapy where they

put little suction cups on my shoulder. The doctor wired me up and pointed me in a particular direction. I sat there, and he walked out of the room quickly. I didn't know that he got Johnnie and told her there was something she had to see.

Johnnie: I go to the door and he tells me to look through the keyhole. I was literally down on my knees looking at Steve through the keyhole.

Steve: All of a sudden I start hearing WGN Radio coming through my shoulder!

Les: You're kidding!

Johnnie: The doctor had turned him to the transmitter.

Steve: The doctor's office was very close to the WGN transmitter. I didn't know that, so I was picking up the station through my shoulder!

Les: Ah. Did you ever walk through the rain next to a fence and hear music coming out of it? Or talking? Did you ever walk under a telephone line and hear talking? We can drive close to (the) WABC (radio transmitter) in New York and when we get close to the transmitter, and the radio is off, the sound will come right through the radio.

Steve: Some people have told us that if they are close to the transmitter, they can hear the station through their toaster.

Les: Electric clock. Through the little speaker on a clock radio.

Johnnie: I loved the story about Lucille Ball supposedly hearing transmissions ...

Les: Through her teeth?

Johnnie: Yes! Through her molars she was hearing the enemy off the coast in a submarine. She claimed she heard top secret messages. Who do you tell? Do you call the government? Who do you tell?

Les: I think I'd keep it to myself! It's like seeing a flying saucer. I thought I saw one, one time, but never told anyone because I'm

Les Paul Archives

*The always curious Les questions astronaut Scott
Carpenter about what it's like in space.*

still … uneasy. I know I saw one out in Texas. I don't push it too far.

**Steve: I would think you'd be the kind of person that if a flying
saucer came down you'd be saying, "I want to see what it looks
like! Can I go on board?"**

Johnnie: I think you'd be the guy they are after!

Les: I'll tell you something that happened down at the Iridium,
or Fat Tuesday's. Scott Carpenter came in, and I had a serious
discussion with him on stage. We had what we have going here. I
said, "I know the people would love to hear you talk about flying
in outer space." In the middle of the conversation I asked him this
question: "You didn't happen to run into a friend of ours when you
were up there did you?" He said, "Are you talking about God?" I
said, "Yeah, yeah." He said, "When you're up there flying, looking
down, and think of the fighting and misery we cause throughout
the world, we just don't understand it." Do you ever think about
that? When he laid that on me that night in that audience, you
could hear a pin drop.

Johnnie: I bet.

Les Paul Archives

ABOVE: *YOUNG Les and his mother, Evelyn Polsfuss, circa 1925*

BELOW: *Les and his mother, Evelyn Polsfuss, on her 100th birthday*

Paul Vrakas

Les: He said, "Up there, you better believe that something that's bigger than us is running this thing. Right?" I don't know … my mother was an atheist.

Steve: Really?

Les: Yeah, she would have convincing arguments about things being fairy tales. Maybe they are fairy tales. Maybe this whole thing starting from a one-cell animal back, back millions of years ago, it's proving itself as time goes on. And you wonder about this whole heavy thing, so I've come to the conclusion I'm going to go where I'm supposed to go. I haven't been able to figure anything out, but neither has Einstein or anybody else. We all come and we go. Whatever we were meant to do on this earth, you just do it. I'm very grateful for everything. When you're 65, you think about it a little bit. At 80, you think about it more.

My mother lived to 101 and a half, and she had her act together. I didn't agree with her. I'm not an atheist, OK? But I do believe this thing is a heavy movie. I haven't figured it out. I'm not going to try to figure it out. I'm just going with it. There's no other way to deal with life. I've talked to a lot of brilliant people, and I don't think they know anything more than I do.

Steve: You're in your 80s and you think a lot about the heavy things. Is there anything you haven't done that you want to do? Not necessarily musically. Anything you really want to do?

Les: I'd like to come back and finish it.

Johnnie: How do you feel when you hear, like tonight at the House of Blues, you're introduced as the only legend on two legs? Us common folk are thinking that's big stuff.

Les: I can't handle it. I can't handle any of that. I've talked to my doctor. I've talked to different people and I've asked, "What's my hang up? Why is it I can't deal with these things?" See, I don't think I did anything that means anything, and yet people come up to me and say such wonderful things. I know I did it. I made "How

High the Moon." I know that Mary and I did this. I know there's a Wizard of Waukesha with all those gadgets and batteries, crystal sets and telephones. I can't figure out the way I feel when I'm at the House of Blues, or being introduced at Guitar Center, or two weeks ago when I was honored at the Smithsonian. I tell them I can't reason it out. I know I did the things they talk about, but what's the big deal? What's the big deal? So I happen to think up a multi-track machine.

The wildest thing — I'll break up this heavy thing — the wildest thing is a couple of weeks ago when I was inducted into the Inventors Hall of Fame. They already put me in one in Jersey, but they put me in the national one. They had to hunt up a lot of data. They hunted up Ampex. They hunted up, that's not a good way to say it, but they did, and they came back with the most astonishing thing. Ampex never patented it and neither did I.

Steve: No!

Les: Nobody patented my Ampex invention. They thought that I did, and I thought that they did!

Steve: So did you run out and patent it?

Les: No! It went to public domain a hundred years ago!

Steve: No!

Les: Yep. They found that out a month ago. And a couple of weeks (later) I found out, and I just can't believe it.

Steve: I'm amazed.

Les: I'm more than amazed. I was shocked. They said, "Why did you give it away?" I said, "What's the big deal? It should be out there for everybody to have it."

Steve: Well, I'm not trying to flatter you when I say this ...

Les: Then don't! (*laughter*)

Steve: Understanding that we all want to make money doing whatever it is we do, but I get the feeling from the times we've

Les Paul Archives

talked to you that even if you hadn't been successful at what you've done, you would have still been inventing these things. It's in your blood to do it.

Les: Absolutely! It has nothing to do with it. When you play music, you play it to enjoy it. It's a selfish thing to love the guitar. Like I said to Mary, "Mary, I've got two loves going. One is to love music and one is to love you." They're different, but real. It's a different thing to love that guitar. When I was a kid living in Chicago, in a room on the North Side for five dollars a week, before I put the guitar up I would shine it, so when I opened my eyes I would see the guitar. I wanted to open my eyes and see the guitar. It was the most wonderful thing in my life and still is. The guitar is a psychiatrist. It's a housewife, companion, it's the greatest pal you could ever imagine. But it's not a love like you have with Johnnie. It's different. How do you explain it?

Steve: I don't think you can to somebody who hasn't experienced it.

Johnnie: Do you name your guitars?

Les: No, no.

Johnnie: So they remain unnamed and inanimate, but there's still that connection.

Les: Yeah.

Johnnie: Speaking of connections, after seeing you tonight, you

are one of two people I've ever seen that is literally connected to the instrument.

Steve: This is interesting. We were watching you tonight and she remarked there was only one other time she'd seen that connection.

Johnnie: I was awed by it, like when I saw Jerry Lee Lewis perform. I said, "Golly, that piano just extends from his finger-tips." It was like that when we walked into your show tonight. The way the guitar sits on your knee, cradles under your arm. It fits you and looks different than it does with every other guitar player. The guitar is a part of Les Paul.

Les: Hmmm … yeah. Did you ever see Eddie South? I'm sure you didn't. He was at the Bar Ritz up on Sheridan Road on the North Side in 1929. I walked in and saw this man, the "Dark Angel of the Violin," Eddie South. Eddie South played the greatest violin. He played a gypsy violin and he made it cry. He was a black man with a smile that would tear you apart. I worked at the Regal Theatre with him, and we became inseparable. He died in '41. Lost at a young age, but he could say more with that violin and you could just sit at the bar and cry. He'd just tear you apart, like Louie Armstrong. In fact, I was with Eddie South at the Regal Theatre on the South Side of Chicago, and I saw Louie Armstrong. I didn't know who he was. At the last part of the song, he missed the last note. He said, "I don't know … my chops ain't with me, let me go back and get it." He goes back and he misses it a second time. He went back and he missed it a third time. So I said to the stagehand, "What's that fella's name?" He said, "I don't know." So I went out and looked at the marquee. It said Louie Armstrong. After that show, I met the man who I learned SOOO much from. You can turn a wrong note into a show stopper. You can go back to do it again and everybody in that audience is with you, hoping you hit that note. After the second and third time, I realized that clam was going to make him stop the show, and it did. We got to be friends after that. I was at 201 N. Wells in Chicago at WJJD. Every time on his birthday in July, he'd have his mother bake the cake and he'd bring it over there to us. Harry Carey was there. Russ Hodges was there. A lot of baseball announcers, a lot of great talent. Louie would bring that cake up and we would celebrate his birthday. He was another man with a heart as big as a house. From Louie I learned to play one note … if it's the right note, that's it. Louie never thought he could sing. I watched him with Bing Crosby so many times. He could get up there with that gravel voice and sing. Equal to Ella Fitzgerald, which technically he never could, but he could sell a song. He could tear you apart.

Steve: During the break we were talking about Mary Ford and her guitar playing and singing. You were saying she was like iron.

Les: She was as solid as a rock. She had that ability once you told her what to do. She would ask me, "How do you want me to play it, or sing it?" And I'd tell her, and she'd say, "OK," and do it. That's it. You'd have to degauss her head if you wanted to change it because once you put it in her head, that was the way it would be. She had that great talent to do that.

Steve: One of the things that always amazed me, along with your extraordinary multiple parts on the guitar, was Mary's ability to do multiple part harmony. Did she have any formal training?

Les: No.

Steve: She had an incredible ear!

Les: Neither Mary or I read music.

Steve: No!

Les: Although we lost her (as we played), she always had the ability to hear the music, that gift. I'd say, "I want to do this in five parts." She'd say, "OK." I'd ask if she was sure and she would say, "Yes, yes, I'm sure." I'd play a fifth part entirely different on the guitar than what she would sing. So (on) my guitar parts, we would always share them because if she sang a fifth part, I'd play

Les and
Mary
in their
home
studio

Les Paul Archives

a fifth part cause you're not going to waste a track. So when Mary was singing I would be playing. Fifth, fourth, third; she had the ability to do that. I was very confident she was going to do exactly what we'd rehearsed, then I'd go out there and ad lib crazy things, and that gave it spontaneity. The surprise.

Johnnie: Did she play before you met?

Les: Very little. In fact, it was in Waukesha, Wisconsin. My brother and father opened a little tavern, the Club 400. They asked if I'd come back. I went there and brought Mary along because we were going to get married. I said to my brother, "Did you get a bass player, guitar player for me? A trio?" He said, "I figured you could tap your foot loud enough. That will do." I said, "No, no, I need a guitar player." We couldn't find one. We found a bass player but couldn't find a guitar player. So I looked at Mary and she said, "Don't look at me, don't look at me!" She said, "I don't know the chords or anything!" I said, "We'll play something you do know." I didn't care if it was "The Eyes of Texas Are Upon You." I told her I didn't care what it was. We could sing "Back In the Saddle Again." She used to sing with Gene Autry. She agreed and reluctantly got up there, and we wrote on coasters, the lyrics. She didn't know the lyrics and she didn't know the chord changes. She only knew a couple of chords on the guitar. But she'd say "What are you doing?" Right on the stage. We rehearsed, and the people loved it. They don't mind if you rehearse, they don't mind if you miss a note.

Johnnie: Because you're human.

Les: Exactly! If I can, after the news, if you will let me, I'll tell you how I learned the third change on the guitar. It's a fabulous little story.

Steve: You don't mind staying?

Johnnie: At least for that story.

Les: I'm hooked! Like all people listening to you. I know that they're hooked on you.

Steve: Oh! He said that just the way we wrote it!

Les: You know that don't you? I bet you have people out there that are so hooked on you that they hang onto every word.

Steve: As we were talking during one of the breaks, the overnight audience is a very special audience. You develop closeness with your listeners that just doesn't exist other times of the day.

Les: They're busy, but at night they can hang onto every word.

Johnnie: And we've got great faces for radio! Theater of the mind. (*laughter*)

Three-o'clock hour, December 3, 1996

Steve: Let me say thank you again to the guy who's sitting in the studio with us, Les Paul, who put on an extraordinary show at the House of Blues tonight, and then was nice enough to come on over to the radio station and hang out with us. I think it's the goodies that Johnnie made that's keeping him in the studio.

Les: It's sure helping, I'll tell you that. It's very good.

Johnnie: You know, Les, I don't think we got around to asking you, when was the last time you were in Chicago?

Les: It's been a LONNNNG time. I've been back here to do a NAMM (National Association of Music Merchants) show, or back here to do a guest appearance. In fact, the last one I did was a disc jockey thing on WIND. For a week to replace ... Howard ... Howard Miller.

Steve and Johnnie: That's right!

Steve: Well, we were both over at WIND, and that station changed formats before we got there.

Johnnie: Oh my, that's been 20 years now.

Steve: Before we got married.

Les: It was in the Wrigley Building then.

Steve: Well, they had moved when we were working there, about three blocks down the street.

Les: Yep, that was the last time I was here. Ralph Atlass called me in Jersey and said, "Would you come back, Les, and do a week as a disc jockey?" I said, "I don't know." Ralph said, "Yeah, come on back. We'll go to the racetrack and fool around." And so I took over the show. At that time I was doing the commercials for Robert Hall stores. Well, I had to do a commercial on the show for Carson Pirie Scott, and I got in trouble real quick. I wasn't on the air for an hour as a DJ for Howard when I said, "If you have a chance on Sunday go down to Carson Pirie Scott and you'll see truck after truck coming in Sunday at night. They'll be bringing in Robert Hall suits (*laughter*), and they're busy picking out the Robert Hall labels and puttin' in Carson Pirie Scott labels. Just don't get caught in the rain in that thing, you're dead!" Well, the manager of WIND called up and said, "You're fired. Right now. You are fired!" I said, "Well, I'm going over to Old Town. Time for me to get drunk!" I went over to Old Town, and they finally found me. Ralph Atlass had been going up and down the streets trying to find me. He had people running into every tavern trying to find me. Well, when they found me, Ralph called up and said, "Carson Pirie Scott, the president, called and said the commercial was great! He loved it!" I was hired back.

Steve: That's funny.

Johnnie: And unheard of!

Les: Yeah, and for me it was the start of pranks and they were not all good!

Steve: You know, we've talked a lot about your music. I think you could be called conservatively a "free spirit." Forget the music. Where did you get this whole free spirit attitude?

Les: Hmmm ... I don't know. Mary and I were driving back from Hershey Park, and I was driving up the New Jersey Turnpike, and I make a mistake and I get off and I'm going the wrong way. Mary said, "What are those lights?" I realized it was the Statue of Liberty. So I said, "Oh, that's a new nightclub. It just opened up over there. One of these days, remind me, I'll take you there." She said, "Oh, OK. I thought it was the Statue of Liberty." I said, "What month is it?" That was the end of it. At the first turn I can make and get back on the turnpike, I did, and didn't say anything to Mary.

And so, Rheingold Beer was having a big thing. We were at the Hampshire House discussing how they were going to launch this whole campaign. Capitol Records was there, a lot of women were there, and we said we're going to be working two or three days on this thing to iron it out. The president of Capitol said "Mary, why don't you take the women and show them around New York?" She said, "OK, I need to find out where the Statue of Liberty is." Someone said, "What do you mean?" Mary said, "You know, they move it around in the summer months." She said, "Les was telling me they move it, they tow it around, and I'd like to find out just where it is." Well, they looked at her like she was ... and Mary said, "Les! You didn't!" I said, "Yeah, yeah, I did." (*laughter*) I think I screwed that up! I think I'm getting tired!

Johnnie: Aw, but, you teased us. You said you'd tell us about

learning a particular chord.

Les: Oh yeah, back in Waukesha, I only knew a coupla chords on the guitar and this friend of mine, Harold, I said to him, "Hey, your old man's got a guitar." He said, "Yeah, but he don't want us to play it." I said, "When he goes to work, let's get it out and see if we can find the third change in 'Darktown Strutters Ball.'" I said, "I keep craving that chord and I don't know it." He said, "OK." So we went over there and his father was putting on his big boots to go into work at the food company where he cleaned the vats out. He had these big rubber boots on. All the way up to his hips. Hip boots, I guess they're called. So we said, "Can we play the guitar?" He said, "No! Don't touch it." We waited till he left. When he was gone and we saw him walking to work, we dashed into the closet and got that guitar out. We started looking for that chord. I'm playing the piano and Harold's trying to find it on the guitar. We're just determined we're going to find it. Then we see hip boots. The old man had come back. He took the guitar out of Harold's hands and said, "You're not going to get that chord. It's mine!" (*laughter*)

He tossed us out of the house. We were walking away from the house in our swim trunks when I said to Harold, "You don't think ... " We turned and looked at the house. There was smoke coming out of the chimney and it was July or August. We ran to the house and into the basement, and there he was, burning the guitar! He's says, "You're not going to get that chord now."

Johnnie: Gasp! That's weird!

Les: Yep, that's heavy. We just wanted that chord and he said, "You're not going to get it now." He burned the guitar.

Johnnie: So how many years before you got it!?

Les: Ha! Gene Autry came to town and he played it. I was in the front row, and every time Gene played that chord, I'd write it down. See my friend, Claude, had a flashlight. Gene would play it, and I put a dot down. Then I'd have to wait again. As I was writing those things down, Gene (stopped and) said, "Wait a minute. Every time I hit a particular chord, a light goes on in the theatre." He hit the chord, the light went on and I'm writing. Claude whispered, "Hey, I think we're on the air." I said, "What do you mean?" He said, "Gene Autry is talking about you!" Gene Autry said, "Hey, what are you doing down there?" I said, "I'm trying to learn that chord." So he called me up on the stage. I went up there, and he said, "Do you play?" I said, "A little." He handed me the guitar. I played it and of course, in my hometown, I'm going to get applause. That's how I got started. I played in my home town, in the theater, and Gene Autry asked me up on stage.

Johnnie: Did you ever perform with any other female singers for any length of time before Mary?

Les: Yeah. Kay Starr, Connie Boswell ...

Johnnie: Like a Doris Day?

Les: ... Dinah Shore. Ah! Doris Day. Absolutely.

Johnnie: I thought Doris Day!

Les: Sure, many a time. See, in the Armed Forces, that was my job. I was the third person in the Armed Forces with Meredith Wilson, and when I was inducted in the Army I was with Glenn Miller. He said, "Would you like to come with the Armed Forces?" I said, "Sure! I'd love to." He said, "You can live right there in Hollywood." Of all things, I lived on the same street, just down the street. Actually, up the street. I could kick off the brake and coast to work. A block away! In the Armed Forces my job was to play for Dinah Shore, Kate Smith, for the Andrews Sisters. W.C. Fields! In fact, I made the only records of W.C. Fields, period! The only recordings. I played guitar and piano.

Johnnie: Was he a son of a gun?

Les: Oh, he was funny. A funny, funny guy. We did these army shows, you know. They were so great because he would come in bombed with a coat on. A long overcoat. We wondered why he had an overcoat on.

Johnnie: In L.A.!

Les: Yeah, in L.A.! He had a saw underneath!! When he was on with Edgar Bergen and Charlie McCarthy (Bergen's wooden dummy), he grabbed Charlie McCarthy by the neck and he pulled out the saw. And I tell you, Edgar Bergen had no sense of humor!

Johnnie: You didn't mess with Charlie!

Les: Not with a saw! Oh, W.C. Fields was a funny, funny man! The Armed Forces was so interesting because I couldn't get to meet all these people that walked up to the microphone. Groucho Marx, all the great, great people. Gary Cooper. So I had an idea. I didn't say anything to Meredith Wilson. I just took the guitar pick and I threw it out by the mic, and Jack Benny came walking out looking at his script. He looked down, sees something shiny, and bent down and picked it up. What would you do if you saw something shiny, picked it up and realized it was a guitar pick? You'd look at the guitar player, right? He did. He came over to me and said, "Is this yours?" I said, "Yeah," and I started talking to Jack Benny. I told him how much I enjoyed his show and wanted to meet him for so long.

Meredith kept saying, "Everybody who walks in here talks to Les first! What the hell does he got going on?" So Meredith comes out one time and sees something shiny and picks up my pick and walks it over to me. When it happened again and he brought it over to me, I said, "Meredith, how am I going to get to meet these people if you keep picking up my pick?" He said, "Is that what you're doing?" I said, "Yeah!" He said, "Throw the pick out. I don't know this guy either!" That's how I was fishing to get the guys to come over and talk to me!

Johnnie: That's a great bit!

Steve: I'll have to remember that one.

Johnnie: Hey, you could meet the girls that way, too.

Les: I don't know if that works for the girls. But I did work for the Dinah Shores, for the Kate Smiths. One time I was late for Kate Smith. She said, "Where is that character?" She was cussing me out! I hear her and I realize, "Oh my goodness, am I gonna catch hell from her!" So I went to a candy machine and I bought four candy bars. When I saw her, I said, "Gee, I'm sorry I'm late, Kate, but I was looking all over for some candy bars for you." She softened and said, "How did you know I was looking for something to eat?"

Johnnie: You're one smart guy! I'm taking notes.

Les: I played for so many, and it was wonderful.

Steve: Les, are you ever going to write the book?

Les: I'm writing one. You were talking about Dillinger and Al Capone.

Johnnie: Yes, in the commercial for Magazine Memories.

Steve: You would love this place. They have magazines that go back to the 1800s.

Les: Well, I happened to play for the Touhy Gang. I was here when Dillinger was killed. I happened to play for Capone. So I've had some wonderful experiences in my time in Chicago.

Johnnie: Strange experiences.

Les: Well, they were.

Johnnie: If Capone asked you, would you show up?

Les: Oh yes, yes. I got out and went to California. Not so with my bass player, who ended up being my brother-in-law. He's now gone. Wally lived over here on Halsted, he was from Chicago. He was a dear, dear friend. Capone and his brother, I guess it was Ralph, loved Wally and wouldn't let him go. So he went down and volunteered so he could get out. He said, "I want to get out and away from here." They wanted him to stay.

Johnnie: Have you ever played for a president of the United States?

Les: Many. Yeah, the first one was in 1939. I played for Franklin D. Roosevelt. Then he asked us to go down to the basement to the bar to play for him privately. It was an awesome experience.

Johnnie: I bet your knees were knocking though! That's some heavy stuff.

Les: That was the most dramatic walk. He had no help, and he hobbled his way up to the stage and then he spoke and electrified everybody. He was something else.

Steve: Who's the most impressive person you've ever met?

Les: Hmmm ... boy ... probably Bing Crosby.

Steve: Why?

Les: Well, mainly because I admired him so much. But I think the most lasting thing in my mind was when he said, "Les, why do the people like me so much?" He never knew. He said, "I don't have anything." I said, "Well, God gave you a great voice and you know what to do with it." He said nothing. I don't think he ever knew. Great, great talents don't know.

Steve: We've had a dozen calls from people who missed you at the House of Blues. Are you going to play anywhere else in the area?

Les: No. I don't think so. I think I'm going to retire.

(Authors' note: In a 2008 interview, reflecting on this House of Blues appearance, Les told us, "I was going to announce this was my last show. I was going to hang it up. The crowd, their reaction, stopped me from making that announcement, that night.")

I've got to stay busy though. If I don't stay busy, I'll dry up and blow away, and I don't want to do that. I've got to do something to keep going. I'm going to write the book. Maybe write a book on electronics for youngsters and technicians who want to know how I did what I did. Why did you do this, and why did you do that, and how did you come up with this idea? Technically, how are these things done. I think it would be a very interesting book.

Steve: Are you still going to perform at the club in New York?

Les: Probably.

Johnnie: That's your therapy.

Les: Yeah, it is, and that therapy you just don't want to let up on it. You just don't let up on it.

Johnnie: How many guitars have you invented? Just when we think we've asked everything, apparently people want to know how many guitars you've invented.

Les: Only the one. It was the solid body. The question was just asked off the air, why did I pick the wood I did to make the solid body guitar? It started out where I looked at the thing and said, "Should it be wood?" Let's start with the softest, and the hardest piece of material, which would be a railroad track. So, I strung a string on a railroad track, and took the earpiece from the telephone and put it under there. The steel guitar, the steel railroad track with the guitar string on it, was the most beautiful thing you could ever imagine. So, I ran to my mother and said, "I got it, I got it! It's a railroad track!" My mother said, "The day you see Gene Autry on a horse playing a railroad track!" (*laughter*) Shot down again! I said, "Don't tell me, Mother, don't tell me!" So she said, "You've got to go to wood." I went to wood, and I kept getting a harder piece of wood, more dense piece of wood, till I found out maple was the thing that really made the notes sustain. The whole idea is (to) not have the guitar top vibrating one way and the string doing something else. Then it's argumentative, it's defeating its purpose. So, we eliminated that by having the sustain as close to a railroad track. That's why the Les Paul guitar is as heavy as it is. But, that's why it gets out there and barks at you.

Steve: Yeah. Yeah, does it.

Les: It's a trade off.

Johnnie: You had something on your guitar. When we walked into the House of Blues tonight, Steve said, "Whoa! Les has a

Bigsby on his guitar!"

Les: Ha-ha! Do you have one on your guitar?

Steve: Yeah. Most of the Les Paul guitars you see don't have a Bigsby on them.

Les: The first one I made was in Springfield, Missouri, out of coat hanger. It was the dumbest, most ridiculous thing I could ever contrive in my life. But it worked. I kept updating it and making it better and better, then finally one day (Paul) Bigsby came into my backyard with Leo Fender. Bigsby said, "What're you going to do with that thing?" I said, "I don't know, it's kind of a dog." And he made one, and that's where the Bigsby came from.

Johnnie: That answers the question I had the other day! "Who is this Bigsby character?"

Les: The odd part about it is there was one prior to that. It was also kind of a bow wow, but it worked. So several had tried it and it didn't quite fit the needs. Finally, this one came along with Bigsby and that one did. Of course, they've made some better, but they've made them with some handicaps like you break a string and you're there for an hour to get this thing apart. So the Bigsby became very popular, and (still) is.

Johnnie: Ha! I guess we should have a jargon alert for those women, those people who don't live with a guitar player.

Les: Well, I'm uncomfortable because I know this whole night is so far away from a lot of people and the world that they are in, this is not very interesting.

Johnnie: Are you kidding?

Les: Although the guitar is a very popular instrument.

Johnnie: If only you knew the lives you have touched in so many different ways.

Steve: If you knew the people who called us earlier in the week and said they would be taping the conversation, you'd

be surprised. In fact, you've got a lot of fans in Chicago. I know we've got to let you get some rest, but people want to know, are there any new albums coming out? When we last talked, you mentioned a three-album set. One was going to be jazz, one country and one was going to be rock.

Les: It didn't materialize. I've got another idea, and it's a crazy idea, but I can't tell you about it because I've got to walk over to Sony with it. Sony has already approached me about doing my life. To record my life. That kind of thing.

Steve: Please do that.

Les: Yeah, they want me to record it chronologically by year. I've got another idea I want to throw at them. If I can play. Tell anybody out there that plays the guitar, "Don't get arthritis!"

Johnnie: Yeah.

Les: I was listening to your commercials, and a lot of the stations I listen to, they have all this taped. I don't know how many people know that you do these commercials, 99 percent of them, live. I'm watching you do them. Why don't you tape the commercials?

Johnnie: They don't want us to. The sponsors pay for us to do the commercials live. That makes us different.

Steve: They want it live, so if we have a comment to make, we can.

Johnnie: If we go off on a tangent, that's fine, too. Something extra for them. Oooo, two minutes instead of one.

Les: Isn't that interesting.

Steve: Speaking of which, when I was doing the Lou Malnati's pizza, Lou-to-Go commercial I thought, you like Chicago pizza don't you?

Les: Sure!

Steve: Well, we're going to send you a Lou Malnati's pizza. Russ, you'll love this, too!

Les: Ha-ha!

Steve: We should mention that Les Paul's son, Russ, has been here over in the corner all night. He's been so nice, documenting this night on video.

Johnnie: Well, Russ was just a little bitty boy when he was last in Chicago.

Steve: I've got to tell you; you have one proud son. I will never forget the phone call I got from Russ when it was announced that Les was being inducted into the Inventors Hall of Fame. Russ was so excited! He was like a kid in a candy store! His dad was going into the Inventors Hall of Fame!

Les: Isn't that something.

Steve: Les, we would keep you here forever!

Johnnie: Ha! Then we'd have to put him on the payroll.

Les: I'm going to collapse. I'm going back to the hotel and collapse.

Steve: When do you go back to New Jersey?

Les: Tomorrow afternoon. Maybe three or four o'clock.

Steve: Can I offer one suggestion? Joe, are you taking them back to the hotel?

Les: Yeah.

Steve: If you've got five minutes, let Joe drive you north on Michigan Avenue and look at the lights. The Christmas lights are just beautiful.

Les: You mean the decorations?

Johnnie: Yes, and for anyone who happens to be downtown this afternoon and they see a crowd gathered around The Chicago Theatre, that will be Les. Russ has every intention of getting you in front of the theatre because you used to perform there. The theatre is still going.

Les: Really?

Les Paul poses in WGN's Studio A.

Paula Cooper

Johnnie: Yes, they just got a new sign put up.

Steve: In fact, this is the first time, because the old sign had some electrical problems, this is the first time they have remade one of those old signs. They actually duplicated the old Chicago Theatre sign. They just put it up last week.

Johnnie: It'll bring back some memories.

Les: Really! We have pictures of it when we were there performing.

Johnnie: Well, Russ has every intention of documenting you back in front of it.

Les: You know what I would like to leave saying? With all the cities I've been to all around the world, if I could choose any place to live, Chicago has been my number one wish. If I could live anywhere, I would live in Chicago because of the people.

Steve: How nice.

Les: Yeah, I can't tell you anything other than the Midwest has its own little magic. Of course, I came from here. Mary would say, "Why are they like that?" I said, "Let's go back and find out!" She said it so many times: If she could live anywhere it would be in the Midwest. It's something about you people.

Steve: Well, when are you moving back?

Les: Ha-ha! At the House of Blues there were a lot of people from L.A., and I'd say, "Wait till you get to Chicago." They'd say, "Better than L.A.?" I'd say, "Absolutely!" Absolutely. I don't know what the magic is. We talk to you on the phone and I can tell it. You've been throwing all kinds of compliments to me and my career. I just want to say the people here are so different. When you go to Brooklyn, boy, you know you're in Brooklyn. (*laughter*) There's nothing wrong with Brooklyn, it's just different. You win us over.

Johnnie: You take care of yourself.

Les: I will.

Steve: Thank you for making this a very special night.

Johnnie: You made our year!

Les: Are you kidding?

Steve: Anytime you get a chance to come back, you have an open door invitation.

Johnnie: Absolutely! Anytime you're up in the middle of the night and stumble across us on the radio, call us up and tell us, "You're comin' in loud and clear!"

Les: Sometimes Canada comes in over you!

Johnnie: Ah, I know.

Steve: We're going to get you that GE Super Radio.∗

Johnnie: It's boxed up. I didn't want him to take it back in his luggage. Do you travel with your guitars? Do you take them on the plane with you?

Les: Yeah, I wouldn't dare let them go. If they go through customs, the guy opens it up and sees a Les Paul and his eyes light up. Then he looks up and sees Les Paul. That guitar would be gone!

Johnnie: I bet. Oh Les, you've been so generous with your time. We can't thank you enough. Look at that grin!

Les: Thank you, too. I'll go down and dig those lights now. Thank you.

Les with his son Russ, *LEFT*, *Paula Cooper and Joe Cooper*

Paula Cooper

Authors' note: In June of 1997, we sent Les a C.Crane radio so that he could hear WGN more clearly late at night. C.Crane radios are known for their ability to pull in far away stations. During our next conversation, we asked him whether he had listened to his new radio. "No," he said. "I took it out of the box and took it apart. I wanted to see what made it work." That was our Les.

Authors' note: We have to share a nice postscript to our in-studio interview with Les. When he and Russ returned home to Mahwah, Les wasted no time firing a two-page fax recapping his visit with us. The first page was a thank you with the proclamation that WGN was now preset as a local station on his radio.

Les Paul

78 DEERHAVEN ROAD
MAHWAH, NEW JERSEY

To Steve + Johnnie
my Favorite Duo
Guitar + accordion —
thanks for the Kind words
Love you
miss you — and —
THE GREAT MIDWEST

_____

The Radio — WGN — is now a
Local thank you
Hi PAULA.   Les + Russ

The second page was a rundown of the events of the evening, complete with comments on the House of Blues, Joe and Paula Cooper, Johnnie's homemade cake, and our show. Les also thanks the man in the sky for getting us together, and includes a reference to how he was going to be looking for a therapist while wearing suction cups so he could pick up WGN. Makes perfect sense to us!

House Of Blues – (Les) – Why don't you
do a phone interview –
    no. I'd rather go to WGN – eye to eye.
Joe escorts us to Paula – outside on the side-
walk – next – Big dish of Johnnie cake – and
Steve & Johnnie – live – not on tape –
    Thank God – He didn't break for lunch –
He got us together – What a super night –
Am forever grateful –
    I'll be looking tomorrow for a thero – just
With suction cups – on my chest to pick up WGN
720 ᴬᴹ
        Love ya !
        /Keep Pickin'! Steve
        /Keep cookin. Johnnie
        Les

Steve holds the black Les Paul Custom guitar that was his Christmas 1996 surprise from Johnnie (and Les).

The Les Paul Surprise

Johnnie: The overnight of December 2 into December 3, 1996, was a big night for us. We had been talking to Les on the phone for five years, and finally, FINALLY, we were going to get to meet him and spend some time with him. Since it was near Christmas, it was the perfect time for me to get Steve the Les Paul guitar he had always wanted. I went to The Guitar Works store in Evanston, Illinois, and looked at two: a Gold Top and a black Custom. The gold was flashy and I'd seen it often in pictures, but the black looked like the one Steve would pick for himself. (I got lucky! He has said many times that if he'd gone shopping for a Les Paul guitar, this is the very one he would have purchased.)

When I bought it, I told Terry Straker, the owner of the store, what I planned to do. Not only would I be surprising Steve with a Les Paul guitar, but since Les was going to be in our studio, I was going to have him autograph it to Steve. Terry prepped the back of the guitar for a signature, and I bought a gold metallic paint pen. Then, I arranged to have the guitar and pen waiting at the station for Les to sign his autograph.

After Les spent three hours with us in the studio, our producer, Paula Cooper, snuck him into the WGN Radio sales office to see the guitar and sign it. Paint pens can be a little tricky to write with, and Paula was wise to give Les a stack of paper to practice on to be sure he could sign the guitar without a problem.

One of the autographs he tossed into the wastepaper basket

The paint pen practice letter that Les threw into the wastebasket. Paula Cooper smoothed it out and framed it for Steve.

became a Christmas present for Steve. Paula pulled it out of the trash and framed it. Of course, this was a present I had to make sure Steve didn't open until he had opened the guitar. To this day, we're so happy she had the foresight to come up with this gift idea. It looked great and, while the guitar isn't out and on display everyday, the framed autograph hangs on our wall as a reminder of the terrific night we'd spent with Les.

When the guitar was signed and Les had bundled up for the cold Chicago night, he said his goodbyes to Paula and our newsman, Dick Sutliff. He left the station with his son, Russ, Paula's brother, Joe, and our overnight engineer, Aubrey Mumpower. Later, Aubrey told us a wonderful story about two young guys, fans, who had driven down from Milwaukee and had been standing in the lobby for hours waiting with their guitars for a chance to meet Les. The lobby security guard called back to the engineering department and told Aubrey about the guys just hanging around, waiting. Aubrey went to the lobby and met the guys and decided to bring them into the station's break room. He made no promises that the two would meet Les, but by being in the studio area at least they would be able to hear the interview.

When Les was ready to leave the building, Aubrey walked him by the break room on the chance that Les could speak to them briefly and sign an autograph. True to his nature, when Les heard they'd driven so far and waited so long, of course he stopped. One of the guys took out his guitar and asked Les if he would sign it. Les was truly honored that they would wait so long for this brief encounter and eagerly agreed to sign the guitar. Aubrey said the other young man was laying back with his guitar still in the case. Les asked if he wanted his guitar signed, and the guy said, "It's not a Les Paul." Les said, "Let me see it." After he signed his name, he handed the guitar back to the wide-eyed fan and said, "Here. Now you have a Les Paul."

When I finally had a chance to see Les's autograph on Steve's new guitar, I wasn't sure I'd be able to keep it a secret for three loooonnnng weeks! But I did. In fact, I was downright sneaky. Christmas morning came and went with the opening of presents, but we had a tradition of always saving a few presents for later in the evening or even the next day. When afternoon rolled around and we were waiting for family to join us for Christmas dinner, I suggested we open another gift or two. Steve opened the first gift, which was a black and white leather guitar strap. He really liked it and jokingly said, "Since it doesn't match any of my guitars, I may have to get a new one ... hee-hee."

That was my cue. I walked out of the living room, picked up the guitar case that I had hidden in another room, and said, "Maybe this will work." He was stunned. In fact, he was so surprised I had to coax him to open the case. When he flipped back the hot pink, satin material that was draped over the guitar in its case, he was trembling. Steve just gazed, speechless, at the gorgeous, shiny, black Les Paul Custom guitar. He pulled it out of the case to put the new matching strap on it, all the while saying, "How did you do this? I had no idea! How did you keep this a secret?"

Then he flipped the guitar over and saw the inscription and autograph from Les. The one thing we both wanted to do at that moment was call Les. We were thrilled when he picked up the phone after a few rings to hear both of us wishing him a Merry Christmas. Les wanted to hear a play-by-play of how the guitar was presented. After hearing the details, Les said that he had only signed the removable plate on the back of the guitar in case someday Steve decided he didn't like him anymore. That way, he could remove the autographed plate and replace it with a plain one!

One of the best memories of a month that started off with an evening with Les Paul was actually talking to Les on Christmas Day to tell him about the surprise. While we gave him the play-by-play of the day leading up to the big surprise, Steve had the new guitar hanging round his neck and nestled in his arms. One week later, on our annual "Cheap Date Life After Dark New Year's Eve Party" broadcast, the Les Paul Custom made its on-air debut.

 A little more Les ...

> The audience, they're not professionals. They just love music. It isn't necessary to play over their heads to be admired. — Les Paul

Les signed Steve's new, black Les Paul guitar with this note: "Steve - you have a couple of new friends - Les Paul guitar + mercy, me." — Les Paul

Chris Lentz

Charlie Daniels and Les Paul
on stage at the Iridium

memories from ...

Charlie Daniels

oing Steve and Johnnie's radio show more closely re-sembled dropping by for a visit with friends than an in-terview stop. The atmosphere was totally laid back, the conversation free-flowing and unscripted, and Johnnie was apt to have brought along some of her fabulous homemade goodies to snack on. All in all, it was a very enjoyable experience.

I didn't realize until my second visit that Steve was a guitar player, which opened up a whole new topic of conversation for the two of us. As guitar players will, we started discussing our favorite guitars, and being the dyed-in-the-wool Les Paul man I am, the conversation drifted around to the man himself and the amazing accomplishments he had made in music and electronics.

Right about then, Steve pulled one on me that I would nev-er forget. It will always be one of my favorite moments in radio. We took some phone calls, and much to my amazement, I was speak-ing to Les Paul!

I must have come off as somewhat flabbergasted, but you have to realize that for me, speaking to the great Les Paul was tantamount to an airplane pilot being able to speak to one of the Wright Brothers. This man had designed and developed the best electric guitar in the world, the one that I have played since I got to the point of affording one, and here I was actually having a conversation with him.

And it didn't end there. Les invited me to come by the Iridium Club in New York the next time I was in town and sit in with him.

You have to understand that there are thousands of guitar players around the world who would trade parts of their anatomy to stand on the same stage with the legendary Les Paul. I took him up on the invitation and spent a whole set jamming with him, an experience that goes into the top drawer of my musical memories.

To say Steve and Johnnie are nice people is a total understatement, and their making it possible for me to meet and jam with Les Paul will always be very special to me.

I love you folks.

A Little More Les ...

When I got my first guitar, my fingers wouldn't go to the sixth string, so I took off the big E and played with just five strings. I was only six or seven. — Les Paul

*Charlie Daniels during one of
his visits with Steve and Johnnie
at WGN Radio*

a little more about ...

Charlie Daniels

"So, is this the guy who went down to Georgia to see the devil?" That was Les Paul's first phone greeting to Charlie Daniels one night when Charlie was in the studio with us.

Charlie Daniels' career is the stuff of legends. One of his first songs, "It Hurts Me," was recorded by Elvis Presley. He had his own recording success with hits such as "Uneasy Rider," "The South's Gonna Do It," "The Devil Went Down to Georgia," and many others. This Gold, Platinum and multi-Platinum, Grammy-, CMA- and ACM-winning "Long Haired Country Boy" member of the Grand Ole Opry has charted and continues to chart his own highly-celebrated path in music history. (We know that was a run-on sentence, but it's not nearly as long as we hope Charlie's career continues to run.)

In between his recording and touring schedules, Charlie even carved out enough time to record a Christmas story that became one of our annual features on WGN Radio. And when he heard about this book, Charlie's fingers quickly hit the computer to write about his time talking with Les Paul in our studio and jamming with him on stage at the Iridium. For that and many other things, we can't thank him enough.

Charlie, the next time we see you, the catfish is on us.

Steve and *Johnnie*

December 2, 1997

9

A Sketcher of Lester

One year after Les was first in studio with us

Steve: Speaking of guitars ... boy, you talk about synchronicity. Speak of guitars and who is on the phone? Les Paul. Les, how ya doing?

Les: Great!

Johnnie: Hello, Lester.

Steve: We've been missing you. We've been thinking about you.

Les: Well, I got your note and I want to thank you. You wished me a happy Turkey Day or …

Steve: Happy Thanksgiving.

Les: And you went to Indiana?

Johnnie: Yep, we were driving to Indiana and said, "Let's just call Les and wake him up to say hey."

Les: Aren't you nice. Well, what are you up to? You're talking about a Danelectro. You're talking about an old Sears guitar?

Steve: We came across this old picture from Christmas of 1959 when I got my first electric guitar, which was a Silvertone electric guitar.

Les: I know it well.

Steve: And some of them were made by Danelectro and Harmony and Kay. I'm trying to get an old Sears catalog to find out who manufactured it. I think it was Harmony.

Les: Can you describe it?

Steve with his new Silvertone electric guitar, Christmas 1959

Steve: It was a red single cutaway. Two pickups.

Les: What did the pickups look like?

Steve: The pickups were rather large pickups.

Les: Then they were those capsules like a Danelectro.

Steve: No, no.

Les: Then they probably weren't Dans.

Steve: It had a rather long pick guard that was white.

Les: Hmm..

Steve: My guess is it was a Harmony.

Les: Yes, Harmony. Those pickups were made by Gibson.

Steve: Really!?

Les: The Harmony pickups, yeah.

Johnnie: Well, changing the subject. You sound good.

Les: I feel good, Johnnie.

Johnnie: Are you just coming in from work?

Les: Yeah, we just got home and I said, "I'm going to call in and say howdy to you guys."

Johnnie: Well, how did your show go tonight?

Les: Oh, it went great. A lot of visitors ... I don't know all their names. The fella that does the drawings, the sketches. Very famous man. My goodness, what's his name?

Johnnie: New Yorker?

Les: Yeah. He was drawing, sketching out a portrait of me while I was playing.

Steve: Oh, that's nice.

Les: He's very famous and I didn't know him. I apologized because I didn't know of him.

Johnnie: Did he give you a copy of his sketch or is he going to do that?

Les: He's going to do that.

Johnnie: Nice.

Les: Oh my goodness is he great. Ah, I can't think of his name. I'll remember when I hang up! If you said it I would remember it.

Steve: By the way, Les, we're hunting around trying to find a new album we understand you're on with … Pat Martino?

Les: Yes, I'm on that one but, there's another one that just came out. They found a collection of 50 songs I recorded right there in Chicago from '35 to '47.

Steve: Really?

Les: It's called *The Les Paul Trio Plus*. It has Georgia White. Me, playing with her with my trio. There are six songs with her. With Bing … with so many.

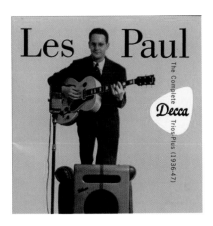

Johnnie: Wow! Who put this out, Les?

Les: Universal/Decca. It's on a Decca label. Decca was sold to MCA. MCA was sold to Universal. Universal called it Decca … again. They put the record out the 18th of November.

Johnnie: Whoa! I know what we're going to buy today!

Steve: We're going to go hunting for this.

Les: Well, I tell you what I'm going to do. I have a friend that found me a Sears and Roebuck catalog. He found the catalog and I found the guitar that I bought from there for $2.98 ... my first guitar from Sears and Roebuck in 1926.

Steve: Oh, boy.

Les: I know if I tell him you are looking for a '59 Sears catalog, he'll find it. I'll tell him we're looking for your guitar. We don't think it's a Danelectro. By the way, many guitar players had the Danelectro; they had a certain sound to them. A sound no other guitar has, and that raunchy sound was a big thing in the early '60s. All of the great guitar players around here, Chicago, L.A., they went to Sears and bought one of their dumb guitars. (*laughter*) Nat Daniel called me and said, "Les do you want to buy my company? I'm going to retire." We went down there with my manager and we looked at it. My manager said, "Les, let's go talk about it. Do you want to be running up and down aisles looking at the fellas doing their work? Do you want to spend your time doing that or do you want to go to a big company and they do all the work? They do the work and you just collect the royalties." I said, "I see your point." (*laughter*) Nat Daniel was a fine, smart man who knew how to take very little and do a lot with it.

Johnnie: Les, what were you playing on stage last night at the Club Iridium?

Les: I was playing my Les Paul Gibson. The same one I played last year there at the House of Blues.

Johnnie: You don't change around?

Les: No! They handed me a new one tonight. They brought it in, it's beautiful. I brought it home and I'll see if it's any good. Nah, I just stick with that old clunker.

Steve: Isn't the one you play the 1981 Heritage model?

Les: That is correct. Boy, you remember.

Johnnie: Les! He knows what you were WEARING that night. Come on!

Les: Well, Steve what are you doing? Are you playing?

Johnnie: All the time!

Steve: Yes, every day. I've written a couple of songs. In fact, you are going to get a tape in the mail in a couple of weeks. I decided I'm going to let you hear how bad I am.

Johnnie: He's written a great little Christmas tune. I rolled over in bed, and there he was with the guitar on his tummy, and I asked what he was doing. He said, "Waiting for the in-spiration." He got it and wrote a neat little tune. So I've de-cided there's room for all three of us.

Les: What's the title of your song?

Steve: The Christmas song is "Christmas from the Roots of Rock 'n' Roll." The other one I wrote is an instrumental.

Johnnie: I titled that.

Steve: Yeah, Johnnie titled that one "When We Were Young."

Johnnie: It's a bittersweet little number. I'm not prejudiced or anything, but I think it's really nice.

Les: No kidding. And you're not jealous?

Johnnie: No! And he would never touch the accordion! That's my terrain.

Les: You really play the accordion?

Johnnie: Ironically, I was going through today's mail and I got a Christmas card from the Dick Contino fan club. Did you know his club is huge?

Les: Is he still around?

Johnnie: Oh yes, he's still around and beloved. Hey, do you have a fan club?

Les Paul and Mary Ford are surrounded in 1952 by fans at The Chicago Theatre who thought they would make a great First Couple.

Les Paul Foundation

Les: Yeah.

Johnnie: Why aren't we president and vice president?

Les: Ha! In fact, our first fan club, Mary and I, was right there in Chicago. When we played The Chicago Theatre, they were there marching around with their signs. It was Dwayne Wadsworth. He now lives out in California. I think he's a bank president. He was just a little kid. Oh my goodness, the memories of the fan club.

Steve: Hmmm, nice memories.

Les: By the way, I just talked to my dear friend who just retired ... Art Van Damme. He was from right there in Chicago.

Steve: Oh yes, a legendary musician.

Les: A great, great accordion player.

Steve: The Art Van Damme Quintet.

Les: Yeah, they were over at NBC. Is NBC still in the Merchandise Mart?

Steve: No, they moved out of the Merchandise Mart and have their own tower east of the Tribune Tower. Just off Michigan Avenue.

Les: Oh, really?

Johnnie: Yep, they filled in some land behind the Trib Tower.

The Merchandise Mart is all decked out in red and green lights for Christmas. The city looks beautiful, Les.

Les: Oh boy, I remember the last time I was there, I drove up and down Michigan Avenue and looked at all the lights.

Johnnie: That's right!

Steve: Do you realize that was one year ago this week?

Les: I didn't realize that.

Steve: Well, when are we going to get you back in Chicago?

Les: They called me yesterday. Robin and Kevin called and asked if I would play the House of Blues, and pick the one I want to go to. I said, "When I get better, when I get to playing better. I'll call you, don't call me." Tonight was one of our best nights and I almost … well, I was thinking about it. So one of these days, Lord willing, I'll go back and play again. I'm playing every Monday.

Johnnie: Two shows!

Les: Two shows whether I feel good or not. Actually, my hands are getting better.

Steve: Wonderful!

Les: The arthritis. The fingers are … frozen. They don't move, and so no fingers on either hand move. The doctor says, "Les, you can't play with fingers that don't move." I said, "I'll figure out a way to do it." I've figured out a way like Count Basie did playing piano. When he played the piano, he only used two fingers, and he played so great.

Johnnie: I didn't know that.

Les: He played the right notes.

Steve: There was a picture I saw in a Guitar Player magazine, and it was your right hand with a pick you have specially taped so you could hold it a little easier.

Les: Oh, I just put, you know what you put in the bathtub so you don't slip and fall down? Well, I got some of that adhesive, 3M ad-

An example of one of Les's picks on which he glued sandpaper to make it easier to hold. The "H" likely stands for "heavy," signifying the thickness of the pick, and allowing Les to quickly distinguish it from medium- and light-weight picks.

www.tinaspicks.com

hesive and sandpaper. It's what you glue onto your woodworking sanding tools. I just get the right grade of sandpaper and I put it on there, and when the sand falls off I put another piece on there.

Johnnie: I know you don't like to hear it, but you really are an inspiration. I know it makes you crazy to hear that. But for people waking up this hour and moaning because they've got to get up and go to work, folks, bound out of bed! Les did and he's just a kid of 82.

Les: Well, you have to have support. I have a honey here that pets my head and sympathizes with my problems. Actually, you have to challenge it. If you don't, you'll say, "This has got me and I'm going to give up." Giving up is easy.

Steve: Are you doing any more recording? I mentioned this album with Pat Martino.

Les: Well, I had a tough time playing anything on that album. I'm playing a lot better now. The reason is when the pain leaves and you don't have movement, at least you know where you can go. I'm having a lot of fun with it. You know the big guys come in and they have no mercy. They come in to beat me up and it's fun, 'cause I have to be just stupid enough to go in there and battle back.

Steve: You know Les, we've had a couple of people email us and ask if there was ever a Mary Ford guitar? A version of the

Les Paul guitar called the Mary Ford model?

Les: No. There never was.

Johnnie: Put that to rest. We did a show last week on collectible guitars and it never ceases to amaze me the thing people have stashed under their beds. They've got treasures.

Steve: Other than the "log," what's the oldest guitar you have?

Les: The oldest one I've got is the original one I gave away to a fella outside of Chicago named Dick Moran. When I left my job at WJJD and I was going to New York, I said, "Here, I'm leaving. From these six guitars, pick out the one you like." He picked one out and I just handed it to him. I handed him my first Gibson L5.

Steve: Wow!

Les: Well, that's worth about a half million bucks right now without my name on it. This one had "Rhubarb Red" on it. Unfortunately, Dick Moran was dying, and he said to his mother, "I know I'm dying and I have a guitar under the bed that rightfully belongs to the fella that gave it to me. Call Les Paul." They couldn't find me, so they sent a letter to Fat Tuesdays where I used to play. The letter ended up in my guitar case. It fell out one night and I saw it floating to the floor, and I picked it up and read it. When I was done, I called a little town outside of Chicago heading up toward Crystal Lake. When I called this 90-year-old lady, his mother, she said she had the guitar and a pair of shoes I had given him. She asked me to describe the guitar and prove it was rightfully mine. I did, and the shoes fit. I got the guitar back, and it had been under his bed. He put it under the bed when I gave it to him and never used it. Like I said, it is worth a fortune.

Johnnie: You mentioned being "Rhubarb Red" here in Chicago. Well, Steve has come up with the name for his next rock group.

Les: What is it?

Johnnie: Rhubarb's Kids.

Les: Ha-ha! You're kidding!

Johnnie: **Really, he announced it the other night and asked if anyone knew why, and right away the phone lines were jammed. They knew.**

Steve: **Actually, Rhubarb's Children**

Les: Wow ... wow. There was a little kid at the show tonight who'd flown in from England with his father. Come here just to see Les Paul. He was down in the front row, little freckled-face kid, and he was playing air guitar. He doesn't have a guitar, he's playing along with me on his imaginary guitar. He was playing what I was playing. He was fingering it the same way. He was picking just like me, and this little rotten kid is down there and I can see he's playing better that I am! (*laughter*) So I stopped the show and said, "What's this rotten little kid doing down here playing my licks?" We got him up on stage with me, and I asked if he had a guitar and he said, "Yes sir, a Les Paul guitar is what I've got!" I had some pictures taken with him 'cause I may never find a kid as much like me as that little guy was. We took pictures and we'll get them to him when he's back in England.

Johnnie: **That's so nice. You know, Les, we started out the show talking about the artist that was at the show tonight, and we may have his name.**

Steve: **Lou, thanks for holding on. You have an idea who the artist might be?**

Lou: Yes, LeRoy Neiman.

Les: That's who it was!

Steve: **It was LeRoy Neiman?**

Les: Yeah, with the mustache! I was bustin' his chops!

Johnnie: **Lou, thanks for holding on! You're half-smart.**

Lou: Just half-smart at this hour of the morning.

Johnnie: **Les, you have to go get your rest!**

Les: I'm going to get my rest, I just wanted to say "Hi."

Steve: Hey, can we talk to you again on New Year's Eve?

Les: Sure, sure … we did last year.

Steve: That's right, we had you on with Duane Eddy. Thank you, Les.

Les: Thank you! (*music out*)

IRIDIUM NY. Dec 1 '97   Les Paul

Courtesy LeRoy Neiman Foundation

LeRoy Neiman sketched Les as he played at the Iridium Jazz Club in Manhattan on December 1, 1997.

Holli Brown/Madame Brown Photography

Doyle Dykes and Les Paul on stage at the Iridium

memories from ...

Doyle Dykes

"Bye Bye Blues"... You can't listen to that song without a smile! Honestly, I don't ever remember not knowing who Les Paul was. My dad was spinning Les Paul and Mary Ford records at our home in Jacksonville, Florida, from the time I was an infant until I left home at 18. Dad, or "Bubba," as everyone called him, was a fine guitarist and was heavily influenced by Les Paul's style. He even had a first-issue 1952 Gibson Les Paul Gold Top guitar. Our family would be asked to sing at various churches when I was very young, and from the age of two to four years my parents would stand me up along with my brother on two folding chairs with my mom on one side, and my dad with his Les Paul Gold Top guitar on the other. Dad would kick off songs using Les's intros to "Bye Bye Blues" and "How High the Moon"! It was fantastic and the folks loved it. In a way, Les Paul went to church every Sunday with the Dykes family!

In the late '90s, I played with Chet Atkins on one of his weekly stints at Cafe Milano in Nashville. Chet told me how he got the idea from Les, who also had a weekly gig in New York City at the Iridium Club. It was one of the coolest ideas for such a legendary entertainer to do, as he could "keep up his chops" as well as keep in touch with his fans. It was then my quest to go up and see Les play in person, and I did on October 2, 2000.

I called my good friend Jon Chappell in New York, who is an avid writer and publisher and had known Les from doing interviews with him, and once even visited his home as they were shooting a video. I had never spent time in New York City, so Jon offered to accompany me. The idea dawned on me that I had never actually owned a Les Paul of my own, so we went to Sam Ash and I bought a used, black Les Paul 40th Anniversary in hopes that he would sign it, which he did. I still own that guitar. Also, I called Tom Doyle, whom I had met at the Chet Atkins Appreciation Society Convention. Tom was also a great guitarist and happened to be Les's sound engineer at the Iridium Club.

> *Oh my Lord! The thought of meeting my lifetime hero and then getting up to play with him was brain overload!*

When we got to the club, Tom immediately made his way over to our table and told me that he had told Les I was coming by, and that Les would probably ask me to get up and play a song or two. That's when I got nervous. Oh my Lord! The thought of meeting my lifetime hero and then getting up to play with him was brain overload!

Soon after we were seated, a young man and woman joined us at our table. They had overheard Tom Doyle call out my name. Well, the woman's name was Denise Rybicki, and she immediately called Steve and Johnnie on her cell phone, as she was their producer at that time on WGN. She happened to be visiting New York to see Les Paul. Right before her trip, Steve and Johnnie had mentioned my name for her to contact as a future guest on their show. I had previously met Steve and Johnnie backstage at the Grand Ole Opry when I was playing there.

Denise gave me her business card, and the rest is history with Steve and Johnnie. They have been like family to me all these years. In fact, they have been that way to my entire family as well. Even my daughter Haley got engaged on their show as I flew her boyfriend, Jake, out from Washington state so he could pop the question on live radio. Also, I have always related Steve and Johnnie with Les Paul in an extraordinary way, and they all hold a very special place in my heart.

The top three guitar legends whose music influenced me more than anyone else's were Les Paul, Chet Atkins and Merle Travis. I was so blessed and honored to have met all three of them. Chet was a quiet and more subdued Country Gentleman, and Merle was like your favorite uncle who happened to play the guitar, and overall, they were both unpretentious, yet confident. Les Paul, though, was quite different. He was an "in-your-face," shoulder-patting, jovial, spirit-lifting, grandfather-like man who almost made you forget that you were standing in the midst of music royalty! Les Paul changed so many things about music that we enjoy every day. He was truly a legendary guitarist, inventor, and entertainer in every respect. His multi-award winning achievements can only be eclipsed by his great personality and warmth. If you never met Les Paul, I believe that through this book, you will feel as though you had.

I went to see Les three times at the Iridium Club, and he asked me up to play every time. He chimed in on some things like "Bye, Bye Blues," or "It Don't Mean a Thing," but mostly he'd just let you play and acted like it was the best thing he'd ever heard. Although his son, Russ, gave me Les's phone number and address and said Les wanted me to come by, I never did. I suppose my shyness and respect overshadowed my opportunity. I remember calling a friend at a vintage guitar store in regards to a '50s Les Paul from my birth year. I figured I would go up one last time to see Les and ask him to sign a guitar that was more like my dad's. Les passed away that very day. Truthfully, the God-given experiences and memories — and of course the music — of Les Paul mean more to me than a hundred guitars.

There was a nationwide commercial where Les had been

listening to a young guitarist getting ready for a set in a club, and went up and asked if he could play his guitar. After Les completely blew the young man's mind, he asked Les his name and Les replied, "It's written on your guitar!" There's a lot behind the name, Les Paul.

Recently, I had my own show at the Iridium Club in Manhattan. Just seeing the amps that Les and his trio used and being in the room where he played once again was a humbling experience. That night, I talked about Les and played several of his songs, but there's one that I still love the most and feel exemplifies his life and work. To me this is the Les Paul Manifesto: "Bye, Bye Blues!"

A little more Les ...

" *Life doesn't owe you a damn thing, but you owe life everything, so get off your ass and do something with it before they put you under the dogwood tree. — Les Paul* "

2007 Gibson Les Paul Custom Shop 1959 Reissue (R9)

©Hans Westbeek

Doyle Dykes with Steve and Johnnie at WGN Radio

a little more about ...
Doyle Dykes

Forget Kevin Bacon, let's talk about Six Degrees of Les Paul. Let's start with the fact that Les Paul's Gold Top was Duane Eddy's first guitar. Then, let's cut to us standing on a sidewalk with Duane one hot afternoon in Nashville and him telling us about this incredible guitarist he had just performed with. Not only was this guy a great picker, but Duane felt he was a pretty amazing person and we would enjoy meeting him.

Next, we fade in to backstage at the Grand Ole Opry, where we finally got to meet this man. Unfortunately, more time would pass, but finally, thanks to our then-producer Denise Rybicki seeing him one night when he performed with Les at the Iridium, Doyle Dykes wound up on our show at WGN for the first of many appearances.

The final shot in this story is of us in the WGN studio telling Les that Doyle had just performed on our show, and Les instantly responding by telling us how much he really enjoyed Doyle's playing. Les's dear friend and Grammy-winning collaborator, Chet Atkins, once said of Doyle: "Doyle is one of the finest fingerpicking guitarists around. I sincerely admire him as a person and as a musician."

Six degrees, indeed. Six strings played so well that even the MASTERS compliment you — yeah!

As our friendship with Doyle has grown over the years, we've come to understand why this world-renowned guitarist's personality is often mentioned in the same conversations that applaud his playing.

Doyle is a man who "walks the walk." Not only should you listen to his music, but if the opportunity ever presents itself, you should get to know the man.

You'll really enjoy both!

Steve and *Johnnie*

A little more Les ...

> I have younger friends who don't work, and they aren't doing so well. My secret is to keep going. Keep working.
> — Les Paul

March 4, 1998

Another Les Paul Surprise

And an invention that changed the world

Steve: Our guest is a man known to play a little guitar, and he's invented a few things that we take for granted today. We're fortunate to call him a friend. How are you doing, Les Paul?

Les: Oh, Steve and Johnnie you make me feel ten feet tall.

Johnnie: Les, congratulations! You're the only guy we know with a stretch of highway named after him.

Les: Oh, well, it has its good side and bad side. I'm afraid everybody will be calling me to fix their tickets. *(laughter)*

Johnnie: I know collectors will!

Les: Yes, can you imagine?

Steve: For those who don't know, we have a copy of the Waukesha Freeman in front of us with a big picture of the stretch of highway named "Les Paul." That's a big deal! Congratulations.

Les: I am so proud. Thank you.

Johnnie: I have the front page of the Milwaukee Journal Sentinel with a big picture of you, and the headline reads "Les Paul Highway a High Note for Guitar Players."

Les: It's hard to imagine.

Eric A. Grosh

Johnnie: And now there's talk of the street signs being shaped like guitars.

Les: They're all pointed this way like you're going to play the G chord.

Johnnie: Cute.

Les: What if it was an accordion? (*laughter*) Are you practicing?

Johnnie: Are you, Steve?

Steve: Ha! Les, notice how she shifts the conversation.

Les: Are YOU, Johnnie?

Johnnie: I'm thinking of taking up the tambourine, it's much more respectable.

Les: You have to have a good ear for that.

Johnnie: Oh, never mind.

Les: Hey, how ya doing doll?

Johnnie: I'm good. How are YOU feeling?

Les: I'm feeling real good and so glad to be able to say that.

Johnnie: Did you work at the club Monday night?

Les: I sure did. Marcia Clark was there. Dick Hyman played the piano. Paul Shaffer from the Letterman show dropped in, a lot of people. We have fun.

Johnnie: And you're still doing two shows every Monday night at the Club Iridium?

Les: Yeah. You know we'd still love to see you guys down there. We miss you so much. My son, Russ, and I were talking about you guys the other day. We've got to get back to Chicago.

Johnnie: Yes! You have to come here and we'll drive up to Waukesha to drive on Les Paul Parkway.

Les: I know! That's the reason I'd go back to crank up the ol' car. Ha! I used to have a crank car, and guitar to go with it!

Steve: We'll come to the club.

Les: I'll fall off the stage if you do! So many come in and say they are avid listeners of yours and hear me on your show.

Johnnie: I'm not kidding. I literally have a box of newspaper clippings about your highway. You'd think we were the local station for Waukesha and Milwaukee. The listeners have been diligently clipping and calling their Congressmen saying, "Make that piece of road honor Les."

Les: Wow.

Johnnie: You were born in Waukesha, Wisconsin. Was it on St. Paul?

Les: Yes, St. Paul Avenue, and that's the highway that's going to be renamed. That was Richard Cook's idea and Ralph North's. They are some of the people that came up with the idea and, of course, I am honored.

Johnnie: Well, your career started there.

Les: It sure did.

Johnnie: That's where you first started playing music.

Les: Yes, I was a young kid and heard a sewer digger on his lunch hour playing a harmonica. I said, "My goodness, what is that?" I stared him out of it! He said, "Here kid, take it." My mother said, "Don't play that thing till I boil it!" So, I waited anxiously and when I got my hands on it I started playing. I told Mom, "I'm going to do something with this harmonica." She said, "You better get something to go with it." So, I tried a drum. Number one, Mother wouldn't let drums in the house. I tried a sax. I tried an accordion. She said, "Harmonica and accordion sound too much alike, and you've got that thing strapped on to your back. I don't like that." I thought, a piano! She said, "You won't find a piano everywhere you want to play." So I considered a banjo, and Mother said, "I don't think so." *(laughs)* Finally, it had to be the guitar. She agreed and we sent to Sears and Roebuck and I got my guitar. Oh, by the way, I have a guitar for you!

Steve: You do?

Les: Steve, yeah, I'm going to send you one of my original, first guitars that I ever had.

*The Sears and Roebuck guitar
that Les gave to Steve*

Steve: You're kidding!

Johnnie: He's kidding.

Les: I'm not kidding! I have it for you, and I was thinking, should I do that? Are you really going to try to practice on this thing?

Johnnie: Les, if you're not kidding, this man is going to have to be picked up off the floor.

Les: Pick him up, it will be sent this week. I'm just telling you, in Waukesha, Wisconsin, this was one of the first guitars that I ever got. I've been thinking about it all night long since I got a message you had called. I said, "What could I do for that guy? He plays guitar, he's got a Les Paul guitar."

Steve: Good grief, Les!

Les: Then I said, "I think I know what he'd like."

Steve: Wow!

Les: It's an old Sears and Roebuck guitar. I'm telling you if you try to play it, your hands will be bleeding.

Steve: Was it called Silvertone at that time?

Les: Yeah, Silvertone ... it's

a round hole acoustic guitar, and I pasted Gene Autry's picture inside it. (*laughs*) So, when I picked it up, I could see him in there.

Steve: Oh Les! I don't know what to say. I'm really touched. That's really sweet.

Les: I'm glad you like it. You'll like it when you get it.

(commercial break ends ... music up)

Steve: That's Les playing harmonica and playing guitar.

Johnnie: And singing!

Steve: Les, that's from a new CD called Les Paul: The Complete Decca Trios–Plus Recordings from 1936-1947. **I just picked up a copy for me and one for my brother. This is great! The last time we talked, you told us about it.**

Les: It was made right behind where you are in WGN Radio. Right there on the lake. They called me and asked me to come over and sing these songs. I said, "Oh boy, I've got a chance to make a commercial record for Decca records." I decided if I did the recording I wouldn't play country guitar. I'd use a pick. So on the record, I foolishly didn't use my fingers and play. It was my ego and wanting to show off. I figured I'd play the other way, with a pick.

Steve: And, there are some great recordings of you playing lead guitar in a way I'd never heard you before, backing the blues singer Georgia White. But you also play acoustic guitar backing her

Les: Yes. That's different now — that fit. That fit that type of music.

Johnnie: Back to what we just heard, I figure you were in your early 20s.

Les: No, no.

Johnnie: Really?

Les: Wait, you can count! I was in my early 20s.

Johnnie: You know what I like about that particular cut? I hear your Wisconsin roots coming through. There was a little polka in that tune.

Les: Oh yeah! I would listen to polkas. Speaking of polkas, I first met Lawrence Welk at the Waukesha Beach. I would walk the streetcar line to the Waukesha Beach and peek through a trestle-type fence. The band would have their backs to me. I was nine or 10 years old when I would hike out there. It was a nine-mile hike, and I'd get there and peek through the lattice work and watch the piano player, or the back of a guitar player. I would see Hal Kemp, Guy Lombardo, and Lawrence Welk. Ted Fio Rito had two guitars. You could imagine how excited I was with that. If I couldn't bum a ride back I'd walk the nine miles back, in the night. Of course, I wasn't old enough to get in, but I loved peeking through the fence and watching. That's where I heard and learned about the polkas and all different kinds of music.

Johnnie: When you played harmonica with your guitar, did you have to come up with something that allowed you to free up your two hands? Did you figure out the doohickey that you could hang a harmonica on?

Les: Playing both is where the name "Rhubarb Red" came from. I admired a man named "Pie Plate Pete," and he played both the harmonica and the guitar. So I was copying him. He played fingerstyle and I had to learn to play fingerstyle. I'd take a rubber band and break the big end off a comb and use that for a pick. Tie the rubber band around my finger with the end of a comb. If I got a blister on my fingers it really worked so I could keep playing. The first pick I got in Waukesha, there wasn't any music store, so I took the last ivory note off the player piano and used that as a pick, too.

Steve: Didn't you also develop a harmonica holder?

Les: Yes, yes, out of a coat hanger.

Johnnie: You were one innovative guy.

Les: No, actually my brother worked for a cleaning company and we had a million coat hangers around! (*laughter*) You talk about the smartest way to hold that harmonica up. I just drilled a hole in each

Les Paul Foundation

end of the harmonica and made the coat hanger so it was a spring-type holder around my neck. I would go out, in fact, the first job I got was in Racine, Wisconsin, playing guitar and harmonica. I couldn't have been more than 10 or 12 years old. I remember the first radio station I ever sang on was at Marquette University in Milwaukee. I made a deal with them. I would sing two songs if they would get my teeth cleaned! (*laughter*) The engineer there had a crystal set and he worked on the cat's whisker till he had the station coming in strong. When it did, I sat on the end of a bed and sang my two songs. First he asked me to pound on the mic, an old carbon microphone. I did, then I sang, "Don't Ever Marry an Old Man," and "Don't Send My Boy to Prison." I'd showed my mother how to record it on a machine I had built. I still have it somewhere. The first recording of me! Isn't that something?

Johnnie: Amazing. Can you stay a little longer, Les? We'll come right back.

Les: Sure!

(out of a commercial break)

Steve: If I sound a little befuddled it's because we're still stunned. Les, I can't believe you're really going to send me your first guitar.

Les: Now it's not the very first, but one of the first. I don't have the first one anymore.

Johnnie: I had to give Steve medication during the break.

Les: Ha! This is old. You realize it is from the '20s.

Johnnie: Geez, a cold cloth will be the next thing I have to get him.

Steve: I'm absolutely stunned.

Les: Be sure to let me talk to your producer so I send it to the right place. Otherwise, I'll send it to Art Bell. (*laughter*)

Johnnie: We don't want that to happen. Steve will be at his house!

Steve: Let me ask you something. You've got that guitar, you really are a pack rat. You've got just about everything you ever used to record with, right?

Les: No, not everything. When my mom sold the house some of that stuff was under the porch and forgotten about. I've got a lot of stuff, but a lot of the real early stuff we don't know where it is. May I change the subject?

Johnnie: Sure.

Les: Harry Caray just died. He was a dear friend of mine, Harry Caray. I used to work with him and Russ Hodges. These guys were before your time. I worked with them on WJJD and WIND. Do you remember those names? Well, Russ and Harry and I went to Gary, Indiana, one New Year's Eve. We went for a good drunk. Russ arranged to have a date we were going to pick up on a corner on our way to Gary. She'd been told what corner to wait by the bank, and to look for us in my yellow Packard. So, as we were getting closer we see this good looking gal on the corner, and she starts to wave. Well, when she waved, her pants, her panties, fell down. She stepped out of them, put them in her pocket book, jumped in the car and away we went. I'll never forget that New Year's Eve! (*laughter*)

Steve: I bet you won't!

Les: Once, we were out running around and had to get back to the station for the next morning. There was a wigwag going on. The snow was coming down like crazy and we're stuck at the wigwag. We wondered where the heck the train was. We finally figured it had to be down the track just sitting.

Johnnie: Wait! Time out. What is a wigwag?

Les: Oh! That's the thing that flashes and tells you don't cross because a train is coming through.

Johnnie: Oh, got it! So, if it's flashing you could be stuck forever.

Les: Yes, and we were annoyed, so we drove along the track a quarter of a mile or so to where the train was sitting. No one was in it. We could see a hole in the fence and what looked like some tracks across the snow to a little joint like a "Dew Drop Inn" where the guys were probably getting a snort. So I said, "Let's move the train!" Russ said, "You're joking!" I said, "No, let's do it, Harry can follow us in the car." I knew all I needed to know to move the train because I lived along the tracks, and my godfather was an engineer. He'd put me in the train and let me watch. So I knew how to start and back the train up. We got the train moving and moved it about a half mile. Hopped out of the train into the car and hit the road back to Chicago. Every time we got together we'd talk about that train ... moving that train. Can you imagine those guys coming out and wondering what happened to their train?

Johnnie: Yes, and I wonder if they ever had another drink!

Les: Yeah, you wonder. That was a beautiful night with Russ and Harry.

Johnnie: That's a great story, too.

Steve: You worked at WGN Radio. Isn't it true you were fired for saying, "Stay tuned for the news," and putting the mic down by the teletype machine?

Les: No. That happened, but that was at WIND. I couldn't pronounce some of the words and names in a news story in a foreign place with killings going on, so I just said, "Stay tuned for 15 minutes of the news," and put the mic into the teletype. I was on notice for some five years. They'd hire and fire me the same day. I remember when I was at WGN and they set me up with Wayne King. They fired me for one of my pranks. Little did I know they'd said, "We've got to straighten this kid out. We don't want to lose him, but we want to straighten him out." Now, I didn't know this at that time. So the music director come over and said, "Red, don't feel bad about getting fired. I think I've got you a job. Go over and see Wayne King, he's right across the street." He was on Michigan Avenue. So I went over to Wayne King's office. It was the only time I ever met him. He said, "Will you play something for me?" Now, I was scared to death. I was so scared I'd gone out and bought a hat. I don't know why, but I was sure it would impress him. So I got the hat and I'm in his office talking to him, and I start pulling on a thread on the band of the hat. Finally, it came apart. I had the brim in my hand and the top was on the floor. I gently kicked it under the desk. Finally, he says, "That's all. I'll let you know soon about the job." I get up to leave and he says, "Aren't you going to take your hat?" I said, "I don't have a hat, Mr. King." He said, "I'm sure you had a hat. I saw you had a hat." I said, "Not me." He said, "Hold it." I said, "Never mind," opened the door to leave and walked right into a closet. Whatever lesson they hoped I'd learn at his office was lost. When I got back with the guys I said, "I won't be working with that guy." I never did. *(laughter)*

Johnnie: You KNOW that story made the rounds at the bars. Les, when you were in the musicians' union, were you in the broadcasters' union? Both?

Les: Well, we were in the musicians' union and it was strict. We weren't allowed to talk to Steve and Johnnie. If I was in Chicago and talked, I'd be fined, so if you were working as a musician you couldn't talk. Ben Bernie was at the ballpark, they announced his name, he got up and waved, and he was fined. That was strict. That was 1941. We played on the radio and if I wanted to talk to the guy playing our records, we could knock. He said, "How ya doing?" and we'd knock back our answer if the mic was open. One for no, and two for yes. You could send a message, but not talk.

Johnnie: They were serious.

Les: Yes. That was one of the strongest unions in the country at one time. It was tough, because a guy like Eddie Fisher could come into a station and plug his record, talk about it all night long. We couldn't. If you were a musician, you were so restricted. We'd actually go over to the union offices and fight them. You couldn't jam with a friend if it was going to be broadcast. If you did, you were fined. It was that way all across the country. I was fined in Chicago, Detroit, New York, L.A. When I went to L.A., I saw my buddy was playing the opening night at the Roosevelt Hotel. I took my guitar over there, he sees me, I get on stage and I play with him. Then I see a guy stick his finger in his ear and I know what he's about to say, "That's the Bud Glenn Trio from the Roosevelt Hotel. This is CBS." I'm thinking, "Oh no, we were on the network!" Sure enough, a fella comes up to me and asks me to do a particular song for him and says, "By the way here's my card. See you Friday morning." It was the address of the union, and I had to be there for my fine. That's how I entered L.A. Landed on a Monday, and Friday of that week I was in front of Spike Wallace at the union. When I got to the office Spike Wallace asked me, "Why are you playing?" I said, "Do you play?" He said, "Of course, I'm the president of the union." I said, "Here's an analogy. When your wife wants to go dancing do you take her to the kitchen, and turn on the radio?" He said, "No!" I said, "When you play guitar, you don't want to play in the kitchen. I have to play where I get feedback from the audience and other musicians. I want to share with other musicians. I don't want their jobs." You know, he let me go and we became close friends after that. Let me tell you how close. After I had the car accident with Mary, I ran out of money recuperating for two years. A year and a half into my recuperation I'm in the hospital when a little hunchback fellow comes in to see me. It was Spike. He said, "Les, I'm glad you have insurance or this could wipe you out." I said, "I DON'T have insurance and I'm about broke." He said, "Yes, you do. You have musicians' insurance. "

Johnnie: Wow! That could have ruined you.

Les: Yes, I was on the ropes already. So, with friends, there's a good side to your life even when it's bad.

(music out of commercial break: "It's Been A Long, Long Time")

Steve: That is Bing Crosby with Les Paul on guitar. "It's Been A Long, Long Time" is on this newly released CD, *The Complete Decca Trios-Plus (1936-1947)*.

Les: I had such a high regard for Bing. That tune can really break me up. I mean, I'm asked to do it at the Club and I have to joke so I don't break up. When I hear that song it can sneak up on me and I have to go to my room and cry.

Steve: He was such an important person in your life. Was Bing the one who first introduced you to an Ampex tape recorder?

Les: No, it's the other way around. I was playing with Paul Whiteman in '46 and Judy Garland and I had to go to New York. It took us 16 hours to fly from L.A. to New York because a snow storm grounded us in Denver. I'll never forget there was nothing more than a shack of a building that 10 or 12 of us had to wait in. Finally, we were able to fly out to New York. When I was there, a little fellow with octagon-shaped glasses came up to me and said, "Sherman Fairchild suggested I meet you. My name is Colonel Ranger and I've just returned from Europe with a tape machine." He went on and explained the machine to me and told me he was in New Jersey and I could come out and see it. I didn't even know where New Jersey was. I knew of it, just had never been there. So Judy Garland was with me when we went to New Jersey and saw the first tape machine. I went back and told Bing about it and said, "You NEED this machine. This is what you've been looking for!" And that's how it happened.

Steve: Wasn't there a point when Bing made you a gift of an Ampex tape recorder?

Les: Yes. A bunch of these machines had been confiscated from the Germans. Hitler had them during the war. That was especially interesting to me because I worked in the Armed Forces, editing President Roosevelt, Churchill, Stalin's speeches. During the war the Germans could edit their speeches so much faster than we could. We thought no one could edit faster than we could. We had three turntables, we could slip discs and edit Hitler to make him say anything we wanted to, and yet the Germans could do it faster. We never understood. Later, I got it when I saw the tape machines and realized that's how they could move so fast. The machines were confiscated, and that's how they ended up in the States. It developed from a wire recorder. They flattened the wire out and put a backing on it. That's how the tape machine came about.

Steve: Is it true that while you were in the service you learned a lot of your editing technique?

Les: Oh yes. We could slip discs set on three turntables. Each turntable had a pair of earphones and a switch. So the three of us had

Chris Lentz

The Ampex tape machine given to Les by Bing Crosby

the same speech of Hitler or whoever, on three discs, transcriptions. We had newspaper under them so we could slip the disc fast. You would hold your finger there when you were reading the script, then let go of your disc, then the next guy is ready with his, then the guy on the end is ready with his, and I now have to move down the script and be ready when it comes back to me. So we chewed up the turntables. We were working on acetate discs. They were actually glass discs with acetate covers. That's how we went about editing. I told Bing how the tape machine would change that. He went to Ampex. He didn't have a deal with them. He went up there and laid down a $50,000 check and said, "I want as many of those machines this will buy." When he got them he came by my house and said, "Les, come out to the car. I've got something for you!" I figured he had a Philco radio or Kraft Cheese for me. A couple of his sponsors. *(laughs)* He opened the trunk and we lifted this great big tape machine out and hauled it into my house. He left the machine there and within two hours I had figured it out. I ran to Mary and said, "I'm so happy! We can take this thing on the road with us and we don't have to take a disc machine!" She said, "How do you know it will work?" Well, she kept on asking that. In fact, we drove from L.A. to Chicago (for a gig at the Blue Note) with the tape machine in the trunk, and the whole time we're driving, she's sure it isn't going to work. She says, "What if it doesn't work?" By the time I got to Illinois, I was sure it wouldn't work. *(laughter)* Mary scared me to death! I told her I'd contacted Ampex. I had them sending me parts because I told them I blew the head. I hadn't, I just didn't want to tell Ampex I had invented this new way of making sound-on-sound with the one tape machine. We could now lay all our parts down, Mary and I, with one tape, mono not stereo.

We get to the New Lawrence Hotel at Lawrence and Broadway to stay while we were opening at the Blue Note. Lo and behold, we're there and in comes the tape head from Ampex. They

LOngbeach 1-2100

New Lawrence
HOTEL

FIREPROOF
1020 Lawrence Ave.
CHICAGO

CLOSE COVER FOR SAFETY

didn't know what it was for, but I said I needed it, I blew a head. I didn't want to tell anybody. My invention might not work. I looked in the phone book and found a guy, a Mr. Goodspeed, and said, "Goodspeed! That's the man!" I called him and he came to the hotel, and I had him drill the holes and we mounted the tape machine. I had Mary say, "One, one, one, one, and hello, hello, hello." I played it back and it came back, "One, one, one, one, and hello, hello, hello." That is where the machine was BORN. I'd had an automobile accident and I was a mess. I threw my crutch in the air and we danced around the hotel room in the New Lawrence Hotel. We cheered and hollered how great it was. We went to work at the Blue Note, and the great thing (was) the tape machine could do multitrack recording for us.

Johnnie: Oh, boy!

Les: Yeah, it was very exciting. Right here in Chicago. You know, the terrible thing is it was the best day with a dark side. You know the name Jim Lansing of Jim Lansing speakers?

Steve: Sure.

Les: Well, Jim Lansing was a dear friend of mine. When I met him in '42, he was on Vine in California. I got to know him real well. Ha! I finally convinced him that playing an electric guitar through his speakers wasn't a bad thing! Well, there we were, Mary and I, dancing around our room celebrating, and that night as we're leaving for the Blue Note I get a call that Jim had hanged himself. It was such a great day, but such a terrible day. I still think of him, because Jim Lansing speakers were sold and eventually became JBL speakers, and they are everywhere now, like at the House of Blues.

Steve: And correct me if I'm wrong, but the way you were doing the sound-on-sound recording then, was, you would do one, then you'd have to do another, but if you made a mistake and you were into the eighth generation ...

Les: The problem was if you make a mistake. We would record in a basement. "How High the Moon" was recorded in a basement in Jackson Heights right next to a fire department. So, the alarm would go off, dang, dang, dang, the sirens would go off, and we blew "How High the Moon." The second time, a plane goes to land at Laguardia and ... we're dead. Start over at one, and the worst part was Mary had to sing the last part first. Otherwise, you would lose (quality) in generations going down. So, Mary sings the fifth part first, I play a line and it's unimportant. A rhythm part. As we work our way to the end, we're on the melody, and the bass line is one of the most important parts. By the time we get there, if we make a mistake it's back to one.

Johnnie: Unreal.

Les: Those days are gone so, Slash, whoever, playing the guitar, George Benson, may take a year, Eric Johnson may take 10 years to get it correct. We had to do it in two hours. "How High the Moon" took two hours.

Steve: Les, this has been an amazing and enlightening conversation. Thank you.

Les: Thank you guys. I love you and I miss the Midwest and I miss snow! We haven't had any, what's going on?

Johnnie: I know. We don't have the weather to complain about! Again, Les thank you for joining us. We love you. God bless you. Now, get some sleep!

For Les, who loved to work, working meant driving, which he also loved. Among the many cars he outlived was this Lincoln Towncar, shown in the driveway of his Mahwah, New Jersey, home. In his later years, Les seemed to "drive" vicariously through his phone calls to Steve and Johnnie when they were on the road.

Chris Lentz

Driving With Mr. Paul

*F*or almost 20 years, we would take our four, and later, five weeks of vacation in one-week increments and head down to our little house in Panama City Beach, Florida. Prior to September 11, 2001, we could leave the radio station after doing the all-night show and cab to the airport with a carry-on bag, arriving in time to zip through security and make the first morning flight, sometimes with no more than a minute to spare. If the planets aligned and everything went as planned, we could be on the beach before lunch that day.

After the events of September 11, the air travel experience changed dramatically. There was no more last-minute zipping through security to rush onto a flight. The new rules required ticketed passengers to arrive hours before a flight. In October of 2001, we decided that flying was becoming too time-consuming for us, so we would drive the 15-16 hours to Florida and try de-stressing en route. We soon found that driving was an excellent way to realize we were actually "on vacation," and the drive became a part of the vacation experience.

A wonderful part of those drives was the phone calls we would get from Les. Either he had called the radio station and found we were on the road, or he was listening to the show and heard us sign off for a week of vacation. After the first of those calls, it was obvious that Les missed getting in the car and just … driving.

Sure, he made the trip to New York City from his home in

New Jersey every Monday to perform at the club, but he longed to do what we were doing: take a "road trip." It seemed as though our conversations — with us on the open road, Les probably in bed — were times when he was vicariously making the trip with us. Over the years on the radio he had fondly recalled the trips he and Mary would make driving from coast to coast. He talked about stopping at radio stations as they drove across state after state.

When he would call us on the road, he wanted details of the trip. Les wanted to know not only the state we were in and the route we were on, but he also wanted a play-by-play of what we saw out the window at that very moment. It could be the flat terrain in southern Illinois, or the hilly stretch of Interstate 65 through Alabama. "Is there a truck stop up along that stretch?" he'd ask, as though he could recall driving that very road decades before. He always asked about the car we were driving. "What kinda' gas mileage you getting?" He'd inquire about the cost of gas from state to state. "Did you stop for breakfast?" "Was it good?" "Did it slow you down?" "When do you think you'll be in Florida?" He always seemed to be impressed that we planned on sleeping in our beds in Florida that very night. After all, we'd just finished up an all-night radio show.

Many times he would say, "I'm like Steve, I relax when I drive." For a while we traveled with a portable CB radio. It was handheld and didn't require a whip antenna on the outside of the car. It was an investment that "saved" us many times. It came in handy listening to the truckers chatter, especially when they became animated because the traffic was stopped ahead. The drivers were then quick with alternate route suggestions. Often we were the rare "4-wheeler" that traveled right along with the 18-wheelers listening closely to our CB as we drove off the beaten path. Les loved those stories and would often ask us to turn up the CB if the truckers started talking back and forth.

In October of '08, we called Les on the air to talk about the news that he was going to be honored by The Rock and Roll Hall of Fame in its "American Masters" series. Even though he was already a member of the Hall, this award was a big deal. The Hall of Fame had also announced that there would be a concert culminating a few days of scheduled events. When we called Les, we not only wanted to congratulate him on the award but also ask if he would be there to perform. He told us, "If I'm breathing, I'll be there and I will perform." The next question was, would he be driving to Cleveland? He said, "That's how I like to travel, so yes, we'll drive."

That question seemed to open up a floodgate of memories. Les said his mother was a driver. Like him, she loved to drive. But, he said, "I'd do anything NOT to ride with Mother when she was driving her Nash Rambler." He said, "You see, it had electric buttons, and when Mother would get in the car in the driveway to back out, she would FLOOR it, foot all the way down on the gas pedal, and reach up and push the Reverse button! I would hold my breath and pray no one was in the road!" He recalled one time she had taken him to Milwaukee for shopping. He said, "Those were the days of the streetcars, and there were signs up and down the road where you would stand to catch the streetcar. Well, Mother was talking to me while she was driving. I mean LOOKING AT ME while she was driving and talking. She hit one streetcar sign and then another. I was so thankful no one was waiting on the streetcar! All she had to say about the scare was I was NEVER to tell a soul, and I didn't, until now!" We all laughed when he was reminded that our listening audience was over the air into 38 states and parts of Canada, and thanks to the Internet he had just told the whole world her secret.

When Les was asked how he learned to drive, he remembered the experience like it was yesterday. He was glad, for obvious reasons, it was his dad who taught him to drive and not his mother. He said he was always thankful that he learned to drive correctly and at a young age, and laughed when he said, "It was harder back then because those were the days of Reverse shift opposite of what we have today." Les's dad would take him down to a frozen lake and lay tin cans out on the lake to teach him to drive around them — an obstacle course on a frozen lake. He said he was always around cars because his dad had a garage. In fact, Les said, "I was born in a garage!" Actually, his family lived above the garage when he was born. In that conversation he proudly proclaimed, "To this day, if I climbed into a Model T, I could drive it without a problem!" We were sure that was true.

If Les was going to "hit the road," he would wistfully talk about his love of doing that at night. A few weeks after our conversation about driving, he called our show. It was the middle of the night and he was, in fact, "breathing," and, as he had promised, he was on the road heading to The Rock and Roll Hall of Fame in Cleveland from his home in Mahwah, New Jersey. He was a wide-awake passenger who was genuinely tickled that the 50,000 watts of WGN Radio and our broadcast was coming in like a local station on his car radio as they traveled across state lines.

The conversations with Les while he was on the road at night heading home from the Iridium, and those times when he joined us by phone as we traveled a thousand miles to Florida, were times that we treasured. We think he treasured them, too, because he seemed really relaxed and reflective about his life.

We were never sure if those calls from Les while we were traveling indicated his itch to get out on the open road again, or simply brought back the memory of a different time when driving meant working, and working was something he truly loved doing.

March 2000

14

Not Just a Guitar

Steve: It is our great pleasure now to welcome back to the show a man who we are very fortunate to call a friend. A man who is a genuine living legend. He is a charter member of The Rock and Roll Hall of Fame and has been known to play a not-too-bad guitar. In fact, for those of you who may have come in late to this ... a mini-history of Les Paul ...

(music montage up)

Steve: This man has been responsible for some incredible music over the years. How ya doing Les?

Les: Hi Steve, hi Johnnie.

Johnnie: Hi Les, how you feeling tonight?

Les: Good.

Johnnie: Isn't it fun to hear your music?

Les: Ah boy, I don't know what to do. Laugh or cry.

Johnnie: When you're listening to your music, do your fingers stay still?

Les: It grabs me.

Johnnie: I imagine you playing air guitar. *(laughter)*

Les: Sometimes I wonder how we did it then. I wonder why?

Steve: One of the things, and I don't say this just to flatter you, those records sound just as good today as the day they were recorded.

Les: Well, thank you. The one thing that bothers me is they're getting farther away all the time. (*laughter*) I don't know if it's further or farther. I just wonder what the people today, the youngsters, what they think of it. You know?

Steve: Well, I can tell you I have a computer, and I frequent a number of Internet sites that deal with guitars and guitarists, and your name comes up a lot. You'd be amazed at the young kids who are listening to your music and wondering, "How the heck did he do that?"

Les: Ha, I'm wondering the same thing when I hear them!

Johnnie: I love the fact, and it's happened many times, you've met a person and they're surprised you're a man and not just a guitar.

Les: Ha, it happened to me the other night. A guy was so happy to find out I wasn't just a guitar. I was a pedestrian … one of us.

Johnnie: In fact, it may ring a few bells for those who remember, that's what happened in a Coors commercial. That was the punch line of the commercial. Some hotshot is playing guitar, and he finds out from you that you are more than the guitar he's playing.

Steve: In fact, Les, are you ever going to do another Coors commercial?

Les: Well, I hear from them, but they never mention doing another commercial. I hear from them all the time. We have a wonderful chat, and I'm not about to ask them why can't I do another commercial, and they don't bring it up. I want to so badly that I decided to stop drinking Coors beer.

Steve: That'll teach 'em!

Les: I know it's going to show on their accounting! They're going to say, "We're weak in Jersey!" (*laughter*)

Johnnie: Smart! Stock will go down, and they'll hire you back!

Les: You know something odd, and I was thinking of it earlier while you were playing the "Tiger Rag" and "Whispering," those things. I did tell you we recorded those at the Sherman Hotel. "Whispering" and "The World's Waiting for the Sunrise," but one of the most important things was Rheingold Beer. The president of Rheingold Beer, he loved Mary and I. We struck a deal to make a Rheingold commercial "My beer is the dry beer, Rheingold beer." I don't know if you ever got it in your area.

Steve: We actually have that. It's on the box set.

Les: So, you did hear it.

Steve: It's wonderful. You were so savvy. That was also an extra plug for Les Paul and Mary Ford.

Les: You know, it actually got Capitol Records so ... psyched that we had a serious meeting about NOT making commercials for Rheingold Beer because it was hurting the sales of our records. I stupidly made the fatal mistake, which I'll never do again, and said, "Well, all the people concerned are here. Let's take a vote." We did. I lost, and the Rheingold commercial was taken off the air. The president of Rheingold said, "I bet you'll never forget the mistake you made today." It was a big mistake.

Steve: You also did commercials for Robert Hall and ...

Les: Listerine.

Steve: Listerine sponsored your TV show for a while, didn't they?

Les: Yes. For seven years. That was a wonderful relationship we had with the Listerine people.

Steve: That show was filmed at your home in Mahwah, New Jersey, wasn't it?

Les: Yeah, we actually lived in Hollywood, and they said "We'd love to do the commercials from your home." I said, "That little bungalow? That's a little $15,000 furnished house that's about to be ripped down." So they said, "Would you consider moving to New Jersey?" I jokingly said, "Where is that?" (*laughter*) They said, "That's where our headquarters are and we can work close together." Well, Martin Black, a disc jockey friend of mine, and the president of Listerine actually cruised around here in New Jersey and found a place they thought would be great to shoot the commercials and do the TV shows. And so we moved from Hollywood here. It's the only reason we would have left there and come here and actually build a home. It was a seven-room house when we got it, and we turned it into 34 rooms!

Steve: That's the house you live in today and your recording studio is there, right?

Les: Yep ... it's a museum now! (*laughter*) It sure did great things for us.

Johnnie: Didn't you go through culture shock? You go from Hollywood where you can hang out with the stars and celebrities to a different world in New Jersey.

Les: It could have been worse! It turned out to be a great move for us. Of course, I wouldn't even think of moving now unless you could put wheels on this thing.

Johnnie: I imagine the thought of moving is terrifying.

Les: I sure don't want to do that.

Steve: Les, have you seen the article that came out last week in the Milwaukee Journal? Listeners have sent us so many copies of it. It was a full-page article with some wonderful color pictures all about you. It was done by David Hinckley. He writes all about you at the Club Iridium in New York. He writes about your band and your new guitar player. Did you ever see that article?

Les: Someone sent it to me. Yes, I have seen it.

Steve: I want to ask you about the band. You mentioned briefly the other night that you have a new guitar player. How did that all come about?

Les: I had a little setback a couple of months ago and had to go into the hospital. I ended up with a month where I wasn't working at the club. I had heard about this guitar player. Actually, 15 years ago he came in and sat in at a little club I was playing in New York. He sat in with me then. I said, "Why don't you all find that fella? By now, he oughta be awfully good." They found him and he went in and filled in for me and the people loved him. I actually hadn't heard him for 15 years, but knew he must be good. I decided to take a chance and hire him. I decided to make it Les Paul AND his Trio instead of the Les Paul Trio. He really is fire. This guy in the group is just great.

Steve: His name is Frank Vignola. Is that correct?

Les: Yes! What he does is, because he studied what I did way back, and he studied Django Reinhardt, he sure does play. Of course, when he gets beside me, that makes me go to work. His playing encourages me. It's just great. He lights a fire! That fourth person, even if it were piano, violin, whatever, would help, but being him on the guitar is just the best.

Steve: One of the things we wanted to do tonight is, I brought in a couple of your records and I don't even know if you know they exist.

Les: Uh-oh.

Steve: When we come back from a break, I'm going to play a bit of these and get your impressions, your thoughts as you're listening.

Les: OK!

(music out of break)

Steve: Les Paul is with us. Les, what you're listening to is part of a series of V-discs that were reissued. This is a whole series that has one album of you and your original Les Paul Trio from back in the war years. A whole series of V-disc records! Do you remember all that?

Les: Oh I remember. I hadn't heard them since I made them till right now. Hadn't heard them since we recorded them … many of them right there in Chicago.

Johnnie: So when they were recorded, they were done for the servicemen, not released to the public.

Les: That is correct.

Steve: Wasn't this during a musicians' union recording ban? The only thing, correct me if I'm wrong, union president, James Petrillo, said all the musicians could do was make records specifically for the soldiers. Am I right on that?

Les: That's right. Yeah. Those were great times. Yes, we had a war going on, but those were the greatest times. I think I could say that for both Mary and I. Chicago is really my home, so I'd always go back home. That's where I got all the breaks and the privilege to work with so many great performers. In Chicago.

Steve: You worked at many of the clubs in town and as we've talked before, you worked at radio stations WGN, WBBM, WJJD under various names. When would you make the recordings? Would you do that during the day or after you finished up gigs at night?

Les: Well, when I wasn't Rhubarb Red. Rhubarb Red was in the morning. From 5 or 6 in the morning, I'd be on WLS, 'JJD or 'IND. After 12 noon I turned into another villain. (*laughter*) I was with the likes of Art Tatum, the gang over at WLS ... it seemed like I was all over that town. With the great talent, the Nat Coles, the Benny Goodmans, all that was happening.

Johnnie: So you really had to look at a clock to determine what persona you were.

Les: In the afternoon I was Les Paul, in the morning, I was Rhubarb Red.

Johnnie: Did you go into recording studios at night when you didn't have a gig? I mean it's amazing to think you went to work early in the morning and literally worked till you went to bed at night.

Les: Yes, it was crazy. Let's say it would be 2 or 3 o'clock and I'd be at the Three Deuces, and I'd be jamming with people like Art Tatum and Roy Elders, and I'd say, "Hey, I've gotta split. I've gotta go to work." Art Tatum would say, "Where does he work, a post office or something?" Someone dialed me up for him, and to Art's surprise, he heard me yodeling and singing hillbilly music. (*laughter*) It was quite a life.

Johnnie: This was during the '30s, right, Les?

Les: The early '30s.

Johnnie: Had you come up with your idea for your guitar and had you taken it to Gibson or did that come about in the '40s?

Les: That came about in the '40s. I did go to Gibson with primitive ideas. That was a hard sell, a very difficult sell ... the idea that you take a guitar and plug it into a wall. (*laughter*) That didn't seem to go over well with ANYBODY, much less the Gibson people. You can imagine an electric guitar. Think about the orchestra that was there at WGN with Bob Trendler. Can you imagine an electric guitar in that? In the midst of these great violin players ... great musicians?

Johnnie: I can imagine the engineers' union back then saying, "I'm not sure I WANT to plug that thing in the wall!"

Les: I got opposition. The most came from other musicians that wanted me to get rid of the electric guitar and go back to the acoustic guitar. Even listeners responded. The jury — I called the listeners the jury — they had a different opinion. Many of them chose the electric guitar over the acoustic. That continued till I left Chicago and came to New York to join Fred Waring. Five years with Fred Waring, and there was a BIG discussion about which was better, the electric or the acoustic guitar. By then, Fred Waring and my trio voted on it, and it was decided unanimously to stick to the electric guitar. It was considered the way of tomorrow, an important instrument because it could be heard. In a nightclub, it was almost an impossibility to hear an acoustic guitar, and in an orchestra, can you imagine sitting in, going to the Grand Terrace ballroom to sit in with Coleman Hawkins (which we did) and great players like that with a live orchestra and no P.A. system? You just couldn't hear that guitar. The guitar was crying ... it needed help very badly. It took a good many years to convince Gibson to go with the idea. They called me the character with the broomstick with the pickups on it. (*laughter*) They laughed about it until it was obvious it was going to be successful. Then the president came to me and said, "I've got a little confessing to do. We made fun of you for 10 years."

Steve: Wasn't Ted McCarty the one that came to you and talked about making the Les Paul guitar?

Les: No, it was actually Mr. Berlin. M.H. Berlin was the chairman of the board. He and I were old friends from the days he had the Chicago Musical Instruments Company. Lyon and Healy was the Gibson dealer and the Martin dealer was Mr. Berlin. He's the one, when he became chairman of the board, to make the decision to "bring that character in here." I flew in from L.A. with the log, this 4x4 piece of wood with some wings on it and pickups. We made the decision on what to do, then we brought Ted in. We had lots of discussions. In fact, I remember when we were discussing color. They said, "What's your first color going to be?" I quickly yelled out, "GOLD!" There had never been a gold guitar ... an instrument like this. In fact, the first complaint was, "Why gold? It'll be turning green on you in a week!" I said, "I want gold." Mr. Berlin said, "That's what the kid wants, give it to him." Then they asked, "What's the other color?" I said, "Black." So they said those are the colors, gold and black, of the first guitars to come out. Those are still the most popular colors we've got in the Gibson line today. I know the gold is.

Steve: Does it amaze you the prices some of those vintage Les Paul guitars will command on the vintage guitar market?

Les: It's ridiculous. I was talking to the president of Gibson and they're thinking of making, contemplating, a Les Paul guitar that's going to sell for as low as $59.

Steve: You're kidding!

Johnnie: Oh wow!

Les: Yes. This has been a dream of mine for a million years. I've said, "When I was young, I had to get a Sears and Roebuck guitar that was like a bow and arrow. It was terrible! I've said kids should have something with a fine neck on it. Make it simple. Make it as inexpensive as you can. Take care of the beginner. You cannot have just the elite, the ultimate, the Cadillac, the greatest. They weren't convinced of doing it for years. They said, "It'll cheapen the line." I've used an example of Sony. You can go in and ask for an audience with the president and she's listening to a Sony Walkman. Very inexpensive. You go into studios and you find the finest equipment in the world. From cameras to TV monitors, video monitors. They don't have a problem doing that, so why don't we do it? Make an Epiphone guitar, use less expensive wood and use workers in the Orient. They didn't like it for years, but they did it. It's Henry Juszkiewicz that listened, and he did it.

Steve: He's the one that really, in recent years, turned the Gibson company around.

Gibson president Henry Juszkiewicz holding a Les Paul at the Gibson factory

John Paulson, *Chasing Sound*

Les: He's done a terrific job. We work very close together and have a great relationship. It's always a pleasure to see him and talk to him 'cause he's always saying, "What do you think, Les?" Great! If you can get a guitar out there without all the bells and whistles for that fellow who just can't afford $5,000 for a guitar — they agreed to do it.

Steve: Speaking of the inexpensive guitars. I'm still blown away by the guitar you sent me, the one that your mom got you from the Sears catalog. Remember we said, "It belongs in The Rock and Roll Hall of Fame?" You said, "You'll show it to people, won't you?" True to our word, everyone that comes to our house has to see it. It still has the Gene Autry picture you left in the sound hole.

> *(Authors' note: A small portion of this interview was deleted because it is repeated in The Wizard of Waukesha chapter.)*

Steve: We've got some people hanging on the phones that want to say hi, if that's OK.

Les: Sure!

Steve: Joe, you're on the air with Les Paul.

Joe: Hello, Les. I'm calling from about 10 miles east of Waukesha in Milwaukee. I have two questions. Recently, NPR radio ran a piece about a recording session where musicians came in to the studio to play into a gramophone.

Les: The Edison machine.

Joe: The story goes, all the musicians came in and played a retro sound, but you said, "I'm an electric guitarist." Is that how the story goes? I think it was in Menlo Park.

Les: Yes. It was an extreme pleasure to be in the place where Edison worked, to be in his office. So the audiences that would come through there on tour, we set up a stage to do a show for those 40 people or so and actually made a recording. We got the horn and the cylinders and made the whole thing. The great part about that was, I think it was great, you could find the horn out of 40 different horns to go with the electric guitar. I knew the frequency response of the electric guitar and the response of what the horn was capable of handling. To do that recording, it was really a kick. I'm sure the horn had never heard anything quite like the electric guitar. I'm guessing Edison wouldn't have liked the electric guitar.

Joe: The other thing is, are you back at the Club Iridium?

Les: Yes, yes.

Joe: Is there any chance of getting an 18-year-old in to hear you? Through me, he knows your name and your music. He's a musician. Is there any chance of getting him in to see one of your shows?

Les: Sure.

Steve: Can under 21 years old get in to see you?

Les: Absolutely!

Johnnie: In fact, you told us of a very young man in the front row playing air guitar along with you.

Joe: That's my son. I'm trying to get him interested in music other than rock and roll.

Johnnie: Then take him to the club. Les is back in business. Two shows every Monday night as of last week.

Steve: Les, I said I was going to play some things I bet you haven't heard for a while. This next piece is from an album that came out about two months ago. It's a Jody Reynolds two-disc set. He had a hit with "Endless Sleep." Some of the cuts on this album are jam sessions. There's a cut on here of you playing along with Jimmy Bryant on "Out of Nowhere."

Les: Oh! I remember that. I just haven't heard it.

Steve: OK, here's a little bit of it …

(music up)

Steve: Was that done at a jam session?

Les: That was done in Palm Springs. Some guy had a tape recorder going and got that and put it out.

Johnnie: It still sounds great.

Les: I can't tell that much on the phone, but Jimmy Bryant reminds me. Do you remember Speedy West?

Steve: Oh, sure.

Les: He was a great guitarist and a dear friend.

Steve: If you don't have a copy of this I have an extra copy. I'll send it to you.

Les: Oh, I'd appreciate it. I'd love to have it.

Steve: I don't think I ever asked you: The time you spent with the big bands, did you take some of the big band arrangement style and utilize that with some of the recordings you made with Mary Ford?

Les: Yes. Yes, I did especially on something like a Count Basie background or … it would depend on what it was. If it was "Tiger Rag" I'd have a different thing going entirely. The wonderful part about Mary and I working together was she said, "Whatever you want, you tell me what you want, and I'll do it." Neither one of us read music, so we made no arrangements. The arrangements would be contrived or conceived driving in the car, or we'd be eating. It could be anyplace that these ideas would come to mind. So if I'm listening to some orchestra, or the piece I'm working on reminds me of Fred Waring, Benny Goodman, you name it, then yes, there was a great influence. When you're going to put together an arrangement, when you have the privilege to be able to do a multiple — even though we were going back to the way it was in the beginning when I invented the thing with tape number one — you're challenged as to how much you could put on there, and it would be just garbage unless you organized it. So that would probably be what you're talking about. Yes, I was influenced very much by Les Brown or whoever.

Steve: Did you always, as you were doing your, particularly,

your early multiples before you were able to do individual tracks, did you always record your lead line last? In other words, put the bass then the rhythm guitar and all that stuff first, then do the lead line last so it would stand out more?

Les: Well, you could only do that as you got used to that type of recording. The problem with those recordings were, if you got to the twentieth part, if you made a mistake you've got to go back to one. So you didn't make a mistake. That's the other amazing part about Mary. If you told Mary, if I told Mary how I wanted a part sung, she'd say, "OK." She'd print it in her head. She had this ability to say, "OK," and then do it that way every single time. Me? I'm the opposite. I do it twice and I'm tired of it and I'm changing it, constantly looking, not capable of doing the same thing over. If Mary were around today, you could say, "Hey Mary, sing 'Smoke Rings,'" and she'd do it EXACTLY like the record.

Johnnie: Is it true that she never really thought of herself as being a genius, having this wonderful voice, able to play the guitar and the capability to do multiple harmonies?

Les: That was a gift that she had, to be able to play the guitar, be able to sing, be able to hear all these harmony parts AND the ability to do it in one take. And, ah, she never thought much about herself as being good, much less fantastic. She just liked to do it. She had no idea the talent she had.

Johnnie: Amazing.

Steve: Les, we have to take a break. Can you stay with us a little while longer?

Les: Oh, if I'm not overdoing this thing!

Johnnie: Gosh, no! Selfishly we've been doing all the talking, and people have been waiting patiently to talk to you, too, so we'll give them a chance.

Les: Oh, I love it.

(music up — Les and Chet Atkins — coming out of break)

Steve: One of the most amazing albums you'll ever hear, *Chester and Lester*. **It was a Grammy-award-winner for Chet Atkins and Les Paul. Les Paul is on the line with us, and I want to bring in one of our callers. Bob, you have a question for Les?**

Bob: Yes, hello Les.

Les: Hi Bob.

Bob: I have so many of your records and listened to these shows for years. I picked up a copy of the *Chester & Lester* album a while back. You just got through playing my favorite cut from that album. I heard somewhere that maybe you and Chet Atkins were going to get back together again and re-record some of that stuff and record some new stuff. Any truth to that?

Les: No, ah, it would be wonderful if that were the case, but, ah, Chet has not been well. He's had a pretty tough time going and I've been threatening to hang up it up. Well, I started to retire in ... 1965! Ha!, I haven't retired yet. I've got to call Chet and see how he's doing. I hear he's doing OK.

Steve: As a matter of fact, Les, we heard from our friend Muriel Anderson that Chet is starting to do a bit of recording again. As you know, Chet had some serious problems with cancer, and it really set him back for a while. Basically, he's had to learn, as you have at different periods in your life, how to play the guitar again. Now, he's starting to get back into the studio, and we wish him well.

Les: Oh yes ... what a talent.

Johnnie: He was apparently seen at Vince Gill-Amy Grant's wedding a week ago Friday. The reason it was mentioned, I think it was in People magazine, was apparently he's still got his sense of humor. He was flirting with Amy Grant and threatening to steal her away from Vince Gill.

Les: Yeah, Chet has a great sense of humor.

Steve: Well, are YOU doing any recording these days? You've got

that big ol' studio in your house. Do you every now and then pick up a guitar and just fool around with recording some stuff?

Les: No, no … although I'm practicing a little bit more now just because of that guitar player I hired. He's bugging me! He's playing too much! (*laughter*) He is really good. Getting back to Bob, if we're physically up to recording together again, if we can, we will. It would be great.

Steve: Did you know at the time you did those sessions with Chet Atkins that it was special? Did it feel special to you? Here's why I'm asking, because most of your hits had been made with you and Mary, and those were all multiples. Here's a different situation, you go into a studio, it's just you and Chet, somebody picks a key and counts it off and you go. No retakes or nothing. What did that feel like for you at the time?

Les: It was fun. It's something that I always like to do, and Mary did too, that is to perform live. Whether it's a recording or otherwise, I would rather play one guitar and say what I have to say that way. It wasn't any problem for Chet and I to do. The thing that happened was when Chet called me with the idea of doing this thing, he said, "You can bring your harmonica and guitar, and you can be Rhubarb Red and I'll be the old Chet and play the violin, and we'll do country and sing." When I got down there with my harmonica rack and got to the studio and run through some things, it was awful. I said, "Chet, what are you known for?" He said, "I guess it's my guitar playing." I said, "Don't you think you better do that?" (*laughter*) I said, "I sure didn't get any Oscar for my singing. I'll just put this stuff aside." He said, "What should we do?" I said, "You know, you don't have to be country, you can do 'Avalon' and 'Lime House Blues,' it doesn't really matter. We're country enough; we'll get the message across." So he agreed to try it. We put a mic up and recorded the rehearsal. The rest is history, because this was on a Saturday, and he said, "We'll get together Monday and we'll do it right." I said, "Nah, I booked a plane back already. This is it." He had to put the rehearsal out.

Steve: Were you surprised at the success of that album? It was huge, and I believe it's the first album you won a Grammy for, wasn't it?

Les: That is correct. I knew that what we had done was a hawkable item and Chet did too, but I don't think either one of us thought it would be that big. See, he's a rather modest guy, and I think I am, too. We don't go around telling too many people how great we are, and we really didn't think, either one of us, didn't think it was all that great.

Johnnie: Thank goodness it's still available and available on CD. The quality is outstanding.

Les: Thank you. It is one of the things I am SO glad we had a chance to do.

Steve: I tell you that this is one of the albums, whether you talk to a 60-year-old guitar player or a 19-year-old guitar player, that is a defining album for guitar players. It's one that I know there is literally not a week that goes by that I'm not listening to that album and trying to figure out how the heck you guys did some of the stuff you did.

Les: If it wasn't easy, we didn't do it! (*laughter*)

Johnnie: Talk about being humble.

A TV screenshot from the 1977 Grammy Awards where Les and Chet won "Best Country Instrumental Performance"

Les: You know, while we're talking here, I was wondering, when I was doing the country thing back there in Chicago from '31 to '37, I wonder where all those people went. We used to get mail, I'm talking about thousands of letters a week. This is the kind of mail we drew back then. Oh, and cookies and cakes and the gals that fell in love with Rhubarb Red ... I wonder where they are now.

Johnnie: They're probably sitting back listening and grinning at the memories.

Steve: For anybody who's never heard, we're talking about the '30s for Rhubarb Red, right Les?

Les: Yeah, it started in '31 at KMOX.

Steve: This is a little bit of Les Paul as Rhubarb Red ...

(music up — Les singing "Just Because")

Steve: That's Rhubarb Red like you would have heard him back in the early '30s.

Johnnie: Back in the 1900s!

Les: Now you know why I changed my name and left town.

Johnnie: It sounds so good today. But correct me if I'm wrong, as much as you loved to play the guitar, you were never really comfortable singing.

Les: No. That's a kind way of putting it.

Johnnie: Oh, I love it!

Les: Here I am with the harmonica trying to play some polka music, and it was my first recording. My mother got so mad at me because I used a pick, and instead of playing bluegrass style, I wanted to become more modern. I used a pick and played my L5 jazz guitar, and I was ... all screwed up!

Art Wachter

Frank and Les on stage at the Iridium

memories from ...
Frank Vignola

I first met Les when I was just out of high school. He had just emerged from retirement and started playing every Monday night in downtown New York City with his trio, which I personally think was the greatest guitar trio ever. I had heard he was looking for a rhythm guitarist, and our mutual friend Rich Conaty set up the meeting. We ate a meal together, and he was so extremely nice and completely down to earth.

I sat in with Les and his trio. He sat me in back on a chair while the three of them sat on stools. He wanted to check me out a bit before exposing me to the public. Les then asked me to take his stool, and proceeded to invite another guitarist up named Vic Jurris. Les then left the stage and had the two of us jam. We had never even met before. Well, we had a ball playing together and brought the house down. Never got to play with Les, but nonetheless it was an amazing experience for a 19-year-old kid.

Later that night, about three in the morning, the phone rang. Of course, Les the night owl. We spoke for hours about guitars, picks, picking technique, Django, etc. We then spoke just about every week until he got sick in the year 2000. His faithful and awesome rhythm guitarist Lou Pallo called me to sub for him. Sub for Les Paul? Really?

After six weeks, Les called and said he wanted to come back, but wanted me to join his trio, making it Les Paul and his Trio. A dream come true! He said he wasn't going to play but maybe sit in for a tune or two. I got to the club for rehearsal and there he was on his stool, practicing away. We played the whole night together. I get goose bumps thinking about it.

To me, Les got better with age. His tone was impeccable. His way of interpreting melody and his ability to entertain an audience was just amazing. I learned more from him than anyone else. Two of the most important things I learned were: play for the people, and appreciate your audience. What always impressed me was seeing Les take sometimes up to two hours after two shows to meet, greet and sign for everyone. He would spend a few minutes with each person, making them feel special. He truly enjoyed people.

One night, on a through-the-night drive I was making to Chicago, I called Les, as I would do if I was up late. We were speaking for about an hour and lost the connection. By the time I got the connection back, I thought maybe I would just drive and leave him alone. About three hours later, the phone rings and there is Les, worried to death because I didn't call him back. Just called to make sure I was OK.

Les used to tell me about Steve and Johnnie's show and how he would call in at 3 a.m. It was such a joy to finally meet them and perform on their show with Tommy Emmanuel.

Frank Vignola

© Kelly Leavitt, Luvduck Photography

Frank Vignola, Tommy Emmanuel, Johnnie, Vinny Raniolo and Steve

a little more about ...

Frank Vignola

S ome guitarists possess a magic that makes you smile when you hear their music. Les had it. Django had it. And Frank has it — in spades. We first met Frank in Nashville at Muriel Anderson's All Star Guitar Night salute to Les Paul. But we didn't really get to spend time with him until he joined Tommy Emmanuel and Vinny Raniolo in our WGN studio one night after we had introduced them at a Chicago appearance. In the hours that followed, we got a close-up view of Frank's exceptional talent.

In the years that followed, Frank made several return visits on and off the radio. Along with gaining a new friend, we came to understand why Les sought him out: This guy can PLAY! Frank is recognized as one of the world's foremost practitioners of Gypsy Jazz, and his musical ability knows no boundaries. He is equally comfortable playing with Madonna, Ringo Starr or Lionel Hampton. Les once named Frank to his "Five Most Admired Guitarists" list for the *Wall Street Journal*.

All this time later, we think Tribune Tower maintenance may still be cleaning up notes Frank, Tommy and Vinny left scattered all around the WGN Radio studio when they played "How High The Moon" as a tribute to Les. Talk about "a beautiful mess!"

Steve and *Johnnie*

Les Paul Foundation

Les Paul and Chet Atkins in the recording studio

Chester & Lester

Chet Atkins' Death
July 5, 2001
2:30-3:45 a.m.

Steve: Hi, Les, we've wanted to talk with you since we heard about your friend, Chet Atkins, passing last Saturday, the 30th.
Les: Oh boy …

Johnnie: We're so sorry, Les. You had a chance to talk to him recently, didn't you?

Les: Oh, it was a while back, yeah. He had a great sense of humor. He was giving me a hard time. He'd say, "How come you're not joining me to make another record?" Seriously, I said, "I don't know if I'm up to it." He said, "How come I'm up to it and you're not?" He'd laugh when he was giving it to me. I sure miss him … well … it's tough.

Steve: Yes, I'm sure. You've mentioned, with all the hits and records you made with Mary Ford, you've mentioned THE album that sells the most at the Club Iridium is the legendary album you did with Chet Atkins.

Les: Yes, over a period of time, you know, we would have different records available and get comments about them. We found that over and over, the one we got the most positive comments on at different times … the one they seemed to like the best was the *Chester & Lester* album.

Johnnie: I don't know if we ever told you, we've sold a few hundred copies of that album!

Les: Did ya? (*laughter*)

Steve: Every time we play something from that album, people call and say, "What is that? Who is that?" Some who are familiar with you, and others, younger people, say, "Who's playing that? It rocks!"

Les: (*laughs*) Hey, thank you.

Johnnie: We were so happy when it came out on CD. We had been playing the vinyl forever.

Les: Great! You know I was thinking while you were playing the introduction to our call, "My goodness, that was done a lot of years ago!" I go back, back, back to when you had to make sure a record was cut. Today you could just turn the music on in the palm of your hand … or on the computer. Things that were so difficult then are so easy now.

Steve: It's funny you should say that. After we talked a few weeks ago, I was mentioning that very thing to Johnnie. I'd just picked up a 16-track recorder from Akai. I'm fooling around with it at home and it's amazing. The thing is the size of a briefcase, as compared to the kind of stuff you had to deal with. That was a HUGE eight-track thing you built. You piled those Ampex machines together to make a recorder that was as tall as the room, right?

Les: Seven feet tall! A seven-foot rack.

Johnnie: Oh my!

Les: With a monstrous eight-channel mixer. Then I look back when the first records I ever made, made in Chicago at the Furniture Mart. We would sit in the studio (and) if I struck a note on the guitar or sang a note, they had a VU meter almost as big as the window you're looking into the control room. Well, with that VU meter you'd say, "Hi," and the meter would react like it was saying, "Welllll … I guess I got to get up and go alllll the way over there!"

John Paulson, *Chasing Sound*

Les next to his seven-foot tall Ampex rack

(*laughter*)

Les: It looked like we were being punished with this volume indicator, VU meter that's going to go, "Ohhhh-kay."

Steve: What kind of stuff do you have at your home studio? I know you have all the old equipment, but do you have any new, digital stuff? Have you updated?

Les: Yes, we have some. We're going into a whole new updated studio. Pro Tools is what so many are using today, but I have a problem: Everything goes in my place and nothing goes out!

Steve: Ah, the pack rat syndrome?

Les: Yes! Whatever it is ... I got it! I can't help but think of the old days when you would walk down a street and see signs on the door with the diseases people would have. You're too young to remember that, but we had those signs and I think I'm going to get signs for the different rooms around my house! (*laughter*) Contagious! Don't go near! You can get an infection and start saving everything!

Steve: Ha! A friend of ours told us he had gas. We said, "OK, we'll bite, from what?" He said, "G.A.S.: guitar acquisition syndrome!"

Les: Yes! That is something! My equipment was recently looked at by the Smithsonian, the Waukesha Museum and the Rock Hall of Fame. They are all quite stunned when they walk into the room with the equipment in there.

Steve: Does it still work?

Les: Yeah, well almost ... almost.

Johnnie: YOU could make it work!

Les: Yes, I could make it work, but if you open the door and there's a draft, you'd have to realign everything.

Johnnie: Sensitive, huh?

Steve: Talking about you and Chet Atkins working together, those records were made in Nashville. Did he ever come out to your studio?

Les: Ah ... his brother was working with me, but, ah, I don't think ... no, he never came to my studio at the house. Either place, California, Chicago or New Jersey. No.

Steve: OK, am I right? All the stuff you did with Chet was recorded in Nashville?

Les: Yes, both albums, and some hasn't been released yet.

Steve: Really?!

Les: Yes, there are three or four cuts that haven't been released.

Johnnie: Les, didn't you tell us about Chet sending you a recording that he wanted you to re-record or tweak? What did you do?

Les: Chet sent me the tape with a letter and notes here and there. He said, "If you feel up to it, there are a couple of little things you could redo." Well, I set it aside and forgot all about it. The tape laid there for a couple of months. Finally, my brother-in-law, Wally, said, "Les, what're you going to do about that tape?" I said, "Send it back." Well, he did, and Chet sent me a thank-you note when he got the tape. He said, "It's great!" (*laughter*) I didn't even open it! So the record was released with the little goofs in there.

Johnnie: I love it!

Les: You know what my thinking was? It felt more normal. Maybe that's not the best English. I just had the feeling if we leave it alone, raw, didn't clean it up, it would feel like what happened when we recorded it.

Johnnie: Nowadays you can clean it up till it's sterile.

Steve: Too perfect.

Les: I didn't know if others felt that way.

Johnnie: Duane Eddy has said when he goes into the studio he says, "Look boys, I want it to sound dirty." He wants it to sound real, even with a little background hiss or whatever so it sounds more natural.

Les: Isn't that interesting that people recognizing the original, like Bing when we were recording the flip side of "It's Been A Long, Long Time," and Meredith Wilson, who wrote it, was sitting there at the session. Bing missed a note, and Meredith said to me, "I don't want to say anything." He was afraid of Bing. "Les, would you mention the mistake to Bing?" Of course, Meredith wanted it perfect. So I said to Bing, "Meredith" — Mare is what I called him, he was my commanding officer — "wants to know if you can take another shot at it." Bing said, "No, we're going to leave it alone, the people want to know we're human. Right?"

Steve: Yeah.

Les: His thinking was, the original take WITH the flaws would be a lot better than if it was perfect. It becomes mechanical, like Johnnie said.

Steve: That's my biggest problem with some music today ... it's so perfect it has no soul. When you're so concerned with getting it perfect, you lose the feeling.

Les: Yes. You know, Steve, when this thing started, making multi-track recordings acetate to acetate, that kind of thing, then came the tape. It was just luck I found sound-on-sound and used that. Then ... one day the alarm went off and I knew what to do and made multi-track recording. Individual tracks where you could go back and correct and tweak. Do anything you wish with the recording. You know, we never, not only did we never have a hit with eight-track, we made some great recordings, just never a hit. The one thing we found we lost was ... feeling. The more the machine could run YOU, the more the creative problems we had. There's something about you have to go for it, you can't do it again and the first time was the most, the best.

Steve: For people who don't know, correct me if I'm wrong Les, the early recordings you and Mary did, every layer was a performance as opposed to something you multi-tracked and you could correct this part or that part of it. All of the early performances like "How High the Moon," you did each track as a performance and you had to get it correct.

Les: That is right. If there are twenty-four tracks and you miss any one of them you had to go back to ONE.

Johnnie: So if it's the twenty-third layer and you goof ...

Les: If it's the twenty-third, it's back to square one. I know I've told you we had to make "How High the Moon" three times in one day because a siren went off, a plane went overhead or a fella was going to relieve his kidneys!

Steve: Ha! Not what you want on your recording! Les, we have to break for news. Can you stay with us for a few minutes?

Les: If you want me to, cool.

(music out of break of Chet and Les)

Johnnie: Stop that! It's unnatural!

Steve: That's two guys having more fun than anybody should be able to legally have! One of those guys is with us now, Les

Paul. Les, it sounds like you guys were feeding off each other in those sessions.

Les: Yes, it was fun. You know I was thinking while you were playing that, that the very last conversation I had with Chet, when he remembered … his wife Leona warned me he may drift a little bit. You know the last thing he said to me was, "Les, we've only got 15 minutes and we're on the radio!"

Johnnie: Oh, no.

Les: Yes, it was so strange. For some reason it seemed it was on his mind that he wanted us to get to the radio broadcast.

Les Paul Foundation

*Les and Chet clowning during
a photo session in 1975*

Johnnie: Wow, you'd taken him back to a place.

Les: Yes, so it seemed.

Steve: You'd known Chet for years. Chet's brother worked in your band.

Les: Yes, Jimmy.

Johnnie: Is that how you met Chet, through his brother?

Les: Well, I knew Chet, maybe fifteen years through Jimmy. Jimmy went down to Tennessee when someone in the family had passed away, this was 1939-40. He came back to New York and I said, "How'd it go, Jim?" he said. "Everything is taken care of. By the way, I saw my half-brother who's playing and the kid's pretty good." I asked, "What's he up to?" He said, "He's playing like Merle Travis, he's got a whole thing going on. I thought maybe you could part with one of your guitars for him." I said, "Hey, I've got one here I was about to toss out. It was made by the Larson Brothers in Chicago."

Steve and Johnnie: HUH?

Les: Yep, and you know Chet had that thing hanging in his basement ... that guitar is so precious! It's the first one I ever designed with 27 frets on it. So I gave it to Jim, and he sent it to Chet. About 15 years later, Mary and I are driving through Missouri and I was telling her, "This is the state I started in, down here in Springfield." I hit the radio dial and said, "I think this is where it was." Well, I hear some country music playing and I realize it's live. So of course, I said, "Why don't we drive over? I hope the owners are still there." We drove to the station and I go up to the studio window and I see a fella playing guitar sitting where I used to sit. Right where I sat when I opened the station way back in the '30s. Lo and behold, it was Chet, Chester. I guess he recognized me, 'cause he came to the window and said, "You are Les Paul!" I said, "You must be Chet Atkins!" He said, "Yeah!" That's how we met, at the radio station ... KWTO.

Steve: When was the first time you guys actually played together?

Les: Ah. Oh! It was at WSM-TV in Nashville in 1950. We were the hosts of the Grand Ole Opry. It was the opening for the television network. That's when Chet and Mary and I met. We'd met, but never played together till that night. Where my spot was, I asked if maybe Jimmy Atkins, Ernie Newton and Chet Atkins would come out and play with us. That's when we all played together for the first time. That was a real kick. Of course, it wasn't videotaped then, so it'd have to have been on kinescope. We've never found it. It was the first night we were in Nashville.

Johnnie: What a night!

Steve: I know one of the tapes I still have I'll never get rid of is a performance you did — this was sometime in the '80s — it was Chet Atkins, Duane Eddy and …

Les: Oh! Garrison Keillor!

Steve and Johnnie: YES!

Johnnie: I think Ralph Emery was the host.

Les: Ralph was off that night and Chet Atkins was the host, so he called and asked me to come down for the show. I wondered who that fella was who was so funny. I had never heard of Garrison Keillor. Of course, everyone knows him now! Oh, by the way, he loved Chet. Garrison Keillor is so great.

Johnnie: It was the first time you'd met Garrison Keillor. Was it the first time you met Duane Eddy?

Les: No, I think I'd met him somewhere along the way. You know, he is cool. Really cool!

Johnnie: Kind of defines cool, huh?

Les: Yeah. You know we did the *Vanity Fair* magazine pictures together. You have those, right?

Steve: Are you kidding? We went out and bought five copies!

Les: It's great to be alive, isn't it?

Steve: You know, I can tell you really feel that way. I just went to the website *redhotred.com*. There's a picture from Monday night of you and your band and a little kid is on stage with you. Who was that?

Les: He's 13 years old. My bass player, Nicki, asked if he could come up and play and I said, "Sure!" I had no idea this fella had a few problems. His problems didn't affect his playing at all. He's only been playing for a few years and he stunned everybody, even though he had problems speaking and didn't want to talk. So we took him to the piano and ... boy! When he played, it was awesome. It's wonderful how things work ... he could have a problem over here, but excel over here.

Johnnie: That's a terrific picture. You have a great smile anyway.

Les: I just do that when they're going to shoot a picture!

(laughter)

Johnnie: I'm surprised the people who make turtlenecks haven't come to you to make you their spokesmodel.

Les: I tell you that turtleneck ... I've got to get one that's a little taller ... come up to my ears! *(laughter)*

Johnnie: You look great! We get tickled when we give out the website where people can see who was on stage with you each Monday night at the club. Invariably, someone will hear the address *redhotred.com* and say it sounds like a naughty site!

Les: Ha! Say, when are you guys going to drop in at the club?

Johnnie: We are ... really.

Les: Yeah, sure. I've got to get back to Chicago and get up to Wisconsin to see that new Les Paul highway in Waukesha.

Johnnie: You do!

Les: Well, you see, I want to make that a toll road. *(laughter)*

Johnnie: And you want 60 percent of the tolls!

Les: Aw, I just want to go home. I know some of the places are still the same. I just want to see if the sewers are still there I'd climb in to go to school! *(laughter)*

Johnnie: If you ever decide to fly into O'Hare, we will be sure you are limoed.

Steve: Heck! We'll drive you to Waukesha! Speaking of that, any chance you'll come back to the House of Blues in Chicago?

Les: I think I just about had it. I'm hanging my guitar on a hook. I'm gonna play here at the Club Iridium. We're making a new Iridium. It'll be close to Times Square at 51st and Broadway. You know 52nd is famous and we'll be one block down, moving toward 42nd Street.

Steve: Are you recording those Monday night performances?

Les: Since 1984 till now we've recorded all of our Monday night guests at the club. We have a lot with wonderful guests. We hope to release some of those.

Steve: That's great news! Les, it's been great visiting with you tonight and talking about your dear friend Chet Atkins. Thank you.

 A little more Les ...

The guitar is just a wonderful instrument. It's everything: a bartender, a psychiatrist, a housewife. Whenever I find that I've got a problem, I'll go pick my guitar up and play. It's the greatest pal in the whole world. — Les Paul

An admitted pack rat, Les saved virtually every piece of equipment he ever bought or built. Above, in the foreground, are the headsets he wore when recording duets with Mary. In the background is the Ampex reel-to-reel recorder given to him by Bing Crosby. Les modified it to allow the first sound-on-sound recording. Below are the volume controls, as labeled by Les, for his and Mary's guitars.

Photos from John Paulson, *Chasing Sound*

19

The 50th Anniversary
of
The Les Paul Guitar

Steve: It was 50 years ago this week the first guitars shipped that forever changed the face of music. It was May 20th, 1952, when the Les Paul Guitar became a reality. The man responsible for that guitar is Les Paul, and he joins us now.

Les: I still have those guitars. They're under my bed ... I pull them out and water them from time to time. (*laughter*)

Steve: Can I take you back 50 years? Do you recall your reaction to those first guitars?

Les: Oh, I flipped out. I remember Mary said, "I can't imagine you playing that thing. It's so tiny." I had been playing this monstrous guitar I'd drag out on stage. To have a small guitar was a whole new innovation. It was like an ironing board with a pickup on it. I loved the fact they were electric, amplified. You could turn the volume up. You could do so many things with it. I know 50 years later there isn't a parent of a guitar player who hasn't said, "Oh, that Les Paul! Thanks a lot!" as the kid is in the basement playing WIDE OPEN!

Johnnie: The Les Paul Standard available today, is it any different than the ones shipped to you 50 years ago?

Les: No, not really. The only difference is the first ones were flat top. The chairman of the board, M.H. Berlin, who lived in Lincolnwood, came to me and said, "Do you like violins?" I said, "I love violins." He told me he collected violins and invited me to his house. He said, "Let's go to my vault." Well, he showed me the most beautiful violins. He said you just wanted to hug them and love them. He said, "Would you consider arching the top of the guitar to make it look like the violin?" I said, "I'd love that!" Of course, today that's what makes it so wonderful, and it is a very loving instrument.

Steve: Wasn't one of the other changes the tailpiece? Someone at Gibson got the tailpiece wrong?

Les: Oh yeah. The first two, you couldn't play them 'cause somewhere along the line the guys at Gibson thought they'd made a mistake and to correct it, what they did was run the strings under, and not over, the stop bar. So, you couldn't lean your wrist on it and mute the strings. That's one of the first things I did, a style they called "chicken plucking." You couldn't do that the way they had it strung. If you string it incorrectly, the neck was way off. So, they took them apart, reglued the neck, restrung them, and sent them back to me. (*laughter*) We got them and I looked at them, and I asked, "How many have gone out that way?" They said about 700, maybe a thousand. So all those rare, rare birds are out there, and they are all "goofs."

Johnnie: Highly collectible goofs, huh?

Les: Yeah, when someone brings a goof in for me to see, I say, "Do you know what you've got in your hands? You've got one we screwed up and it's worth a fortune." It's cool ... a mistake paid off.

Johnnie: Now, I'm guessing there are over 100 variations of Les Paul guitars.

Les: You know, I don't know. I was just with the president of Gibson and I said, "So many ask, 'How many Les Paul guitars have gone out in the last 50 years?'" He said, "We have no idea."

Johnnie: Oh, my gosh!

Les: But it's got to be a staggering number. I told my brother-in-law — we were sitting on the steps outside the house for him to have a cigarette — I said, "You know, Wally, the guitar has been good to me. It will probably be gone in a few years. I'm happy the kids like them." That was 40 years ago! Shows what I knew. (*laughter*) Isn't that unbelievable?

Steve: For anybody who doesn't know, this isn't exaggerating. The Les Paul Guitar is the most successful celebrity guitar endorsement in the history of music, in the history of the world, ever!

Les: And I'm a lousy businessman. That's the only thing I ever did in business that I'm real happy about. When we finish a show and I see a line of 30 or 40 people waiting to meet me, occasionally the wives are along, each guy has a guitar with him. The guitar comes first. Sometimes I even ask the wives or girlfriends, "How do you handle his other love?"

Johnnie: I bet you look at a group like that and you see all ages. In fact, we have a package a 15-year-old sent us. He was assigned to write about someone who's had a profound effect on his life and he chose you. He's been babysitting since he was 13, and he's saved enough money to buy a Les Paul guitar, and not a cheap one. He bought himself a really good one.

Les: When was that?

Johnnie: Recently. The guitar has changed this young man's life, and he chose you to do his theme paper on.

Steve: He put together a scrapbook as if he were you. He wrote about your life story, how you started, all about your hit records, everything.

Les: Isn't that something.

Johnnie: It'll break your heart. It's a wonderful tribute to you and he got a good grade. He sent us the original to send to you.

Les: Oh, I'd love that!

Johnnie: Buckle up. It brought me to tears. This kid put a lot

of blood, sweat and tears and love into it.

Steve: We'll send it to you and maybe we can get you both on the air sometime.

Les: Great, I look forward to that.

Johnnie: You know, it's exciting to think with his drive you just know in a few years he'll be taking that guitar to gigs, thanks to you.

Les: I probably won't see it, but bet he will do just that.

Steve: I won't be surprised when he's old enough he'll be standing in line waiting to meet you in person. I'm looking at pictures of you from Monday and you look great at 87. You look healthier than most people half your age.

Les: Oh, that's thanks to Chris, my photographer, and Russ, my son. They make me look good! I remember there was a gaffer that lived across the street from me when I lived in Hollywood. He did all the Bette Davis stuff. He knew just how to make her look good, and she wouldn't have anyone else do the lighting. He did it so wrinkles wouldn't show and the photographer could get great shots. That's what the guys do for me now. I tell Russ, "BACK UP, BACK UP! I look better from back there." (*laughter*)

Steve: Chris Lentz also does these shots of you on the website each week.

Les: Yes, he's good and a nice guy. So talented. He's the one that says, "I'm going to get you a computer for your birthday." I said, "Just the power of suggestion and I already have carpal tunnel!" (*laughter*)

Steve: I'm amazed you don't have a computer. Of course, you'd be tempted to take it apart.

Les: I'm afraid I'm going to love it and spend too much time on it. Right now I'm spending a lot of time on what will be a beautiful book. This Cochran fella has been out a few times and coming back this weekend to take pictures of my guitars. It's going to be a coffee table book.

Steve: Like the Chet Atkins book?

Les: Yes! The same guy is doing mine.

Steve: That's wonderful.

Les: Have you seen the Chet book?

Johnnie: I bought it for Steve's birthday last year.

Les: Oh, it knocked me out, and Chet got to see it before he passed away. He signed one for me. When I was exercising tonight I was thinking of him.

Johnnie: What kind of exercising?

Les: I have to walk to the bathroom sometimes! (*laughter*) I sometimes think while I walk.

Steve: Both?! (*laughter*)

Les: I was also thinking about how cool it was that "Sitting On Top of the World" was recently played for the astronauts who were fixing the Hubble Telescope.

Steve: Wasn't one of the astronauts on the mission recently at the Club to see you?

Les: Yes. I got him up on stage. They all came and brought me an autographed picture. Of course, I was honored to be asked to wake them up. I said, "All right you guys, wake up and aim that thing down on me in Mahwah, New Jersey. You'll know it's me; I'll be out watering my trees." (*laughter*)

Johnnie: Just when you think you've done everything, an opportunity like that comes along.

Les: Oh yes! You know several of the guys were very serious. Scott Carpenter stops by the show all the time, and he is just a sweetheart.

Johnnie: Are any of the astronauts musicians?

Les: I know Scott is. He plays a little guitar — enough to want to play more. I think that's probably better than the guy who's so obsessed with playing he's pained when he doesn't get something exactly right. Monday night, there must have been 10 or 12 guitarists on stage with me. One tried to play better than the last guy. It's like they were fightin' it out, and I was thinking, they're going to go home and say, "I wish I'd done this or that, or why didn't I play better?" The reality is, one guy may be able to play what the next guy can't, but don't beat yourself up. The things you can do on a guitar are unlimited ... make it your own.

Johnnie: We just had a guy in the studio who had just come from performing with you at the club. He's become a good friend. He's Doyle Dykes.

Les: Oh, isn't he good!?

Johnnie: He looks like the guitar is an extension of his arm. He makes it so natural, punctuating his conversation with a little Chet licks, or a little Les.

Les: Yes, yes, he is so good.

Steve: I've got to tell you there's a guitar we are both, Doyle and I, are looking for: The Les Paul Recording Guitar.

Les: You can't find them?

Steve: No, and I just got a call this week from Doyle, and he found one with a Bigsby. It's a '73. He said, "If you don't want it, let me know 'cause I will get it."

Les: And, if he doesn't take it, I will!

Steve: That's what you play on stage now, right?

Les: Yes, I play a Les Paul Recording and guitarists have commented so often on the different sound I get.

Steve: It's the low impedance pickups that make the difference, right?

Les: The low impedance pickups go back to the beginning when I started in Waukesha and did a hysterectomy on Mom's telephone. The low impedance pickup idea came from Ma Bell. I took the phone apart and held the earpiece under the string. I just lifted the diaphragm of the phone off and put it underneath the string and plugged it into the radio. That's when I heard my first electric guitar. That's going to be part of the display they're putting together at The Rock and Roll Hall of Fame. I told them all about it, and the piece of railroad track I used, so they had to find a surplus piece of railroad track and get someone to cut it off to two-and-a-half feet long. They'll think it's crazy that someone's going to make a guitar out of it.

Johnnie: That's a great story, Les.

Les: I remember running to Mom and saying, "I got it, I got it!" She said, "WHAT?" I said, "This piece of railroad track ... it's perfect! It sounds great." She said, "The day you see a cowboy on a horse playing a railroad track, I'll believe you." And with that, she ran me out of the kitchen.

Johnnie: What kind of strings did you use?

Les: I only needed one. That's all I needed to know it would work. Hey, if it'd work with one, I knew it would work with five more. *(laughter)*

Steve: That's the key to the Les Paul Recording guitar, right? The same theory as the telephone.

Les: Well, that was the most important thing. All the intricacies, the size wires, the wiring — all that was from a 1915 phone. I think Mom let me attack it in the '20s.

Johnnie: Did you ever injure yourself doing those experiments?

Les: Hell, lifting a railroad track wasn't easy!

Johnnie: I have visions of you messing with electricity and curling your hair!

Les: Oh yeah, I spent well over a year out of the playing business because I stuck my hand in a transmitter with the guitar in my other hand. I lit up! (*laughs*) It was a shock, no pun intended. I went to Mayo Clinic because I was desperate to get the use of my hands back. They said I was like a person who'd been hit by lightning. My symptoms were similar, and they warned me the numbness in my hands may take a year to go away, or may never go away. You don't know how much of my inability to play was from the actual shock, or the anxiety of never being able to play again, the daily stress. I remember going back to the first person I ever worked with in jazz, Eddie South, The Dark Angel of the Violin. He was playing on Sheridan near Montrose at the Bar Ritz on the North Side of Chicago. I went in there during the time I was recovering from the shock, '41-'42, and I hung out with him. That's how I ended up in Chicago the second time. I wasn't playing, but I worked as the music director at 'JJD, 'BBM and WIND.

Johnnie: We never knew the reason you ended up behind the scenes in radio.

Les: I had to quit playing and was seriously praying I'd recover. I went to the Mayo Clinic, and they said, "This must be celebrity day." In fact, one doctor said, "Are you the fella with the band?" I said, "No, I'm not Les Brown!" I still get that today. I asked, "What other celebrity is here today?" The doctor said, "Eddie South." Eddie was there with tuberculosis. He didn't make it. The last time we talked was at the Mayo, and we actually went back to the days at the Regal on the South Side of Chicago with Louie Armstrong.

Johnnie: Wow! It's amazing how your lives crossed paths over the years.

Steve: Did you ever record with Louie?

Les: No. Oh, yes, I did, but they were live army broadcasts. Not a commercial record yet. We were with the same record company. Mary and I were in Chicago to play the Blue Note. I came in with a sport shirt on, loafers, checked socks, and Mary was wearing a gingham dress. I had a bass player — we were a trio then. Well, we got fired after that first night. (*laughter*) There was a phone on the wall right off the stage, and I heard the manager call New York and say, "Get me someone else, not these hillbillies." The three of us got fired that night. I was doing comedy, talking to the audience. Well, the story goes, the New York offices told the manager they would send Louie Armstrong, but he couldn't be there till the next week. It so happened there were a lot of "pencils" in the audience that night writing reviews. I had decided since Louie couldn't be there for a week, we would go out and get a gown for Mary, a tux for me, a comb for my hair, a tie for the bass player, and new strings for the guitar. We showed up at the club that afternoon and told the manager we were ready to work that night because Louie can't start till next week. He said, "Have you seen the reviews of Monday's show?" I said, "What reviews?" Well, it turned out the reviews were wonderful. We were called refreshing, not stiff, not the same ol' same. We were new and different. So the manager called Louie and told him not to come to Chicago. We were told we were staying, BUT we couldn't wear the new clothes! (*laughter*)

Johnnie: That's a wonderful story. The classic case of agents and managers telling you what you have to do to be marketable, and surprise, surprise, the public wants the opposite. The public wants something new.

(commercial break)

Johnnie: Oh my goodness, during the break I opened a package that arrived today. Steve hasn't seen this. It's a package from a listener named Nicky or Micky Clemmons in Waterford, Wisconsin. It's a 10-inch copy of the *Bye, Bye Blues* album.

Steve: Wow! It looks brand new! Thanks, Micky. Is that a book with it?

Johnnie: It's sheet music of "The Carioca."

Les: That's great. You know, Mary and I did the *Bye, Bye Blues* album in one day. And I'll never forget a hot summer night we decided to drive over to La Guardia to watch the planes land. We didn't live far from the airport. We got there, parked, rolled down the windows, and started playing our guitars. Mary was playing rhythm and I played "The Carioca." We played it over and over. We had no idea anyone was listening or could even hear us. Well, we stopped playing, and horns started blowing. People loved it and wanted us to play more. I've never forgotten that.

Johnnie: A nice memory.

gibson presents
muriel anderson's
**All Star
Guitar Night**
featuring
LES PAUL

20

Muriel Anderson's All Star Guitar Night

S ince the first time we visited "Music City" we have loved
Nashville. Even though the lion's share of our time in
broadcasting has been based in Chicago, "The Athens of the
South" has been a very welcoming place for us. We've been fortunate enough to host concerts at the Ryman Auditorium and share
that fabled stage with such greats as Brenda Lee, Duane Eddy, Peter Frampton and others. So, while we were not novices to this
legendary structure, this time was different.

The date was Friday, July 18, 2003. Muriel Anderson was
presenting one of her legendary All Star Guitar Nights at the Ryman and THIS time it was a special tribute to Les Paul. The concert
coincided with the summer National Association of Music Merchants (NAMM) show in Nashville, which meant that a lot of very
talented musicians would be in Music City, many of whom would
be participating in the tribute to Les.

We made the drive from Chicago to Nashville with our
longtime Chicago broadcasting friends, Gary Schroeder and his
wife, Sue Berg, a voice-over actress. The morning of the show, Muriel Anderson called and asked if we could give her a hand. She was
going to be co-hosting the second part of the show with Les and
had a special guitar player's chair that she needed help getting to
the Ryman. So, along with Gary and Sue, we drove out to Muriel's
house, wrestled the chair into the trunk of Gary's car and chauf-

feured it to the Ryman.

It was mid-afternoon when we walked into the auditorium. A small group of people were gathered on stage doing a sound check. We quietly found seats in the back row and watched and listened as Les and his group went through some songs, preparing for that night's show.

A bit of background is in order.

Along with some of the other medical problems that SHOULD have compromised his ability to play, Les Paul was dealing with hearing loss. He wore not one, but TWO hearing aids. As he told us in a couple of interviews, in addition to constantly tinkering with guitars, sound recording techniques and various electronics, he was working with Shure Incorporated on some hearing aid improvements.

So, although we shouldn't have been, we were surprised when, in the middle of one of the numbers during the sound check, Les stopped the song, talked to the sound board engineer in the back of the auditorium, and asked him to make a few tweaks to the sound of Les's guitar. Now, you have to understand that Les was not leaving it up to the engineer to decide what adjustments to make. Les was politely, but firmly, telling him exactly what adjustments to make and exactly how many decibels to raise this or that fader.

The adjustments were made, and Les played a little and asked for a few more tweaks. Each time, we could hear a distinct improvement to the sound. Whatever special sauce Les had added to his hearing aids, we're here to testify that it worked! After a few more tries, Les had the sound he wanted and the settings he knew would sound best in Nashville's most revered music hall.

When the rehearsal finished, we made our way to the front, and as we walked on stage, Les was talking with a few people. But when he saw us, he quickly walked over to welcome us and gave Johnnie a hug.

Chris Lentz

Les's soundchecks were legendary for their length and his pursuit of perfection. ABOVE, he and his trio warm up before Muriel Anderson's All Star Guitar Night tribute to Les in 2003 at Nashville's Ryman Auditorium.

We talked for a few minutes and waited while Les was called over to the side of the stage to take a couple of formal portraits that were going to be used for upcoming articles in the Nashville press. At one point, a father brought his young son up to Les and tentatively asked if Les would mind having his picture taken. Without hesitation, Les agreed and started talking to the boy as the picture was taken. Someone made the remark that the boy was probably too young to realize the significance of what was happening, but in coming years, he would be happy to have this treasure.

With the pictures and sound check completed, Les needed to relax a bit. It had already been a long day that included some meeting and greeting, and the show was still ahead of him, so we headed to his dressing room, just off the Ryman's stage.

Les settled onto the couch and asked about our trip to

Nashville, how we had been, and, as was his norm, he started sharing war stories about past trips to Nashville and points beyond.

We had only been talking for a few minutes when we heard the first of what would turn out to be a steady series of knocks on the door, signaling another interviewer or fan wanting "just a couple of seconds" with Les. Then a PR person from Gibson Guitars needed Les to follow him upstairs for a meet-and-greet. Tired as he must have been, Les just smiled and obliged.

We were both a little surprised that some of the people who pulled Les in various directions were not more sensitive to the fact that, regardless of his seemingly endless supply of energy, Les was not a young man. He was certainly not the "Energizer Bunny" they seemed to expect, and he might have needed a little time to recharge his batteries.

When Les returned from the Gibson meet-and-greet, it was obvious that he was a little beat. And even though the first half of the show had started — featuring such greats as Nokie Edwards (of The Ventures), Victor Wooten, Bela Fleck, Seymour Duncan, Hubert Sumlin, Thom Bresh, Johnny Hiland, Peter Huttlinger, Dave Pomeroy, and more — there was still a constant flow of traffic at Les's dressing room door. So Johnnie took over, acting as the "gatekeeper" as we did our best to make sure Les got a bite to eat and a little time to rest.

A couple of the knocks at the door couldn't be ignored. One was a British radio host who had journeyed across the big pond to record an interview with Les on the occasion of his All Star Guitar

Night tribute.

Another knock was one of those moments that we were privileged to have fly-on-the-wall seats to see.

After the knock, someone said "Scotty's here."

"Scotty who?" asked Johnnie.

"Scotty Moore."

For the uninitiated, Scotty Moore is the man whose guitar helped a young truck driver from Memphis change the face of music when Elvis Presley kicked open the door to rock 'n' roll.

Scotty and his longtime business partner and companion, Gail Pollock, were quickly welcomed in, and Les and Scotty wasted no time sharing tales, tall and otherwise, from their singularly impactful careers that have cast the kind of long shadows on the music industry and popular culture few can claim.

As beat as Les may have been moments earlier, Scotty's arrival and conversation seemed to rejuvenate him. And, although we have had more than our fair share of moments with celebrities, Steve was practically levitating. Being invited to spend this very special occasion with Les was more than enough, but having another of his guitar idols join the festivities was the icing on the cake.

Les with Scotty Moore backstage at the Ryman Auditorium

Chris Lentz

Steve with
two of his
guitar heroes:
Les Paul and
Scotty Moore

Chris Lentz

So of course, a picture had to be taken.

As Les started to get up from the couch to take some pictures, he asked Johnnie if she would give him a hand. She bent forward to give him both hands to pull him to his feet, but like a child, he reached up to be lifted off the couch. Johnnie bent all the way over and he put both arms around her neck. As she was lifting him up he chuckled and whispered in her ear, "I may be old, but I'm not dead!" When he was on his feet, his arms were still around her neck as they both busted out laughing. We think that was the first time Johnnie called him a rascal, but she would find many an occasion to call him one in the future!

After a few more pictures were taken, it was getting close to show time for Les. So, after making sure that he was comfortable and making plans to see him for a few minutes before his talk the following afternoon at the Country Music Hall of Fame, we left Les's dressing room with Scotty and Gail.

When we got back to the seating area, at Les's request, one of the Ryman's ushers made sure the four of us were sitting just a little off to the side, but close to the stage. From that vantage point, even in the darkened auditorium, as video highlights from Les's career showed on a big screen, we could see Les and his band taking their places. When the movie ended and the large screen raised to reveal Les and his band, the whole place erupted into a standing ovation.

During the show, Gibson Guitar CEO Henry Juszkiewicz presented Les with a specially-made replica of his famous "log" guitar, and *Guitar Player* magazine's editor, Michael Molenda, presented Les with the first-ever *Guitar Player* "Legend" award.

We have to confess that finding ourselves sitting in the Ryman with the legendary Scotty Moore as we watched Les Paul weave his magic was far from your everyday concert experience. Although it was a night of highlights, the one that totally surprised and REALLY stood out for us, was when Les started talking about his memories of being in Nashville and the times spent in Music City that meant the most to him. Times with Mary Ford and dear friends like Chet Atkins ... "and Steve and Johnnie from WGN."

We knew that, over the years, we had developed a very real and very special relationship with Les, but to have him include us that way on that night ... well, we were stunned. And we were glad

The view from Steve and Johnnie's seats at the Ryman

that the seating area of the Ryman was in the dark because we both got a bit tearful when Les followed up those words with a beautiful version of "Somewhere Over The Rainbow."

After the show, we went back to our hotel, which was located just across from the Country Music Hall of Fame and Museum. "A Conversation with Les Paul" was scheduled for 2 p.m. the following day, and while we didn't have tickets to this sold-out event, we'd planned on seeing Les for just a few minutes before his appearance to say our goodbyes.

When we walked over to the Hall of Fame, there was already a large crowd to see Les, so we got in line with them. Overhearing snippets of conversations, we could tell that, like us, many of those in the crowd had been to the All Star Guitar Night show and were still basking in the afterglow of that memorable event.

Finally, we saw Les entering the building with an entourage from the Hall of Fame that included his son, Russ, and his photographer and close friend, Chris Lentz. As he was walking up to the Hall's auditorium, Les saw us standing in line, came over and pulled us out of the crowd, saying, "Come with me. I want you two sitting in the front row close to me so I'll be able to look up and be sure to see some friendly faces."

For the next two hours, sitting next to what appeared to be a floating box with the replica of his "log" experimental guitar inside (shown on the next page), Les answered questions and enthralled the audience with his stories. That "Conversation with Les Paul" is now part of the archives at the Country Music Hall of Fame and Museum.

When the Hall of Fame appearance ended, Les came over to us and wanted to know how we thought he did. Of course, we were enthusiastic, but Les wasn't sure. This wasn't false modesty. As much as he followed the show business axiom of "leave them wanting more," Les frequently seemed to feel that he should have said or done more.

After making plans for Les to join us by telephone on our show the following Monday night for a recap of the weekend's events, Les gave Johnnie a hug, and we said our goodbyes and headed back to Chicago.

A little more Les ...

If I have to go around telling everyone how great I am, then there's something wrong with my act. — Les Paul

Muriel Anderson and Les Paul during one of many performances that began with their introduction on the Steve and Johnnie Show

Chris Lentz

memories from ...
Muriel Anderson

*I*t was sometime between midnight and one o'clock. I had just finished playing "Nola" on guitar on Steve and Johnnie's show. Steve said, "There's a caller for you on line one. It's Les Paul." I was trying to think of which of my friends was playing a joke on me as I took the call. "This is Les. I'm listening on the radio I built myself. Listening from New Jersey," he said on the air. "I really like your playing. If you're in New York on a Monday night, come, sit in." I did, a number of times.

One day, I was backstage at the Iridium and Les told me about a time he was doing a show with Judy Garland, when a little man with glasses walked up to him and said, "I have an invention you might be interested in. The Germans were using it during the war and I think it would be good for music. It's called 'audiotape!'"

After getting to know Les and hearing his stories, how, in his lifetime, he saw and participated so much in the rise of the recording industry as we know it, I thought it was appropriate to give him a proper tribute. I had been producing my All Star Guitar Night shows for many years and had arranged to rent the Ryman Auditorium for my upcoming show. I decided to dedicate the show as a tribute to Les and his contributions to music. I told him my plans and asked if he would like to attend. "Yes, but I won't play unless you hire my band," he said. "You'll play in the show?" I asked, not anticipating even the possibility.

It was a beautiful thing. Gibson Guitars set up a reception

for him in their showroom. That night at the Ryman Auditorium, Les and his band played a fine set and a dozen or so artists performed and gave tribute to Les. A great time was had by all. Les and I co-hosted the show, and in introducing each artist, Les, true to form, never missed an opportunity for funny and colorful patter on stage!

He wasn't just a great guitarist and entertainer, he was always an inventor, innovator, and an inspiration.

Muriel

A little more Les ...

> *I got out of the car and there was a knife in my neck. The guy says, "Don't move." And the drummer got out of the car, and he got a gun in his head. This was my entrance to the South Side of Chicago. But it was necessary, because I wanted to play jazz. — Les Paul*

a little more about ...

Muriel Anderson

*I*n her own way, Muriel Anderson has carried on Les Paul's legacy. Years ago, a young and tiny Muriel picked up a guitar and fell in love with it. Her small stature didn't get in the way of her desire. Years later, in one of her many appearances on our show, we marveled at the way her still small hands were able to brilliantly move over the large guitar. We asked, "How on earth did you ever learn to play that big guitar?"

She quickly responded, "Well, nobody ever told me I couldn't."

Just as Les Paul innovated and blazed paths, Muriel has never been comfortable with being a follower. She is the first woman to win the National Fingerstyle Guitar Championship. She is the founder and host of the legendary All Star Guitar Night® concert series, an annual guitar-centric event bringing together the finest pickers on the planet. ASGN not only delights standing-room-only audiences, but raises money for the Music for Life Alliance charity, which Muriel founded so that disadvantaged children can have access to instruments and music instruction in their schools.

Muriel's award-winning double CD *Nightlight-Daylight* is the first CD to incorporate interactive fiber optics. And all of that is just the tip of the Muriel Anderson iceberg.

A seasoned world traveler taking her music to all corners of the globe, Muriel has been known to pause in the midst of her travels to give us a call. Maybe just to say hello, or to share her latest pastry discovery from a restaurant in Paris. She's also been known to have some serious "guitar pulls" at her house, and join in at our house, too.

We're lucky to have her in our life. Les felt that way, too. Here's what he once said about Muriel: "Just one hell of a great player ... a great personality, and what I like is the touch that Muriel has on the guitar. The way she plays is like we all wish to play."

Steve and Johnnie

Muriel Anderson, Steve and Johnnie at WGN Radio

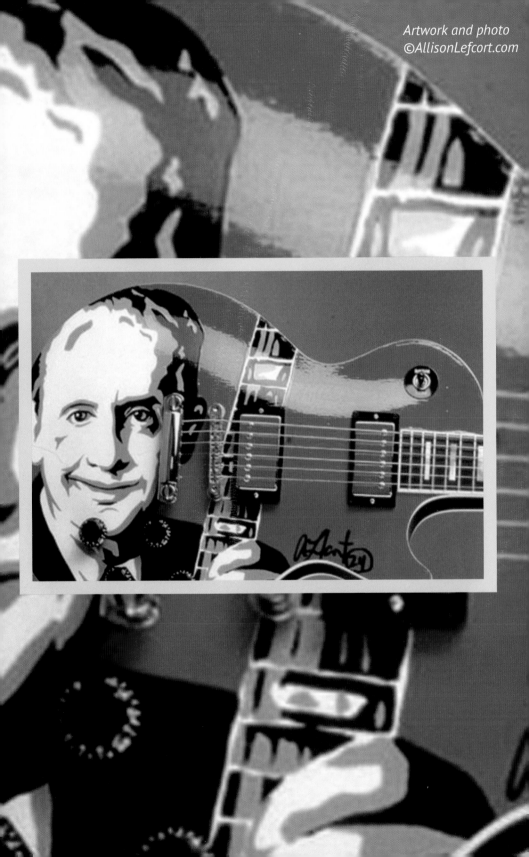

Artwork and photo
©AllisonLefcort.com

April 16, 2008

"It's Been a Long, Long Time" in the Making

Les: Thank you guys for inviting me on for National Guitar Month. So many people come down to the club, say they drive all the way from Illinois and Wisconsin to New York, come to the show and turn around and drive back.

Johnnie: They make a pilgrimage to see you!

Les: Well, so many tell me they hear me on your show and that's why they've come to see me. They all talk about Steve and Johnnie!

Steve: We pay them well! Les, when you were young, was there any performer you'd drive out of your way to see?

Les: Yes, Bing Crosby, the most important person I ever worked with in my life. As far as Bing being a talented man and someone you'd look upon to think, "Someday I could be half as good as that guy." Bing was always so nice to me. He called me the night before he passed away. He told me he wanted to come see me. He said, "You know you made an album with some hillbilly. I was on a plane flying to Europe, and I listened to the thing over and over, all the way over. It is priceless." This is the one I did with Chet Atkins. He said, "Would you do that with me?" I said, "Bing, I'd love to do that!" Bing went on to say, "I'll come over on flight so and so." And I said, "I'll never remember, can I tape it?" He said, "Tape it." So the last conversation the night before he passed away, I taped. He talked about what time he would come in, on what flight, songs we'd do, how we'd chat, kid around, kibbutz like Chet and I did.

Les Paul Archives

This photo of Bing Crosby with The Les Paul Trio is interesting for a couple of reasons. One, it appears Bing is reading the sheet music for "Whose Dream Are You." As you'll read in the accompanying transcription, neither Bing nor Les could read music. Also, "Whose Dream Are You" was written by Les's friend Meredith Wilson, and was the "B" side of "It's Been a Long, Long Time" when the 10-inch 78 rpm record was released in 1945.

Steve: Oh boy, that would have been extraordinary. Les, I want to play a bit of your first record with Bing. That was "It's Been A Long, Long Time," right?

Les: Yes.

(out of the music)

Steve: That was back in the days of the Les Paul Trio. Les, I don't know if I ever asked you … I always had the impression Bing was very easygoing, laid back. Was he like that in the recording studio, in person?

Les: Oh yes, he was REAL laid back. In fact, when he called me the night before we recorded that song, he said, "You like to do a number with me tomorrow?" I said, "Sure, what time?" He said "Eight o'clock." Well, I thought he meant at night, but he meant that next morning. So, I went over to the Paramount lot real early where he was doing *Going My Way*. I was watching him until he took a break and he and I had a chance to talk. Finally, he handed me the music and said, "Play this thing for me." I said, "Geez, I'd love to, but I don't read music … I can't read it!" He said, "We got a problem. I can't read either!" (*laughter*)

So, a gaffer hears us and comes down off a ladder and said, "I play a little piano, I can give it a try." He played the song through something like it was written. We went over and we kinda made up a melody, so the writers had to make changes before the record came out!

Steve: I never heard that story, Les!

Les: Once, Bing told me, "Get in the car." So I got in his car and we went up and down Sunset Boulevard. He kept pointing at different buildings and he'd say, "You like that building?" I'd say, "It's a beautiful building." We kept driving and he showed me another place, another and another. Finally I said, "Bing, I don't get it. What are we looking at all the buildings for?" He said, "There's something I want you to do. I want to buy a building … I want to build something for YOU … The Les Paul House of Sound, OK?" He went on to explain that he wanted the place to be where I could teach kids how to play guitar. The place would cover the evolution of recording all the way to the present … like a museum. I listened, but didn't even think about it long before I said, "Bing, I just want to play my guitar." Well, I went back home and two friends, Vern and Lloyd, were waiting there and said, "How'd it go with Bing?" I said, "It went fine, but he's on this kick where he wants me to go into business like Fred Astaire Dance School, but teaching guitar." They said, "Why don't you do it?" Again, I said, "I just want to play my guitar." The two guys said, "We'll help you build this in your garage right here, turn it into a recording studio," which we did. Later, Bing came over and checked it out. He was standing in my backyard when he said, "This is the best sound I ever heard." He said, "I insist you do the House of Sound." Well, I never did, until about three months ago, I got a call. I can't give you details yet, but there IS going to be a Les Paul House of Sound!

Johnnie: What?

Les: Isn't that a shocker?

Steve: Les, that's wonderful!

Les: Yes, it is wonderful and in my lifetime I never thought I'd do it. I just want to credit Bing with the idea. The great idea.

Johnnie: Well, if you met Bing in the '40s, this idea is 60 years in the making!

Les: That's right! It only happened a few months ago when some people came to me, people with heavy pockets. They came in and said, "Hey, we've got to do something about you. We want to cover all of your inventions from the beginning until tomorrow. We want kids to be able to go in, learn, play the guitar, even record. Do the same thing you did and are doing, and even play along with you! We'll have the display cover recording from Edison till now."

Johnnie: That's wonderful!

Les: You're the first people outside of the folks behind this idea I've told. Tomorrow, we'll have a conference call and start working it out. We'll get trucks here to get all the stuff and move it to the location. By the way, it's only a short distance from where you are in Chicago.

Steve: So this is going to be some of the things in your home studio moved to the House of Sound?

Les: All of it!

Steve: Wow!

Les: From the beginning. The first inventions. The first guitars. First recording lathes right on through the multi-track tape machine. Even have a recording studio so people can go in and hands-on make their own recordings.

Johnnie: And it really does all go back to Bing. Not just the idea and name of "The Les Paul House of Sound," but Bing gave you that first Ampex recorder.

Les: That's exactly right.

Johnnie: Your life was forever changed along with the success of a song like "It's Been A Long, Long Time," your own music and your inventions. As you moved into the '50s you were a household name.

Les: Now you know why I picked Bing as my favorite person.

Steve: Les, what kind of equipment are you using these days in your studio?

Les: We've transitioned to digital equipment. The Library of Congress is coming here to take everything I've recorded, everything I've done, and it's all going to be in the Library of Congress. All the stuff will be stored after it's restored and kept so it doesn't deteriorate. In the meantime, we've found a home for all the equipment up in Waukesha, Wisconsin, where it all started for me. The past, all the way up till tomorrow. We've got some new guitars coming out, too.

Steve: I've seen the Les Paul Robot.

Les: Yes, that's one. The Robot is a guitar that tunes itself. There's the new digital guitar, and the one with five pickups buried. These are the future of guitars. I think they are ahead of their time.

Steve: Les, of all the things you've invented, if you had to pick just one, what's the coolest thing you've ever invented?

Les: Mary! (*laughter*)

Johnnie: How did you meet Mary, and was she Mary Ford when you met?

Les: No, she wasn't Mary Ford, she was Colleen Summers.

Johnnie: And what a knockout.

Les: Oh yes, and what a talent.

Johnnie: I've seen film of her singing with Jimmy Wakely.

Steve: There's a video where she was doing harmony with him in some old black and white movie.

Johnnie: So good, and a voice that could melt you.

Steve: Les, you had good taste.

Les: Boy, oh boy, I have a lot to be grateful for and Mary is one of those things.

Johnnie: Back when you were working solo, what was it like playing the clubs up and down the North Side of Chicago?

Les: Oh, it was wonderful. You could go from club to club and whoever was on stage they'd ask you to come up and sit in.

Johnnie: I assume you weren't getting rich doing that.

Les: Money wasn't the important thing. It was fun. It was all about sharing. I learned something new every Monday night. You know, a guitar could be a deadly weapon. If you walked into a club with it under your arm you could get on stage and mow 'em down!

Johnnie: Ha! You sound like a Chicago gangster!

Steve: Les, I want to play a lesser known piece by you.

(music out of break)

Steve: That was "Big Eyed Gal."

Les: Yep, I wanted to do something different. I wanted it to sound a little like a polka.

Steve: That was from back in your days with Columbia Records and it's still available. Do you have any idea how many companies have released your albums?

Les: My goodness, last Monday night at the Club Iridium, people came in with — it must have been a dozen albums for me to sign — and I've never even seen them before!

Johnnie: So you actually see albums come in and you don't even know where they came from?

Les: Sure. You need to get out your accordion and we'll make one.

Johnnie: Lester!

Les: Come on, big eyed gal! *(laughter)*

Johnnie: Les, we have an email from Lorraine who says back in the early '50s, she worked at the Woolworth store downtown and she played the Les and Mary music so much she was almost fired. You remember that place, right?

Les: Sure.

Johnnie: Les, she wants to know if it's true you got the famous echo effect from Mary singing in a tiled bathroom?

Les: Yes, I used to do that! I have a funny short story about that. Mary and I were in New Mexico. We stayed the night in a motel and that next morning, I said, "Mary," — I'd get her coffee and a donut. I left to go to the office where they served the breakfast, the continental breakfast, and it was crazy outside our room, all around the motel. There was a movie being shot. We didn't know that when we checked in the night before, but that morning there were horses, Indians, arrows in doors and Gary Cooper! It was crazy, just crazy. I got the coffee and rushed back to the room to tell Mary. When I walked in, she was in the shower and she was singing. I realized then that was a sound I had been looking for. That's the sound that I like. I tried to remember it so that when I got to Chicago, I said I'm going to make a room exactly like that bathroom. I had plans to recreate that tile bathroom so I could get that sound with Mary's voice. It would be just perfect. OK, I was going to build a shower, bathroom, that whole motel room to get that sound. Years went by, time passed, and I never did it. Many, many years later I was traveling with another gal going through the same town in New Mexico. I remembered the Log Cabin Inn near Albuquerque. I told her I had to stop at the motel. I went to the desk and rented a room … I gave the clerk a fake name, probably Mr. and Mrs. Smith. I told him we HAD to have room 62 and I'm only renting the room for about ten minutes. Well, he looked at me real funny, and I said, "By the way, I want you to come with us." (*laughter*) Then, I said, "Oh, can you bring a tape measure, flashlight, and paper and pencil?" (*laughter*) He was probably thinking, "Boy, I've got one here." Ha! I got him to go with me while the gal was waiting in the car. We walked in the room, Room 62, and we've got the tape measure, flashlight and pencil and whatever it is. It's only going to take 10 minutes. I went in there and I couldn't believe it — they'd changed the whole room, redecorated it. I couldn't believe it; my echo chamber was gone. I turned to walk out and never even told the clerk what I'd been planning to do in there.

Johnnie: But, your reputation lived on!

Les: I know if that guy is still alive, he STILL wonders what in the world did I need with that tape measure and flashlight? (*laughter*) I never told him it was the best echo I'd ever heard in my life.

Johnnie: So, from then on you were on the hunt for the perfect echo chamber in bathrooms across the country.

Les: Yeah, yeah, and my gal couldn't figure me out, either.

Johnnie: I guess!

Steve: That's a great story.

Les: A WEIRD story, that's for sure!

Johnnie: There are so many people who want to talk to Les. What a great opportunity to get him on the radio a little earlier tonight. When he's joined us over the years it's usually after his show at the club in New York, and we're always conscious of the fact he's on the East Coast and it's an hour later. So we'll hush up and let you folks talk to Les Paul. Nick, thank you for holding on. You're on the air with Les.

Nick: Les, with all the musicians you've worked with over the years, was there ever that one musician that you thought was destined for greatness and they did become big?

Les: Yes, in fact, there's going to be a special tribute to him soon. It's Art Tatum. He started the Three Deuces in Chicago. I played with him for years; he was a very dear friend of mine. He's passed away and they're donating his piano to the Apollo Theater. I'll be up there to give a little yak on his behalf. I'll talk about how much I loved him, and how much time we spent together. How flawlessly he played the piano. He was just one of THE greatest musicians of all time.

Steve: Wow.

Johnnie: We were so fortunate to have him here in Chicago. I believe he's in the documentary, *Chasing Sound*.

Les: Yes! He's in there!

Johnnie: Honestly, that was the first time I'd ever seen Art Tatum. He seemed like such a big, lovable guy.

Les: He was. He was also blind. I enjoyed going to his home when he would rehearse, and I would just sit there and listen to him. We'd talk about when and what he was going to record and NEVER did I ever hear a record of his that justified how great a player he was. You had to hear him in a speakeasy kind of joint at four in the morning. The greatest I ever heard Art — this is weird, but, believe me this is true — it was in a mortuary over in New Jersey. You had to go through the mortuary to get to the back room where there was a piano, and there were all the great piano players just waiting to take Art on. Well, when I brought him through, I said, "Art, come on, follow me." He had his arm through mine and we were walking through to the back. He said, "What's that I smell?" I said, "Oh, that's some fella on the drain board. You just follow me." I got him in the back, and here's Leo the Lion, Don Lambert and ... three of the great piano players. They were playing as hard and as good as they could, and Art is sitting there and says to me, "How many keys are going down? Are there five keys going down?" I said, "Yeah, they stick as you go down ... you've got a problem." He said, "Can you bring me another beer?" So, I go to the washtub and get him another beer out of the ice. I open it for him. He drinks it and finally says, "I'm ready. Take me up there." I took him up on the stage and he played about 50 choruses of whatever the song was, but he played way beyond what you would normally hear on a two- or three-minute record. In other words, when Art played, it was like he painted a picture and that's it. This is where you dig deep and you play things in your soul you didn't even know you had. Those were the days. I remember Art Tatum when he was BEYOND anything that he ever recorded.

Steve: There are some performers that are like that, aren't there Les? They freeze up in a studio, but you get them in a live setting and they really come to life.

Les: Yes. That's one of the things that happened when Chet and I recorded. We'd just come from breakfast, and I asked if he'd go with me again. We went back the second time alone, and that's when I suggested, "Why don't we speak to the people on the records so they can hear our personalities. What we're like out of the studio without a guitar," Chet said, "Well, I don't have much to say." But Chet was great. He had a dry sense of humor. He was quick. It was just great to have a microphone between the two of us so we could carry on a conversation. The first one was one where I say, "Did ya ever hear of Mel Bay?" (*laughter*) That was the first one out and the audience was the guys in the band. But when we pull that first joke, "Did ya ever hear of Mel Bay?" Chet says, "Yeah, he teaches guitar or something." I said, "Don't you think we should send for him?" (*laughter*)

Johnnie: Speaking of seeing raw talent in someone, isn't it true you saw Jimi Hendrix performing in a bar and knew there was really something special about him?

Les: Oh yes! I was on Route 46 taking a record back (to Columbia Records) of Simon and Garfunkel. I was working talent then. I was taking them the master tape and they were going to release the record. We're driving down Route 46 in New Jersey, and we drive by this little beer joint. I said, "Stop here for minute." I got out of the car and I went in there, and there was some guy watering down the drinks for the few people in this joint in the afternoon. But there was this fella on the stage. He was auditioning for a job. This left-handed guitar player was ALL OVER that thing. He had it turned wide open and he was playing. I went back to the car and I said to my son, "There's a guy in there playing guitar and he's a wild man. He's GOOD!" I wanted to get this guy a break, get someone from the record company to check him out. We left and delivered the tape of Simon and Garfunkel to Columbia in New York — I think it was The Sounds of Silence. We made the delivery, got back in the car and went back to New Jersey. I asked the bartender, "What happened to the fella that was here auditioning earlier, the wild man?" He said, "I think they threw him out. He was too loud." I said "What was his name?" He said, "I really don't know." He was actually working under a different name, Jimmy James or something, not Jimi Hendrix at that time. I told my manager about this great player I saw all by himself in this dark room playing his heart out. I asked him, "Would you look for him? I don't know his name. He plays left-handed and he's a wild man." He finally, he came to me one day, my manager did, and said, "Les, that left-handed player you had me looking for, that fella died in a fire, smoking a cigarette. He's gone." I gave up looking 'cause he was gone. He gave up looking for this wild man. One day, a guy named McGuire, Matt McGuire at London Records, asked me if I would come out of retirement. This was in the mid-'60s, I think. He said, "You can record anything you want. I'd just like you to make one more record before you throw the towel in." Finally, he got me on a weak day and I said, "OK, I'll do it." I go to make the record, but I said, "Find me some of the music they're playing today. Things are different than when I was playing with Mary." I wanted to hear some of the guitar players that were good and making music then. He dug some out, some I knew, like Eric Clapton. I'm looking through the albums and there, on one of the covers, is a picture of Jimi Hendrix, a BIG hit in England. Well, I called my manager and said, "Hey, you know that left-handed guitar player that died in a fire smoking a cigarette? He's number one in England!" That's how I met Jimi and, of course, he bought Electric Lady in New York, and we became friends.

Johnnie: That's a wonderful story, and we're talking to the wonderful Les Paul. Les, your fans want to talk to you. Can we ask you to stay with us a little while longer?

Les: Sure!

(out of break with music)

Steve: Les, I never told you, that is one of my absolute favorite songs you ever did, "Jazz Me Blues."

Les: Aw, thank you. Did you know that was number one for us when we were playing The Chicago Theatre? It was number one.

Steve: Really? And I've seen pictures of people outside The Chicago Theatre holding signs "Les and Mary for President."

Les: Yes, those were wonderful days. Of course, coming from that area of Chicago, that's where I got all my training. That's where I got the breaks.

Steve: Speaking of your past. Let's go to a caller. Camille.

Camille: Thank you. Mr. Les Paul, I just wanted to say my great-uncle was Karl Davis of Karl and Harty.

Steve: Karl and Harty.

Les: Of course, of course, of the Cumberland Ridge Runners.

Camille: Yes and my uncle Bill, who is still alive, was telling me in the old days you had another name of "Rhubarb Red."

Les: That is correct.

Johnnie: Did Karl and Harty work at WLS Radio at that time?

Les: WJJD.

Johnnie: Steve, you knew Karl Davis at WLS.

Steve: Yes. Les, in later years, when WLS went to a rock 'n' roll format and they still had members of the musicians union, Local 10, working as record turners, I was there and got to know Karl Davis, who was a wonderful man.

Johnnie: He was your record turner.

Steve: He was.

Les: Back in the day, he played mandolin.

Steve: Yep.

Les: And Slim Miller played the violin.

Johnnie: You were "Rhubarb Red" when you were what, 13 years old?

Les: I started out as "Red Hot Red" in Waukesha, then changed my name in St. Louis to "Rhubarb Red."

Johnnie: Did you change it, or did someone come to you and say, "Les, there's someone out there who's got a name real close to yours"? How did the change come about? You were just a kid.

Compliments of Cumberland Ridge Runners
Rhubarb Red, Harry McTigue and Peruna
Reading left to right—
Rhubarb Red, Karl Davis, Slim Miller, Hartford Taylor, Doc Hopkins, Harry McTigue

Joel Paterson Archives

Les: Exactly right. They said there's a guy out there you sound like. He's called "Pie Plant Pete." They said, we'll call you "Rhubarb Red," like "Pie Plant Pete."

Johnnie: "Pie Plant Pete" was on *The Barn Dance*, right?

Les: Yes.

Johnnie: So you were able to hear *The Barn Dance* in Waukesha?

Les: Yep, on my crystal set I made. I used to listen to them all the time.

Johnnie: Camille, thank you. That was a great name from Les's past.

Les: Those were all my teachers. That's where I learned to do everything, in Chicago radio and all around in Michigan, Missouri, Wisconsin, the whole Midwest circuit. That was my stomping ground.

Johnnie: Well, Les, I don't think I ever asked you ... I know your mother was supportive of your choice of show business for a career but, what about the fact you should have been in school? You were a kid and should have been in school. Did

she say, "Lester, you can do this, but only in the summer?"

Les: What Mom said, one day while we were making the bed — by the way, Mother was born in Wisconsin, she was German. My grandparents spoke German, but not Mother. She was an ultra-neat woman. I was making the bed with her, and she was showing me how to fold the corners when I told her that Joe Wolverton from KMOX in St. Louis asked me to come down and join him. He said he wanted to make up a team. I told Mother, "I realize I'm young and I have more time to spend in school, but it really wouldn't mean as much to me to be in school when I could be with someone like Joe Wolverton." I had already decided I wanted to be an entertainer. She said, "Lester, it is up to you." She did not stand in my way. In fact, she encouraged me. She wasn't one of those mothers that wanted to be my manager or promote me. She wasn't on an ego trip.

Johnnie: She was never a stage mother.

Les: Never a stage mother. She said, "Lester, it's up to you. There's going to be rough days, you're a kid around grown people." I went on to St. Louis and, like any homesick kid, I'd go to town on Sundays when everything was closed. I remember sitting at a newsstand that was closed, and I'd cry. I missed my mother, my friends, Waukesha. But I sweat it out. I was with older men and I had to learn very fast what it meant to be a grown man. I was just a kid, so it was a little hard to adjust. During that time, I had my mother run my machinery at home so she could record the shows I'd be on. One of the cutest things that happened was the first week I was in St. Louis, I told Mother what number I would be singing for her and she was going to record it. As luck would have it, the show I was to be on that night was canceled, but the next week, Monday or Tuesday, the program director came to me and said, "You know, you drew more mail than any other artist that we've ever had, AND it all came from Waukesha!" (*laughter*)

Johnnie: And you weren't even on!

Les: Everyone in Waukesha wrote to say how great I was, and the show had been canceled!

Johnnie: Busted!

Les: Yes, my mother was working for me.

Johnnie: Oh, that was a great story! Camille, thanks for taking us down that road.

Camille: Quickly, may I ask if you remember Shelby Jean Davis?

Les: Yes. Of course I do!

Camille: Well, that's my mom.

Les: That's your mom! Tell her I love her and, my goodness, she was just a little tot singing.

Camille: She was the "Little Mountain Sweetheart."

Les: That was *The Suppertime Frolics.*

Camille: Yes, it was.

Johnnie: My goodness, Les, you have such a memory. You had no idea Camille was going to throw that name at you!

Les: Oh, Doc Hopkins, too.

Camille: Yes, Doc Hopkins and Harty Taylor, too.

Les: I remember them well.

Camille: I'll tell them you said hi.

Steve: Thanks, Camille. Les, I pride myself on having most everything that you ever made or were on that's available, but Johnnie unearthed an Art Tatum CD from '34-'44 and it says, "Guest artist Les Paul."

Les: Oh, yeah.

Johnnie: It's just been re-released on CD.

Les: Did they?

Johnnie: Yes, and it's not inexpensive. It's priced at 50 dollars.

Les: My goodness, those are wonderful memories. I was so lucky to meet great guys like Art and play with them.

Johnnie: We're also lucky people had the wherewithal to save these recordings, as you have. You have your own history saved and we can go to YouTube now and see you performing in the '50s all the way up to last Monday night.

Les: And you know what? I've got more gals now than I did when I was a kid. *(laughter)*

Johnnie: Let's sneak in another call for the wonderful Les Paul! Todd, you're on the air with Les.

Todd: Oh Les, it's an honor. I'm an avid guitar player.

Les: Fire away!

Todd: I have an ES-335.

Les: That's a great guitar.

Todd: I got it from my brother with a clipping from when you were at Guitar Center downtown and at the House of Blues.

Les: That's where I met Steve and Johnnie.

Steve: That's when Les ducked out on the Gibson people and came over and spent three hours with us on the radio.

Todd: I was wondering what year that was.

Steve: I remember it well: 1996.

Todd: I heard your doctor told you to keep working, keep working. You are an icon.

Johnnie: A listener emails and wants to know if you play guitar every day preparing for your Monday night shows?

Les: No. I wish I could. I'm spending a lot of time writing a movie.

Johnnie: WHAT?

Les: Yes, I want to do a movie about my life. I won't be in the movie. It's interesting because I could write for months, a book's worth, and I'd just be in my ninth year. I'd like to start from the days when my mother was bathing me in the sink.

Steve: Les, if you were casting the movie, who would you pick to play you?

Les: I don't know. I would leave that up to the director.

Johnnie: Did you ever see the movie *Sweet and Lowdown*?

Les: Yes, I did. I enjoyed it.

Johnnie: I loved the heart of the movie, but Sean Penn chose to not even learn how to HOLD a guitar, much less how to play it.

Steve: That drove me nuts and was a distraction from the story.

Les: I agree, I don't know why he didn't even try. It was such a good movie goofed up by that. The message was still there, though.

Johnnie: It was the story of Django Reinhardt; it was loosely based on his life.

Steve: Les, I've always wondered why no one has actually done a movie on Django. His life story is fascinating.

Les: Oh yes. I was with Django just before he died, and we swapped guitars. I gave him one of mine and he gave me one of his. I came back here, flopped down on the bed, and the phone rang. It was a call to tell me Django had passed away. I took a flight the next day and went to Paris. I still have the tickets and pictures saved. When I got to Paris, I found that he lived on the sixth floor of a rundown building. I was told there were times when they had no electricity, running water or heat — nothing. I climbed those stairs and was welcomed into his apartment, and found he didn't even have a phonograph — a record player or records. He and his wife and son lived in this small, almost like a one-room apartment. I left there and met up with a publishing friend of mine in Paris and said, "I want you to do me one favor. I want you to find all the songs that Django wrote and the publishers. I want you to get them all together for a meeting here on Saturday." He said he would do that. You see, Django hadn't received any money for the songs he had written. I wanted to see that changed. We had the meeting, and we were able to get the money for his monument and money that was due him for his family. Of course, with his death I'd lost one of my dearest friends.

Johnnie: What a story, what a life he lived.

Les: You know, we were riding in the back of a taxi when he asked me if I could read. I told him no. He laughed like mad and said, "I can't read either." Then he asked me, "Am I playing right or am I playing bad?" Can you imagine that? I told him, "I idolize you and think you might be the finest guitar player in the whole world." During that conversation he asked a third question. He asked me, "Do you think I should change anything?" You know, when we swapped guitars, his plan was to try going electric. When he passed away, he had been playing the guitar I gave him. We were so close. The one thing I always wanted (was) to bring him back to the States with the right situation. Bring him here and let everyone hear how great he was. Not only a lovable, talented guy, but he had a great family, too. They were poor, but happy. He was happy as long as he could play his music, but he was always confused that when he played in America he wasn't received the way he thought he would be received. He was always wrestling with that.

Johnnie: Now he's an icon in the States. You see kids wearing T-shirts with D-J-A-N-G-O on them, and you wonder how they came to be such big fans. You also have to wonder what Django would make of that.

Steve: In closing, Les, we need to know if there are any plans to come back to Chicago.

Les: I'll be passing through on my way to the Rock Hall of Fame. They're honoring me for something.

Johnnie: Ha! Something ... maybe you can do something before they honor you.

Les: Yeah, or maybe they'll stuff me and put me on display in there! (*laughter*)

Steve: Oh dear!

John Paulson, *Chasing Sound*

Johnnie: Les, we talked to Dusty Rogers last night, and he told the story of Roy coming home and telling Dale that Trigger had passed and he was going to have him stuffed for display. Dusty said Dale seemed horrified and asked if Roy expected her to do that to him when he passed! (*laughter*) **We started talking about Dale Evans getting her start in Chicago and wondered if you had ever crossed paths.**

Les: Of course! She sang in my trio!

Johnnie: Oh, come on!

Les: She did, and so did Fran Allison from Kukla, Fran and Ollie. She did a show with me. I had a lot of friends in Chicago.

Johnnie: And your reputation lives on here. Hey, is that why you don't come back to town more often?

Les: Ha! I love you guys so much. Thank you, thank you.

Johnnie: I hope you can feel a great big hug from all of us.

Steve: You know we love you, too, Les.

Les: Thank you. Good night.

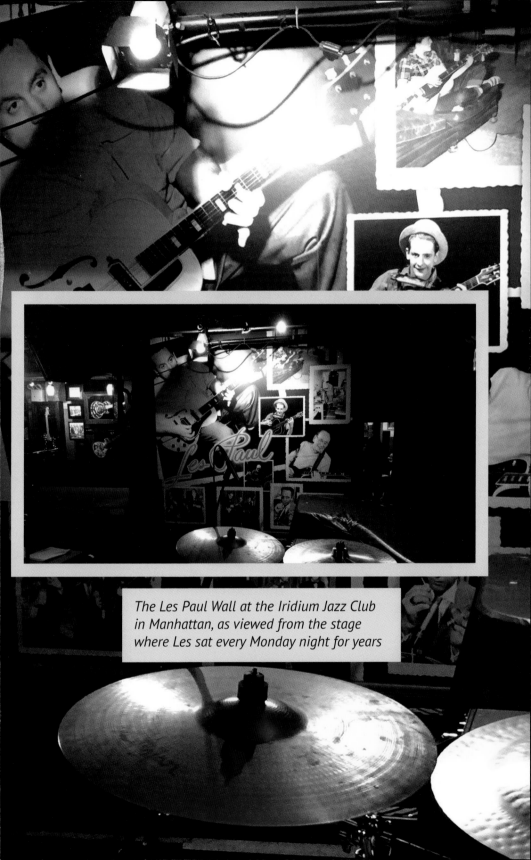

The Les Paul Wall at the Iridium Jazz Club in Manhattan, as viewed from the stage where Les sat every Monday night for years

Chris Lentz

Tommy Emmanuel and Les Paul at the Iridium

memories from ...

Tommy Emmanuel

C het Atkins handed me the phone at his studio and said, "Here, talk to Les." That was the first time I spoke with Les Paul. Well, he was funny and kind of lovable, and didn't even know me. Then Chet and I played a show at the Hard Rock Cafe in Nashville that was supposed to feature Les on his 80th birthday. But poor Les had had a stroke of some kind and was in a hospital, so we sang "Happy Birthday" to him via a phone and a speaker beside his bed.

Fast forward many years from that event to me being a lucky guest on Chicago's WGN Radio with Steve King and Johnnie Putman. They were so kind to me, and after we talked and I played awhile, they got Les on the phone and we chatted for a long time, on air! I got the invite to come and play with Les and his band down at the Iridium Jazz Club where he played two shows every Monday night. I was so excited to be coming to New York to play with one of my heroes and get to hang out with everyone backstage!

I got there early, met Les and his fantastic band, and talked with Tom Doyle, who was doing the out-front sound. I set up and checked my sound in two minutes flat, then we all ate dinner and discussed what we would play. Les said to come on up stage and just play the hell out of it!!

In the first show, I was really trying to hold myself back and started to play a slow tune and got Les and the band to join in. I repeated this and then we played "Birth of the Blues." Les and I traded solos but I kept it pretty reserved from my side as I just felt, out of respect for Les, that I should go easy. The crowd loved it and I came off to wonderful cheers and applause.

In the break between shows, Les came up to me and said very sternly, "Don't you ever do that again. When I say GO, YOU GO! Don't you dare hold back because you think I'm old. I'll whip your ass out there for ya!" We laughed and I agreed to hold nothing back next show.

> *"Don't you dare hold back because you think I'm old. I'll whip your ass out there for ya!"*

I came out for the second show to wild applause and tore straight into a fast tune which ended in screaming, yelling and a wild standing ovation! After a long ovation, Les says to the audience, "That guy makes me sick. He waits until I'm old to come and beat me up!" Then we all roared laughing! He really did a number on me that night and we became instant friends. I had so many great nights talking and playing with Les after that, including his 90th birthday show at Carnegie Hall in New York City. I played as often as I could with him when I was in New York, and I felt he played his best in the 94th year of his life! What an inspiration, what a prankster, what a pal!

I'll always be grateful to Steve and Johnnie for hooking us up!

Tommy Emmanuel cgp

a little more about ...

Tommy Emmanuel

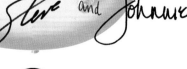

We call him "Tigger." It's the most appropriate nickname for the force of nature that is Tommy Emmanuel. The level of energy Tommy brings to his shows once caused a cardiologist friend of ours to say, "Just WATCHING Tommy perform is a great cardiac workout."

This, combined with his nothing-short-of-amazing guitar playing ability, caused an immediate bond to be formed between Tommy and Les. If you have never seen the performance video on the *Chasing Sound* DVD of Tommy and Les jamming together on "Blue Moon," do yourself — and your heart — a huge favor and fill that gaping hole in your musical education. ASAP!

Along with sharing a stage with Les many times, Tommy was the recipient of one of only four "Certified Guitar Player" (CGP) awards ever presented by Chet Atkins.

Like Les, Tommy never really learned to read music. Or, as Chet often joked, "Not so much that it hurts my pickin'."

Steve and *Johnnie*

ABOVE: Tommy and Clara Emmanuel, Steve and Johnnie

BELOW: Tommy and Les performing "Blue Moon" at the Iridium

John Paulson, *Chasing Sound*

Tommy with Steve and Johnnie at WGN Radio

Steve and Johnnie with Paul Harvey, 1997

26

Good Morning, American ...
This is Paul Harvey!

his will probably sound corny, but sometimes we really
can't believe how lucky we've been to not just encounter, but become friends with some of the real giants of
the broadcasting and entertainment arenas. Of course, this book
is about Les Paul, but there is another fellow named Paul who became not just a co-worker, but a dear, dear friend — Paul Harvey.

In another missive we'll relate the story of how Mr. Harvey
helped save Steve's life (really!), but for the moment, we'll stick to
the road this book is traveling and tell you of the times Les Paul's
and Paul Harvey's planets aligned.

While WGN Radio was Paul Harvey's Chicago radio home
for decades, his broadcasts originated from a building just across
the Chicago River from our studios in the Tribune Tower. In fact,
Paul's refusal to relocate to New York was the reason the ABC Radio Network maintained a Chicago office. As was the case with Les
Paul, Paul Harvey's Midwestern roots were on display throughout
his career. So was a very strong work ethic. Even though very few
ever saw Paul Harvey in the studio as he delivered his daily broadcasts, he always came to work wearing a suit and tie. He was also
a very early riser, driving in to his office shortly after 2 a.m. Quite
frequently, we would get off the air to find a voice message or a

note from Paul or his long-time assistant, June Westgaard, regarding something Paul had heard on our show as he was driving and might want to include in his broadcast. Over the years, we developed a friendship with Paul that not only found us sharing a table at one of the National Radio Hall of Fame broadcasts, but sharing many other things, like recipes and a love of music, particularly that of Les Paul.

In June of 2005, a few days prior to Les's 90th birthday, we got off the air to find a message from Mr. Harvey. He'd heard us mention Les's upcoming birthday and wanted to include a tribute to him on that day in both his early morning and midday broadcasts. Being the scrupulous researcher that he was, Paul wanted to make sure he had his facts right and, since he was more than a little aware of our friendship with "The Wizard of Waukesha," asked if we could write something about Les, including what we thought were significant highlights. We were happy to help out and went to work putting together a couple of pages about Les and emailed them to Paul.

Now you have to understand that in the time we've spent inside your radio speakers, we've experienced some events we can look back on and say were real highlights. Right up there near the top was hearing Paul Harvey read exactly what we wrote, without changing a word, as his birthday tribute to Les Paul!

WE WERE GHOST WRITERS FOR PAUL HARVEY!

Later, Les, whose day would start around noon, told us that he woke up just in time to hear Paul Harvey's midday broadcast and was completely knocked out to hear his birthday tribute.

August 30, 2005, was a very important date for Les and another opportunity for the Paul planets to align. This was the release date for his first rock 'n' roll album, Les Paul & Friends: American Made, World Played. This album featured Les collaborating with Jeff Beck, Sam Cooke and many more world-renowned artists. We had Les on to talk about the album.

LES PAUL & FRIENDS
american made world played

BUDDY GUY·JOE PERRY   STING·ERIC CLAPTON·KEITH RICHARD
KE·BILLY GIBBONS·RIC   JOSS STONE·JEFF BECK·STEVE MILL

Johnnie: We're talking with Les Paul. Today is a really, really big day for him because his new album is out today.

Steve: His first new album in 27 years, *Les Paul & Friends: American Made, World Played*, features Les jamming with people like Sting and Joss Stone and Kenny Wayne Shepherd and Edgar Winter and Eric Clapton and Peter Frampton and Jeff Beck and Buddy Guy.

Johnnie: And our favorite, Steve Miller, "Fly Like An Eagle."

Steve: Oh, absolutely!

Johnnie: You told us about six months ago that you really, really wanted to have a record on the charts in your 90th year and we said, "Doggone it, we're going to do our part to see that that happens."

Les: Well I, I just said I, I don't know what I'm gonna do, but I'm gonna do one for my own 90th birthday. I wanna do, I want to record one more time. I didn't say five, I just said one, ya know. Now if I can get Paul Harvey to just autograph it for me in Chicago.

(*laughter*)

Steve: He may be listening.

John Paulson, *Chasing Sound*

One of Les's ribbon microphones used in the "old days" of radio

Johnnie: Well you know what, we could do him a favor and we'll take one of your CDs, have you autograph it, and we'll turn him on to some good rock 'n' roll music, too. (*laughter*)

Les: Well you know I was talking to someone the other day and I was, I don't know what I was explaining, but I says, "A very good example would be"... Oh! I know what it was: it was in the old days of radio when I was Musical Director or Program Director in Chicago. And my job was to pick an announcer, and the announcer went into the studio and he had a ribbon microphone in front of him, and he had to have that nice, rich, beautiful sound. And that was important that he could read well, and that he had that sound on that mic. OK? And they said, "What kind of a mic did we use in those old days, did you use?" And I said, "The same one that Paul Harvey uses today." Isn't that amazing?

Johnnie: Yeah.

Steve: Wow.

Johnnie: I'll bet he's listening, too and he's grinning.

Les: And you guys are using the same mics.

Steve: You know how you were just talking about Paul Harvey?

Les: Yep.

Steve: Les, say good morning to Paul Harvey.

Les: You're kidding!

Paul Harvey: Good morning, American! (*laughter*)

Les: Oh, my goodness! You're my favorite!

Paul: Oh, dear Les.

Les: You're my favorite!

Paul: You have been a star to steer by for such a long time.

Johnnie: Well, I think you heard us say that today is a big day for Les because he's releasing his new rock 'n' roll album today, and we're going to get you a copy of that album.

Paul: Oh, thank you. I've been sitting here making notes. (*laughter*)

Les: I listen to you, "and here's the rest of the story." (*laughter*)

Johnnie: In fact, I gotta tell you, Mr. Harvey, it was about a week ago, you had mentioned Les in one of your noon reports, and Les, didn't I happen to call you just as you woke up to that and you said, "Isn't that a weird feeling when your radio comes on and you wake up and hear your name, and your name is being said by Paul Harvey?"

Les: Yeah.

Paul: Well, I've got to mention this new album, today.

Johnnie: Oh, how nice.

Paul: The first in 27 years! We've wasted a lot of years there.

(*laughter*)

Steve: Absolutely right.

Johnnie: And, Mr. Harvey, the next one's going to be country, and then bluegrass, and jazz, and blues ...

Paul: Oh, man!

Steve: He's only getting started. (*laughter*)

Johnnie: Well, we know you're terribly busy. Thank you so much for stopping by.

Paul: Well, thank you all, and Les ...

Les: Thank you, Paul.

Paul: As the politicians say, many happy returns.

Les: Thank you, thank you, thank you.

Paul: Bye bye, buddy.

Johnnie: Bye, Mr. Harvey.

Steve: Thank you. You know after all these years, Les, we still have to call him Mr. Harvey. He is such a special man.

Les: I guess I'm the only one that could get away with it, right?

(*laughter*)

Authors' note: There is another Les Paul and Paul Harvey story we want to relate. It's a story that takes place in a crowded ballroom on the night of Thursday, May 10, 2007, at Les Paul's Waukesha Homecoming Concert. It has to do with Paul helping us surprise Les. But you'll have to turn to "The Wizard Returns to Waukesha" to read "the REST of the story."

A little more Les ...

When you just get mixed up and there's too much going on, then it's time to pick up your guitar. — Les Paul

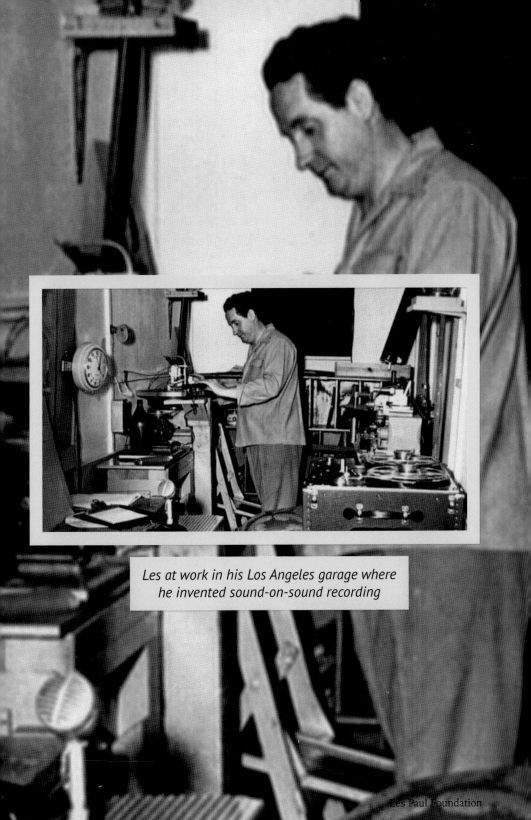

Les at work in his Los Angeles garage where he invented sound-on-sound recording

Les Paul Foundation

Edward Butkovich

Les attends the world premiere of Chasing Sound *at Milwaukee's Downer Theatre in 2007.*

27

Chasing Sound

*I*n our 2006 telephone conversations, Les started telling us about a movie that was being made about his life. From the first time he mentioned it, he talked about giving his full support to the crew making it because he "got a good feeling from them," and thought they would do his story right. He talked about being shadowed by filmmaker John Paulson and thought we might like to meet the man behind this new documentary.

John Paulson had been a filmmaker with Smithsonian Productions, and — after Les introduced him to us — we had John on our show multiple times. During the early interviews, we talked about his vision for capturing Les on film, which included spending a lot of time with Les at the Iridium filming his stage performances, interacting with guests who dropped in to visit and perform, greeting fans, and spending a great deal of time with him at home. Each time we talked to either John or Les to get an update on the progress of the documentary, it was obvious they were both excited with the way the film was developing.

John was kind enough to send us an advance copy of *Les Paul: Chasing Sound*, and it blew us away. Even after our years of conversations with Les, we still learned new, exciting, and sometimes funny things about him from the film. Some of our favorite segments showed Les at home in Mahwah, New Jersey. We paused the video at one point because we couldn't believe the shot of a (no doubt very expensive) Les Paul guitar leaning by its neck against an open kitchen drawer. There were guitars on the couch, on countertops, and around every corner. A terrific scene took the viewer into

LEFT: As shown in the Chasing Sound film, Les's Mahwah, New Jersey, home

BELOW: Les in his "Austin Powers" bedroom

Photos from John Paulson, *Chasing Sound*

BELOW LEFT: Chasing Sound *showed the rows of guitars in Les's bedroom.*
BELOW RIGHT: Each guitar had been labeled by Les with clues to its unique story.

Les's bedroom, which looked like a scene from an Austin Powers movie. The décor was retro cool, and the walls were lined with guitars in cases. Each guitar was labeled, and each had its own story.

When the DVD became available for sale, we once again interviewed John on our radio show to tell listeners how to get their hands on a copy. One of the things that Les was really excited about, aside from how pleased he was with the finished product, was that he could attend the world premiere of the documentary in Milwaukee. An enthusiastic sold-out house cheered the film, and Les, at the Downer Theatre on May 9, 2007.

Edward Butkovich

In July of that year, the documentary aired on PBS in its *American Masters* series. It was again broadcast in October, 2008, on BBC Four as part of its *Guitar Night*.

Over the years and our many hours of conversations with Les, we would eventually get to the subject of "sound." Talking to Les and not talking about sound would be like talking to Muhammad Ali and not talking about boxing. After we'd seen *Chasing Sound*, we asked Les about the scene with the guitars lining his bedroom wall. He said that scene reminded him of being a young boy who would sing in the bathroom, loving the sound of the echo, but realizing it was too much echo. He said, "I went into my bedroom with curtains and a bedspread, and the sound was dead, so I got a chair and moved it between the bathroom and bedroom, and I would play my guitar. I would keep moving it until I found that 'sweet spot' with just enough echo. I was chasing sound as a kid and that search for the 'sweet spot' is how reverb would eventually come about."

When we asked Les about the sound he heard when he was playing on stage, he explained that, unlike many performers, he did not like stage monitors. He said, "Lou (Pallo), my guitarist, doesn't like 'em either. My piano player had one and eventually said to take it away. If it's the right stage, like that 'sweet spot' between the bathroom and bedroom, you don't need monitors." Les was asked if this went back to the early days of performing, and if now, like then, he liked interacting and really listening to the other musicians on stage with him. He said that's what made each performance different, listening to the other musicians.

During that same interview, Les talked about Andrés Segovia: "Doesn't get any better than him when it comes to classical guitar." He said Segovia had confided in him that he wanted to design an electric guitar with Les. He said, "But Andrés didn't want it to be seen or recognized as being an amplified guitar."

Les felt that not all changes in sound technology were necessarily for the better. He remembered being in the renowned Carnegie Hall before his 90th-birthday concert. He said, "I was there to see Ella Fitzgerald, and she was singing though a P.A. system. I think I changed seats 10 times! I was either in front of the woofer or the tweeter. This beautiful Carnegie Hall was filled with speakers that didn't give the audience the sound our ears could hear. I sat there and longed for the good ol' days."

Les Paul stops to greet Steve and Johnnie as he makes his way to the stage for his homecoming concert in Waukesha, Wisconsin, on May 10, 2007.

Kevin Harnack, The Waukesha Freeman

28

The Wizard Returns to Waukesha

*E*very time we talked with Les, both on air and off, the conversation would return to his Midwestern roots. Ever since his appearance at the Chicago House of Blues in 1996, he had expressed a desire to return to the area. Also, without fail, the question our listeners would most often ask Les during his appearances on our show was, "When are you coming back?" It took about a decade, but during one of his phone interviews on our show, it was a very happy Les who announced that, yes, he would be coming back, but not to Chicago. Instead, his return concert would be a true homecoming in his birthplace of Waukesha, Wisconsin.

Les's "Homecoming" appearance was set for the night of Thursday, May 10, 2007. The location was the Milwaukee Marriott West Hotel in Waukesha. Les, who would turn 92 on June 9, was scheduled to play a complete set with his trio at the event. The concert was part of a fundraising effort for *The Les Paul Experience*, which was planned to be the largest exhibit for the Waukesha County Museum.

Even though it was on a Thursday — a "school night" for us — there was no way we were going to miss out on Les's appearance, so we happily agreed to co-host the concert along with Steve Palec, a well-known radio personality from Milwaukee's WKLH.

We had never been to Waukesha, so the afternoon of the

concert, we left early enough to make the several-hour trip north from Chicago and still avoid Milwaukee's afternoon rush hour traffic.

When we arrived at the hotel and were checking in, we ran into Paula Cooper, our former producer who was now doing news on our show, and her brother, Joe. Like us, "school night" or not, she was not going to miss out on Les's homecoming show. After getting settled at the hotel, we headed for the night's performance and ran into Les's son, Russ. Russ was as excited as we were about his father returning to his hometown for this special performance. This "lovefest" for Les was good medicine for Russ in light of his own recent medical challenges, including the loss of a few toes to diabetes. Russ enthusiastically recounted the previous night's *Chasing Sound* premiere, and this day's celebratory events, reunions with old friends, and several interviews that had already taken place.

Show time was quickly approaching, so we made our way into the ballroom and found our table, where we sat with our friends from Guitar Works, Terry Straker and Bill Takatsuki, Paula and Joe, photographer Angela Morgan, Steve Palec and "Popcorn" Edward Butkovich. "Popcorn," whose nickname stemmed from his time as a movie theater manager, is a longtime friend and photographer who also functioned as an "off-site producer" for our

Edward Butkovich

FROM LEFT: Bill Takatsuki, Terry Straker, Steve and Johnnie, Paula Cooper, Joe Cooper, Edward Butkovich, Steve Palec, Angela Morgan

Les hugs WGN producer Paula Cooper as Steve and Johnnie look on.

Joann O'Hare

show. While listening at home, Popcorn was always scouring the Internet and would frequently email Paula or us with information he found that might be relevant to something we had mentioned on the air. Anytime he found a story with Les's name attached to it, the story would quickly find its way into our email inbox and sometimes result in a call to Les for a comment or clarification.

After consulting with Steve Palec about what we were going to be doing on stage prior to introducing Les, and going over a surprise we had planned for Les with the sound engineer, we made our way back to our table. The members of Les's trio entered the ballroom and sat at a table just off the side of the stage. We went over to say hello to Lou Pallo, Les's guitarist, and Nicki Parrott, who played bass and functioned as a female foil for Les's jokes, some of which could be raunchy. We had last seen them at Muriel Anderson's All Star Guitar Night tribute to Les in Nashville. We were also introduced to a recent additon to the trio, John Colianni, a brilliant pianist. After Steve spent a little time talking guitars with Lou, we returned to our seats.

Just as we sat down, Les walked in and, along with everyone else in the ballroom, we were on our feet giving him a standing ovation. As Les made his way over to the table where the trio was sitting, he was taking his time, stopping for pictures, recognizing old childhood friends and cracking jokes along the way. When he saw us, he walked over to our table with a big smile on his face as he called out our names. Johnnie and Paula jumped up and he gave them both big hugs. We kept our hellos short, knowing the show was starting soon. And the sudden infestation of video and still cameras capturing Les's every move didn't make the moment right for an extended conversation. Eventually, Les was able to make his way through the crowd and join his trio at their table.

As the show began, some local dignitaries made a few comments, and we joined Steve Palec on stage. As we looked out at the packed ballroom audience, we recapped some of Les's history, and then said we had a surprise for him. Les had no idea where this was going and looked up at us quizzically.

Johnnie said, "Les, there is one other person who desperately wanted to be here tonight. He is a huge, huge fan of yours, as you are of him. Now, he's 88 years old and needs his beauty sleep, but he wanted to send you an audio tribute." We signaled the engineer and the instantly recognizable voice came booming through the ballroom's sound system.

> Good evening, Americans! May I share sixty seconds of this historic celebration? From my earliest remembering, I have near worshipped the care and the keeping and the shaping of fine wood — fine wood. I can be closer to God in my tiny wood workshop than in a cold church — just handling and smelling and shaping the ever-living texture of fine wood.
>
> Les Paul has made a wood box sing. And Stradivari never, ever did it better. Thank you, Les! That we get to see you, and know you, and hear you ... now that is a lasting legacy beyond price. Thank you, my treasured friend. I'll see you in a few miles.
>
> Good day!

Watching Les's face as Paul Harvey's voice filled the room, we could easily tell that he was moved. After Les joined us on stage, he was still shaking his head, saying he couldn't believe that Paul Harvey took the time to say all those nice things about him. After a few minutes of back-and-forth kidding, we left the stage and settled in to watch what we knew would be a special performance.

It was!

Les was in fine form and obviously pumped, after all those years, to be playing in front of his hometown crowd. At various times throughout the show, he reflected on his early years in Waukesha. He would talk about several boyhood friends who were in the audience, relate a story, and play a song that had a particular memory for them. As with every show, he had the crowd in the palm of his hand. Les's playing and showmanship took his audience on a journey that far exceeded their already high expectations, but this time, perhaps because of the night's significance, it seemed Les was experiencing some of the same emotions they were. "Somewhere Over The Rainbow," always a highlight of Les's shows, was especially poignant on this night with so many of Les's old friends attending this "homecoming" event.

At one point in the show, New York bluesman Jon Paris, who was also a Wisconsin native, and a favorite of Les, joined Les on stage for some songs and presented him with a sign designating Les Paul Parkway.

When the show was over, we returned to the stage to announce that a table had been set up in the lobby and Les would be signing autographs. However, because of the size of the crowd and the number of guitars and other memorabilia they had brought for him to sign, we had to ask that the audience remain seated until their table number was called. This attempt at crowd control proved only partially successful. Even though many remained seated until it was their turn, a long line of autograph seekers stretched through the hotel's lobby.

Les always loved interacting with his fans, and this special

Edward Butkovich

Fellow Wisconsonite and New York bluesman Jon Paris presents Les with his Waukesha street sign.

night was no exception. If anything, he was even more conscious of this crowd's expectations and was thoroughly enjoying renewing old acquaintances while he signed autographs and talked with fans and friends, old and new. However, the long day, concert, and more than an hour of autographs and handshakes were starting to take their toll. Les's right arm and arthritic hand were starting to ache.

The story behind that pain, which Les recounted on our WGN Radio show, goes back to 1948, when Les tried to shield Mary during a winter storm car accident in Oklahoma. He wound up with a shattered right arm and a crushed elbow, along with many other serious injuries. After several surgeries, Les's right elbow was replaced with a piece of bone from his leg. This left him without an elbow joint. His arm would have to be fixed in one position. Les told us what he instructed the doctor: "Put my

Edward Butkovich

forefinger in my bellybutton when you set my arm. That's how I hold the guitar, and I'll still be able to play." The resulting cast is shown below.

Unfortunately, not all of Les's fans knew of that story and some, even if they did know, in the excitement of meeting Les would forget and start aggressively shaking and pumping his hand and arm. So as much as he wanted to continue, Les, apologetically curtailed this autograph session.

When we heard that he was going to head back up to his room, we quickly gathered up our things and caught up with Les to say our goodbyes. As he stepped in the elevator, Les turned to us and said, "Get in, get in!

Les Paul Archives

You're coming up to my room, aren't you?" After making sure that we wouldn't be imposing, of course we said, "Yes!" and joined Les, Russ, Chris Lentz (Les's close friend and photographer), Michael Braunstein (Les's manager, who we'd met earlier in the evening), and Sue Baker from The Les Paul Foundation, in Les's suite.

When we got to the suite, Michael made sure that Les was comfortable and had everything he needed, then confessed to being a little tired after the long day they had all had, and left. Les immediately went over to a comfortable chair and asked for a cold bottle of beer. When he was handed the bottle of beer, Les told us that he didn't want it because he was thirsty. He wanted to hold it. He'd found out that just holding a really cold beer bottle was good therapy for his aching, arthritic fingers.

Along with Sue, we sat down as Les started asking us how we thought the night had gone. The next several hours consisted of some of the most personal conversations we ever had with Les. Although we always enjoyed any occasion where we could spend some time with him, it was as if a very warm afterglow from the night's long overdue homecoming put him in a particularly relaxed place. This wasn't a dressing room before a concert or a radio studio with commercial break interruptions. This was just friends sitting back, hanging out, and having a good time. Along with wanting to know how we were doing and asking questions about our personal and professional lives, Les freely — sometimes wistfully — reminisced about his days in Waukesha and Chicago and told stories of friends and events, some of which he'd never mentioned during our interviews.

After a while, Sue said she was getting tired and was going to leave. We were going to follow her cue, but Les still felt like talking and since both Russ and Chris appeared a bit drowsy, we stayed. Les enjoyed having some fellow "night owls" to talk with and told us that he planned to check out a few more of his old haunts during the day on Friday. We later found out that one of the places he wanted to go was Prairie Home Cemetery to pick out his

Chris Lentz

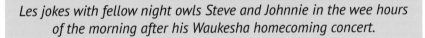

Les jokes with fellow night owls Steve and Johnnie in the wee hours of the morning after his Waukesha homecoming concert.

burial plot.

Sometime after 3 a.m., Les still seemed full of energy but we didn't want to overstay our welcome. Gentle handshakes and hugs at the door, accompanied by promises to make sure it was a much shorter time between in-person visits, put the cap on what was a very special day and night full of wonderful memories that will stay with us forever.

James Joiner

Les, with his hand firmly grasping Johnnie's, tours Les Paul's House of Sound. *The idea for the exhibit was first presented by Bing Crosby.*

29

The House of Sound

Saturday, June 21, 2008, was a very important day for Les. Decades after Bing Crosby first offered to build it, *Les Paul's House of Sound* was finally becoming a reality in Milwaukee. The afternoon grand opening ceremony was to be followed that evening by a concert at The Pabst Theater benefitting the *Les Paul's House of Sound* exhibit at Discovery World. The concert was billed as "An Evening With Les Paul and Friends — His 93rd Birthday Celebration."

Les wanted to make sure we were going to be there and also wanted us onstage with him. Hearing that, we were more than a little surprised. Les explained that, to give The Pabst Theater stage a more intimate feeling, he wanted it set up like a nightclub with his friends sitting at the tables. We were honored and, of course, said yes.

After several more on-air conversations with Les prior to the event, we also talked with Joel Brennan, president and CEO of Discovery World. Joel sounded like a kid let loose in a candy store when he told us of visiting Les's Mahwah, New Jersey, home for the first time along with Paul Krajniak, former executive director of Discovery World, to get a look at Les's guitars and other artifacts for possible inclusion in the "House of Sound" exhibit. As Joel recounted, "At one point early on in the conversation, Les pointed to a handsome guitar that was propped up by an open drawer that held all the silverware in the kitchen. 'Right there is Les Paul Number One,' Les said. 'That is the first Gibson Les Paul ever made in 1952.' Paul and I looked at each other in amusement and mild disbelief, cognizant that an errant elbow or a misplaced kitchen knife could transform this precious piece of history into twisted metal and broken wood. But this episode exemplified the real genius and essence of Les — everything about him was right in front of you, without pretense, for everyone to see and to enjoy."

Longtime Les Paul fans, Joel and Paul wanted *Les Paul's House of Sound* to be a high-quality undertaking that Les would be proud to have his name associated with. "We worked together to build an exhibit that reflected both Les's contributions to music and sound technology, and his lifelong commitment to innovation."

After months of hard work, opening day had arrived, and Les was in town to perform and see the results. As we arrived, Discovery World, already a stunning presence on Milwaukee's lakefront, was made even more so, beautifully bathed in the afternoon sun's rays shining down from a crystal clear sky. It was a more-than-fitting natural spotlight for that afternoon's and evening's events.

We were ushered upstairs to *Les Paul's House of Sound*. A crowd, augmented by press with cameras, was gathered outside the exhibit, waiting for some opening remarks from Les and local dignitaries. We found Paula Cooper, her brother Joe, and their parents, who were also huge Les Paul fans. A few minutes later, Les walked in to applause from both fans and press. After opening remarks, *Les Paul's House of Sound* was officially open, and Bing Crosby's suggestion to Les had become a reality.

When he saw us, Les smiled and motioned us over, and he quickly took Johnnie's hand. A public relations person walked up and asked, "Les, are you ready to tour the exhibit?" He replied "Sure," and, without letting go of Johnnie's hand, said, "Let's go." Getting that kind of really personal guided tour of Les's history is something we will never forget.

Even though all of the guitars, tape machines and other artifacts were his, and even though he readily offered background stories on many of the items, Les appeared to be excited to see them in this context, almost as if he were seeing them for the first time. He seemed moved by the phone booth, where you could pick up the phone and hear him in conversation. Les enjoyed seeing the young lady in the black wig portraying a desk clerk. As we continued walking through the exhibit, it seemed that around every corner and in every cubbyhole, there was a part of Les's life on display. He really loved the way the guitars were displayed and commented that he thought they looked like art.

We stopped at a glass booth in the center of the exhibit showcasing "The Log." Les said he was pleasantly surprised that it was displayed lying down in a glass case rather than hanging on a wall. This way, he said people could get closer and see how he made it. He wanted to linger at this display. Les was quiet until he chuckled, seeing his quote in the glass case:

> *"They called me the character with the broomstick with pickups on it. It was another 10 years before they saw the light."*

James Joiner

"The Log," one of Les Paul's first electric guitar inventions

Les's entire life was laid out before him in this beautiful, bright exhibit. Yet, it seemed like the icing on the cake was the interactive display where a guitarist could sit down and play along with a virtual Les. He said he imagined young kids would get a kick out of that. In fact, this was just one example of the cross-generational impact Les had. As we walked through the exhibit, it was fascinating to observe many fans old enough to have grown up with Les's music rubbing shoulders with much younger converts to the magic of "The Wizard of Waukesha." Throughout the afternoon, Les was more than willing to stop, take a picture, talk a little, and sign autographs for all who asked. As excited as they were to see Les, he was equally happy to see them and, though he'd already had a long day and still had a concert to perform that night, it was obvious that this interaction with his fans was like a very good medicine that kept him energized.

After taking in the exhibit, we arranged with Les to go dir-

James Joiner

Les happily took time to visit with fans of all ages during the grand opening of Les Paul's House of Sound.

ectly to The Pabst Theater and meet him backstage. As we got to the parking garage, away from the crowd, Johnnie said that there were times she was concerned that Les was a little overwhelmed by everything. Not so much by the people, but from seeing his whole life on display.

And it was on display all over Milwaukee. As we drove to the theater, it seemed that everywhere we looked there was an image of Les or one of his guitars. Milwaukee had gone all out to hail the arrival of the "Wizard of Waukesha." When we arrived at the Pabst, we saw that this grand old Milwaukee landmark had also been "tricked out" to celebrate Les.

We found Les, his son, Russ, his close friend and photographer, Chris Lentz, his manager, Michael Braunstein, along with Les's trio and some of his regular New York guest performers who would be a part of the night's show. They were gathered in a backstage dressing room area having a pre-show bite to eat. We were warmly welcomed and were pleased to see Les relaxing and warming up in his own unique way by happily sharing stories from his

The city of Milwaukee and The Pabst Theater went all out to welcome Les and his fans on his 93rd birthday and the grand opening of Les Paul's House of Sound.

Photos by Edward Butkovich

early Wisconsin days.

Les introduced us to some of the people from the Pabst Theater and, always the gracious host, found seats for us on the couch. Les and Russ started recapping some of that day's events and talking about the night's concert. The relaxed conversation was interrupted every now and then by the entrance and introduction of a few select fans, who were thrilled to get the chance to say hello to Les and share a private moment with him before the show started.

After a while, Les said he wanted to change for the show. Johnnie kidded him about traveling with a vast selection of different colored turtlenecks. He said that he did because turtlenecks were his friend, and he hadn't decided which color he was going to wear.

Before the show started we went out into The Pabst Theater's auditorium and lobby to check on some friends and family members who were attending the show. On a very personal "full circle" note, after having introduced Steve to the "Wizard of Waukesha's" magic at a very young age, Steve's brother, Lee, and brother-in-law, John, had driven up from Indiana to see the show. Knowing that we were going to be on stage with Les Paul was a pretty far cry from the day Lee had first shared that little two-record 45 rpm extended-play album with Steve.

WGN Radio's vice president and general manager at the time, Tom Langmyer, a big Les Paul fan, had made the trip from Chicago, as had our producer, Dan Sugrue. Dan had gotten to know Les through their off-air conversations while Les was waiting to go on with us. In fact, we wouldn't be surprised if Dan decided to write his own book about some of the things that transpired in those conversations. Several people who were part of our show's "cast of characters" were in attendance. We'd had to act quickly to make sure they all got tickets to this sold-out show.

Since it was getting close to showtime, we returned to the backstage area and were quickly ushered to our onstage seats. True to Les's request, with tables and roving waitresses, The Pabst Theater's large stage had been transformed into a nightclub. Even though this beautiful landmark theater with its two balconies was capable of seating close to 1,500, the stage area now resembled the intimate feel of Les's New York home base nightclub, the Iridium.

As we had witnessed in Chicago, Nashville and Waukesha, Les was greeted with an enthusiastic ovation from the sold-out crowd. He quickly settled into some of his favorite standards: "Get Happy," "I Can't Get Started," "Lazy River," and "Brazil," and it was easy to see that, once again, he had the crowd in the palms of his hands. Actually, from our onstage vantage point it was much easier to see, because rather than looking up at Les, we were looking out at the audience. Even though we knew Les fed off interaction with his audience, seeing the looks of appreciation, adulation and amazement on faces of all ages, and the number of lips that mouthed "Wow!" as Les played, made us understand even more how much he was nourished by this experience.

As we've mentioned, playing guitar with the kind of medical stumbling blocks that were now a constant in Les's life was not an easy thing for him to do, but playing and the feedback he experienced on a night like this was something he had to do. Even on nights when his hands might not want to fully cooperate, he willed them to. For him, the payoff was more than worth the pain.

Much has been written about Les's guitar prowess and inventiveness. Not nearly enough has been written about Les as an entertainer who had the ability to read his audience and respond with the kind of timing that can't be taught; it has to be learned over the years. It was all on display on the Pabst stage: the jokes, the stories, the saves, and the onstage savvy that provided the icing on the musical cake.

The tables on the stage were peppered with people who would be joining Les at various points in the show. One of them was an eight-year-old blues guitarist from Wisconsin named Tallan "T-Man" Latz. Wearing sunglasses that made him look like a mini-Blues Brother, Tallan was, not surprisingly, a little nervous when Les introduced him. Without missing a beat, Les put him at ease

Edward Butkovich

Eight-year-old Tallan "T-Man" Latz jammed with Les at The Pabst Theater.

with jokes and questions and jammed along on "Green Onions" and two other blues songs. By the third song Tallan was laughing along with the audience as Les put on a pair of sunglasses handed up from the audience so Les would match Tallan's look.

After his last song, Tallan exited with Les encouraging him and saying, "Next time I come through town I want to hear a lot more from you."

After a few more songs and a guest appearance by one of Les's New York favorites, singer/actress Sonya Hensley, it was time for an intermission. With the promise of returning in just a few minutes, Les started walking to the back of the stage, talking with people as he went, but when he saw where our table was, he turned and headed right over. After asking how we were enjoying the show, he jokingly asked Johnnie if she had brought her accordion. We laughed and Johnnie told him the story of how she actually burned an accordion onstage, Jimi Hendrix style, while Steve sang and played Johnny B. Goode during a WGN Radio charity fundraiser.

> Speaking of us bringing instruments, allow us to insert here the one regret we have from Les's Pabst Theater show. The night Les called in to tell us about the show, he said he wanted us on the stage and that Steve should bring his guitar. Unfortunately, until the night we got there, we didn't know that Les wasn't just kidding, but actually DID want us onstage and that Steve really SHOULD have brought his guitar. Even though he probably would have been more nervous than Tallan Latz, to this day Steve regrets having missed the opportunity to play a song with Les.

Les said we would be the first guests he invited up to start the second part of the show. We asked him what he wanted us to do, and he said, "Do anything you want to do." After a little more conversation, we all headed our separate ways to freshen up for the show's second half.

When the intermission was over, Les casually wandered up to his chair at the center of the stage, sat down and began softly playing a slow version of "How High the Moon." Gradually, the members of his trio joined in until Les quadrupled the tempo for the song's signature riff. Of course, the audience loved it. Paul Krajniak came out next to talk a little about the opening of *Les Paul's House of Sound,* and to thank everyone for attending, for their support, and for helping to make this benefit performance a huge success.

Then, it was our turn.

As we walked out after being introduced, Les smiled and Johnnie leaned over and gave him a kiss. Les quickly deadpanned to the audience, "When I kiss her, I feel like a condemned building with a new flagpole on it." The crowd went nuts.

Edward Butkovich

Any backstage jitters we may have felt quickly faded away as we fell into an easy onstage rhythm with Les, laughing and putting a few twists on some of the stories he'd shared with us about his time in Chicago at various radio stations, including WGN. Steve related some of the tricks Les played on the air. Johnnie got a little emotional being onstage with Les at this historic event, but she got the crowd roaring again as she described Les as "a man who is a guitar, a man who is a sound, and ... a man who is a RASCAL!" Les laughed as hard as anyone in the audience.

A few more jokes and more back-and-forth kidding with Les, and we wrapped up our portion of the show. As we were walking past Les and exiting the stage, Johnnie again leaned over and gave Les a kiss. Although they hadn't talked about it, Steve had an idea and had the feeling Les would know what to do. After Johnnie's kiss, Steve said, loud enough for the audience to hear, "Oh, what the heck" and leaned over as if he was going to give Les a kiss, too. Les leaned up as if he was going to reciprocate but, at the very last second, turned away looking at his guitar. Once again, Les's timing was perfect, and the crowd loved it.

Opposite: Les was clearly receptive to Johnnie's kiss.

Right: Les played Steve's faux attempt at a kiss to comic perfection.

Edward Butkovich

We returned to our table to watch the rest of the show. As the evening progressed, it was easy to see and hear that the audience was having a great time and they were in no hurry for it to end.

As Les did each Monday night at the Iridium, he was happily playing ringmaster, integrating some of his friends from New York into the performance, like Wisconsin-born bluesman Jon Paris. Finally, although obviously much too soon for his appreciative audience, Les played the evening's final notes to a standing ovation, then took off his guitar and stood on the stage, waving to the audience and shaking hands with his fellow performers. After several minutes of applause, the crowd gradually started to leave the theater. Before he left the stage, Les, joined by his manager, Michael Braunstein, walked over to our table. Les put his arm around Johnnie and, even though it was a little hard to hear through the din of the exiting crowd, we spent a few minutes talking about how the evening had played out and made plans to talk more a little later.

Les wanted to pause and catch his breath for a few minutes

James Joiner

Les and Jon Paris on The Pabst Theater stage.

before he planned to come back and spend a little time with VIP ticket holders at a special 93rd-birthday celebration event that was tied in to the night's "House of Sound" benefit performance. A lounge adjoining the theater was the birthday event location. A special guitar-shaped birthday cake had been prepared, and Les stopped for a few seconds to admire it.

After Les left the stage area, we spent a little time talking and exchanging contact information with some of the performers. Then, seeing that most of the crowd had filed out, we made our way through the theater to the lobby and spent a little time talking with listeners, some of whom had driven through several states to get the chance to see Les.

When we got to the birthday party, the lounge was close to being filled. Even though we had the proper "Les Paul and Friends VIP" tag, some people were being turned away, and we weren't

Les checks out
the birthday cake
prepared for his
93rd birthday

James Joiner

sure we'd be able to get in. Eventually, we made the cut and went inside to find Paula, Joe and Dan Sugrue. All of us were still very buzzed from the night's show and amazed at Les's stamina with the kind of full schedule he'd been keeping that day.

Knowing Les was a night owl, none of us thought much of it when the hour got later and he still hadn't arrived. After a bit more time passed, some of us began to get a little concerned. When the door finally opened and Michael Braunstein walked in with a serious look on his face, we knew that Les was not going to make another appearance that night. Michael said that after a full day, Les, very regretfully, would not be joining us.

Although we would have more on- and off-air phone conversations with Les in the coming months, sadly, these precious moments with him on the Pabst stage would turn out to be the last time we talked in person.

A post-show chat on *The Pabst Theater* stage was the
final time Steve and Johnnie saw Les.

A little more Les ...

*I never stop being amazed by
all the different ways of playing
the guitar and making it deliver
a message. — Les Paul*

Les Paul, guitar virtuoso, dies at age 94

NEW YORK (AP) — Les Paul, the guitar virtuoso and inventor who revolutionized music and created rock 'n' roll as surely as Elvis Presley and the Beatles by developing the solid-body electric guitar and multitrack recording, died Thursday. He was 94.

Known for his lightning-fast riffs, Paul performed with some of early pop's biggest names and produced a slew of hits, many with wife Mary Ford. But it was his inventive streak that made him universally revered by guitar gods as their original ancestor and earned his induction into the Rock and Roll Hall of Fame as one of the most important forces in popular music.

Paul, who died in White Plains, N.Y., of complications from pneumonia, was a tireless tinkerer, whose quest for a particular sound led him to create the first solid-body electric guitar, a departure from the hollow-body guitars of the time.

His invention paved the way for modern rock 'n' roll and became the standard instrument for legends like Pete Townshend and Jimmy Page.

He also developed technology that would become hallmarks of rock and pop recordings, from multitrack recording that allowed for layers and layers of "overdubs" to guitar reverb and other sound effects.

Paul was inducted into the National Inventors Hall of Fame in 2005.

Vaya con Dios

O ur crazy five-night-a-week, five- or six-hour overnight radio broadcast schedule was made even crazier by the fact that we would sleep in two shifts. When we got home from the radio station in the early morning hours, we would unwind, often watching an hour or so of television and then collapsing for a few hours of much-needed sleep. For years, we tried to sleep more than three or four hours at a stretch, but we were never able to master that. So we gave up trying. Our routine was to be up in the afternoon hours to work on that night's show. We would use that time to book the show, line up a guest or two, and catch up on the day's news. Around dinner time, we would grab a few more hours of sleep before getting up to leave for the radio station to do the show.

The morning of August 13, 2009 was no different for us. After our show, we came home and slept for a few hours. When we crawled out of bed, one of us looked at the answering machine on the headboard to see if any calls had come in while we slept.

The answering machine read 22!

Seeing that 22 calls had come in during the three hours we had been sleeping woke us up fast. We both dreaded hitting the play button on the machine because we knew it was no doubt going to be bad news.

The first of the messages was so soft we both leaned into the machine to better hear what the caller was saying. It was Russ Paul, Les's son, calling to tell us that his dad had passed away. Russ said, "The news is reporting that Dad died today, the 13th, but he actually died the 12th." Russ said he and other family members and friends were at Les's side when he died of complications from pneumonia.

We continued to listen to the phone messages while we processed the news of Les's death. Each of the 21 other calls was from a friend or a family member sharing the same news. We had calls from California, Florida, Indiana and New York, and calls from people we hadn't heard from in years. We were genuinely touched that people who knew of our relationship with Les Paul wanted us to hear the sad news of his passing from a friendly voice and not from a newscast while wiping sleep out of our eyes.

We can't say we were terribly surprised by the news. The last time we had spoken to Les was on June 9, his 94th birthday, when he said he had literally just come home from a hospital stay. When we ended the conversation, we both said on and off the air that we were concerned that he sounded so weak and more fragile than he had ever sounded in all the years we had talked to him. After we hung up, hoping that he would indeed be able to get some rest, we recalled the time we were in the middle of a conversation and he casually said, "Oops, my pacemaker battery just went out!" We were understandably rattled and wanted him to hang up and do something, anything, but he refused. As he said, "It's not like I can get a replacement in the middle of the night, so let's talk."

The conversation on his birthday was obviously going to be short. He sounded weak, and he actually agreed to hang up and roll over and try to get some sleep. Resting and sleeping at night seemed foreign to Les, but that night, his birthday, after wishing him a happy birthday and telling him we loved him and sending him off to bed, it was clear this time he wasn't the Les Paul who was going to magically come to life after midnight.

After getting the news of his passing, we knew the focus of our show that night would be to remember and celebrate the genius of Les Paul. It had already been a long day for Les's friends and colleagues when we spoke with them after midnight. In most cases, they had already done a number of interviews and were still processing what Les's passing meant in their lives. Even though they were weary, each of them, without hesitation, agreed to stay up late to join us on live radio to share their thoughts and still-raw emotions on the loss of a man all of us were privileged to call our friend.

Lou Pallo

(music out of break)

Steve: What you're listening to is *Les Paul from Cinemax Presents: Les Paul & Friends* **from 1988. The man sitting alongside Les playing guitar is the same man sitting alongside Les playing guitar at Fat Tuesdays, the Club Iridium, and anytime we were fortunate enough to see Les. At the tribute night down in Nashville at the Ryman, at his homecoming in Waukesha, and at the Pabst. The man is Lou Pallo. Lou joins us now. Lou, thank you for joining us, and first of all, please accept our condolences, our sympathies, on the loss of your dear friend.**

Lou Pallo: Yes, thank you. He was a very dear friend, and a great musician.

Johnnie: Amen. Lou, how many years did you work with Les?

Lou: I worked with Les 25 years.

Steve: How'd you meet?

Lou: Going back to when I was a teenager I played Les Paul and Mary Ford's "How High the Moon" on the jukebox, and it just knocked me out. I said, "Wow! What a sound. What a sound!

Lou Pallo, background, with Les Paul

Chris Lentz

Unbelievable!" And I just played it over and over, maybe 50 times, and at that time it was five cents to play the jukebox. It was a 78 (rpm record) then. I just idolized him. Then in '60,'61, I was at a bar in Greenwood Lakes, New York, and he was sitting at the bar. I didn't know it was him. He called me over and said, "My name is Les Paul." And I said, "The Les Paul?" He said, "Yes." I said "Oh my God, all my life I've wanted to meet you." He gave me his phone number, and I went to his house the next day, and from then on we became friends. But to work with someone you really idolize? That's an honor.

Steve: When was the first time you worked with him professionally?

Lou: I was working a gig in New Jersey in 1975. I was by myself, I was a single and he would come in. In fact, one year he came in 80-something times. We counted. He would come in with his guitar — he lived up the street from where I worked — so he would bring his guitar and sit in with me, and it was just fabulous.

Johnnie: I bet you were just pinching yourself saying, "This is just too cool."

Lou: Oh, exactly. He just knocked me out. He was great. He was a great man. I really feel so bad today.

Steve: His sense of humor always shone through, not only in the conversations we had with him on the air, and conversations he had with other people, but the musical conversations he would have. There were times when he would play these licks and he'd be looking at you, and I could tell the two of you had these little musical jokes going on, didn't you?

Lou: Yes, yes, we did. I was always looking at him and he'd look at me, and I knew exactly what he was thinking of. I knew just where he was going with all the experience of being with him.

Johnnie: And even though he'd done thousands of shows, when he was going to do a show he was there for the show. Ready to perform, focused, in the zone.

Lou: Oh yes, yes. In the 25 years, we did two shows every Monday. We'd get to the club at four in the afternoon, and we'd be on that stage from four till show time. We said he WAS a perfectionist, yet he said he wasn't. He was a perfectionist.

Johnnie: I remember we were sitting in the auditorium at the Ryman for the sound check, and even though the man wore hearing aids, he knew the sound he wanted and he worked with the sound crew until he got the sound he wanted. That was his m.o. He came to work and he was going to do his job right.

Lou: Exactly.

Steve: Lou, I know this has been a long day for you, but if you could, put into words not only how you think Les will be remembered, but how will you remember Les?

Lou: I'll never forget him, I can tell you that. Every time I pick up a guitar he'll be there next to me. Thank you for remembering him in Chicago, and continue to do that.

Johnnie: We certainly will. Tonight we celebrate his life and you were the perfect person to start out with, so thank you, Lou. Good night.

(Lou Pallo disconnects.)

Steve: I remember when we saw Les in Waukesha, I was so impressed with Lou's guitar, and it's a Les Paul. I got a chance to tell him how much I loved the sound of his guitar, and he said, "Les does too! He's always trying to buy this guitar off me."

Johnnie: Lou was such a big part of the show. Not only because of his skill as a guitarist, but he's a great vocalist, too.

Steve: One of the fun parts of the show was when Lou sang "Makin' Whoopee" and Les would sit with his arms folded over top of his guitar, and when Lou got to the line "makin' whoopee," he would stop, and Les would hit just the right notes and the crowd would go nuts!

Johnnie: Yes! He knew just the right notes for the punch line and the audience would be like putty in his hands.

Ron Sturm
Owner, The Iridium Jazz Club

When you talked about Les, you had to talk about the fact that at age 94, he was still gigging at the Iridium. The owner of the 200-seat venue near Times Square is Ron Sturm. Ron, born in the '60s, was raised on rock 'n' roll, not jazz. It was during his college days at Boston University when Boston was hopping and jazz was hot that Ron caught the jazz bug. In 1994, the Sturm family decided to open a club in New York, and Ron suggested it be a jazz club. He chose the name of the club for its associations, ranging from a silvery white metal, to a word that refers to rainbows, to the story that saxophones are lined with iridium. The family liked the name, and the club was opened. It has developed a great reputation as a jazz club in New York.

Johnnie: Ron, how many years did Les work at the Club Iridium?
Ron: A little over 12 years.

©Thomas Hawk

Steve: How did that start?

Johnnie: Was he out of work? *(laughter)*

Ron: Les was like the Lou Gehrig of music. He had been working at a place in town called Fat Tuesdays for 12 or 13 years. I was a punk kid that had heard of Les Paul, but didn't know exactly who he was. I called a critic at the New York Post and said, "Can I have Les Paul's phone number?" He gave it to me, and I called Les and invited him down to the club. He came in one night wearing a windbreaker and jeans and hung out in the back. He did that a few times. He just wanted to check out the whole scene. I just knew from a business perspective that, wow, he is important. He's been playing at a club for 12 or 13 years already, and we should have him here. We got him, and this amazing man became a big part of my life.

Steve: Have you had a chance to think about how you want Les remembered at the club? Is there a special tribute planned?

Ron: Yeah, we intend to do a number of things that are in the planning stages. A lot of people think of him as a cartoon character or untouchable icon. They really don't know the human being behind the guitar, the amazing, amazing human being. Lou Pallo spoke of the music genius side of Les, I want to be a spokesman for the human side of Les. I want to say that you can toss around accolades about him as genius, a virtuoso, but I can talk about the wonderful human being Les Paul was. I want to perpetuate that he was a great man. He loved me and I loved him. He loved people. He was fascinated by them and the world. From when I first met him till today, he was the hippest guy you'll ever meet. We are not going to mourn him. We're going to celebrate him, and every note played on the guitar from now and forever will have Les Paul's imprint on it. He was that important to music.

Steve: Absolutely, Ron.

Johnnie: You'll get no argument from us!

Ron: Yes, I'm preaching to the choir.

Johnnie: We said tonight we'll be celebrating his life, because every time we talked to him we'd come away talking about what an inspiration he was and how he made you feel so darn good! You, Ron, were so spot-on when you said not only did he love people, but he was always interested in what they were up to, and everything going on around him. Forever curious.

Ron: He was a tinkerer. Les could talk to everyone, common man to rock star to U.S. president. He was meat and potatoes, yet he was a genius. He also knew exactly who he was. It wasn't existential stuff. It wasn't like, "Look at me, I'm Les Paul!" He knew who he was and honestly, so few of us can say that. He was happy with his life.

Johnnie: He certainly was, Ron.

Steve: It's been a long day for you.

Ron: I could talk for hours. I just want to leave with: Not only was Les Paul a great human being, but every note that is ever going to be played will have Les's spirit in it. We knew a true icon of the 20th and 21st centuries. People can't even fathom how important he was. Those who didn't get to know him, at least they'll hear his music. Always.

Chris Lentz

Ron Sturm, LEFT, *with Jose Feliciano,* CENTER, *celebrate Les's birthday at the Iridium.*

Nicki Parrott
plays with Les
at the Iridium.

Chris Lentz

Nicki Parrott

Steve: As we remember the life of the extraordinary Les Paul, it's nice to talk to the people who had the good fortune of working with him. The lovely lady you would hear singing in Les's trio was the lady who had an INTERESTING onstage relationship with him. She has an extraordinary voice and played bass in Les's trio for years.

Johnnie: Nicki Parrott is an internationally-acclaimed bass

player and joins us now.

Nicki: It's a pleasure to be talking to you about our dear friend Les. I've been up and down all day. Quite sad at times, and overwhelmed sometimes at the thought I'm not going to see him again. He will be missed and I will definitely miss him a lot.

Steve: You had a wonderful onstage flirtation with Les.

Nicki: Really? I never flirted with Les! (*laughter*)

Johnnie: Right, and it was obvious he loved every minute of it.

Nicki: How could you not flirt with Les? He was adorable!

Johnnie: Yes!

Steve: How did you first meet him?

Nicki: Actually, I was playing in a group with two wonderful guitar players, David Spinozza and John Tropea. We were a trio working professionally in and around New York and New Jersey. I think it was John who said, "We should go down to the club and see if we can sit in with Les Paul. We've got our act together." I agreed and said, "I've never even met Les." So, we went down on a Monday night and he invited us up on stage to do a couple of numbers. We did them, then Les said, "You guys sit down, but leave the girl up here." I was very nervous. I was sure he was going to roast me on stage. But he picked all the tunes I knew, thank goodness, and I started to loosen up. He was very nice, and then he started making cracks about a girl musician, and I went right back at him with cracks about old men. It was like an instant back-and-forth connection. I felt he saw it, too, the way he was looking at me. Like he thought, "We may have something here." So, he gave me a chance to fill in for the other bass player for three weeks. After three weeks, Les said, "We'll see you next week." I said, "No, actually the other guy is back." He said, "No, no, no, we'll see you next week." He made it happen for me to have the gig. That was nine years ago.

Johnnie: And two shows every Monday night.

Steve: One of the wonderful things about Les is when you see him perform, you realize his musicianship, and also his showmanship.

Nicki: Oh, he was a showman!

Steve: His sense of timing was impeccable.

Nicki: Absolutely. He had a great sense of humor. He was sharp till the end. He was so witty, too. It was hard to outwit him. He was always able to have one up on you. He knew exactly what was happening around him at all times. He was a showman. He lived to perform for an audience.

Steve: I would assume you'd agree that, even though we all know his health wasn't the best, you never counted him out. He had bounced back from so many health challenges. We always thought, and even this time thought, he'd wind up back on stage.

Nicki: Exactly. He had bad health through the years, but would only take a couple of Mondays off and be back. I always thought he'd be back. It's only been in the last couple of days I had the feeling that maybe this time he wouldn't be back. He was happiest when he was on stage.

Johnnie: Nicki, every time we saw you perform with Les it was pure entertainment.

Nicki: Thank you. He was a total pleasure to work with. It was a unique gig. Once he said to me, "Don't you do anything else besides play the bass?" He brought me out of my shell. It was a great experience. I'm very fortunate.

Johnnie: And we're fortunate to have this time to talk with you about our friend Les.

Nicki: Thank you very much.

Tommy Shaw

Les and Tommy Shaw (with his "bra shirt") at the Iridium in 1996

Courtesy Tommy Shaw

Steve: Les loved music. Yes, Les played jazz, Les played country, he could play rock 'n' roll with the best of them. I'm looking at the MTV website where he's being remembered by Slash, Joan Jett, Joe Satriani, and joining us now is ...

Johnnie: From Chicago's own Styx: singer, guitarist Tommy Shaw. Tommy, thank you for joining us. I'm smiling looking at pictures of you with Les on your website. When did you first meet Les?

Tommy Shaw: I met him in 1996. That was the first time I went down to the Iridium Club and I jammed with him that night. I didn't know what to expect. He was such a huge personality, and besides being the great guitar player, he was a teacher. He was just larger than life. He really made me feel welcome. He brought me right up on stage and we played quite a few songs. I believe it was that night a local girl got up and sang before I went up. Well, he stopped right in the middle of her song and said, "What are you doing?" He was schooling her right there on stage. He wasn't trying to embarrass her, he just felt she had a better performance in her and she wasn't giving it.

Johnnie: That's a theme we hear from professionals, that Les was in heaven when he was on stage, and he wanted you to give all you had if you joined him on that stage.

Steve: He wanted performers to do their best, never hold back on him.

Tommy: He did. I've been doing this since I was 10 years old and I'm telling you, waiting to get on that stage was one of the most nervous times of my life, just waiting to play with him.

Johnnie: Did you have one of your Les Paul guitars with you?

Tommy: No, I played one of his guitars.

Johnnie: Did you? Oh, that would be even more nerve wracking!

Tommy: Yeah, but, for some reason we got along great. We laughed. We came up with silly stuff right there on stage. And he didn't take me to school! (*laughter*) I was so relieved.

Johnnie: I bet! Now, you have played a Gibson Les Paul guitar over the years, right?

Tommy: Yes, the guitar I played when I joined Styx was a Gibson Les Paul. I was making payments on it to Roselle Music.

Johnnie: Ah, I thought so. Like in "Grand Illusion," you're playing a Les Paul guitar.

Tommy: I just got another new one, just two gigs ago.

Johnnie: I've always said, for people who think being a musician, a rock star, is easy work, pick up a Gibson Les Paul guitar!

Steve: That is a heavy sucker.

Johnnie: So, when you're out there on stage playing two, three hours, holding that much weight around your neck, that's working, isn't it, Tommy?

Tommy: You know, I've had one around my neck so long, I can't wear shirts with horizontal stripes because they kinda go at an angle from having that Les Paul on my shoulder for so many years. (*laughter*)

Steve: Well, speaking of shirts. You sent us a picture of you and Les. You're backstage at the Club Iridium, and what happened?

Tommy: We were backstage talking, and my wife, who is a really pretty woman, was with me. Les was focusing on her while I talked, and he turns to me to take that picture, and I was wearing that shirt which was a black pullover with cool scrolling stuff on the top of it. I hadn't paid much attention to it when I put it on. Well, we took the picture and Les turns back to me and says, "Is that a bra?" *(laughter)* When you look at the picture, sure enough, it kinda looks like a bra. Well, I never wore the shirt again.

Steve: Always working that wicked sense of humor.

Tommy: He was funny! And tireless! I was amazed at the long shows he would do. Two of them, with guests and a full house, which meant he was available to greet everybody as they were leaving. He would take time to talk, take pictures, sign autographs. He'd look at the memorabilia they would bring. I saw him talk on the phone to their relatives. He would talk and meet every single person till they were all gone. Then they'd bring in a new audience for another long show, and another meet-and-greet afterwards.

Steve: And Tommy, the norm was after he did all that, he'd get back home to Mahwah, New Jersey, and he'd call us on the air at three or four in the morning, our time. It's like he needed to talk and unwind.

Tommy: Yes, because he loved that gig. It was all Les. It really was a fun gig for the audience and musicians if you were lucky enough to share the stage with him.

Johnnie: He's going to be missed at the club. He's going to be missed in New York on Monday nights. We know many people from Chicago, from all over the Midwest, who made a pilgrimage to New York to see him. And if you're a musician and you're in New York, you had to find time to stop by and see him just to be in the presence of this music legend.

Tommy: Oh yes, and I'm so glad I did that. I just wish I'd done it more. I guess he was just one of those guys you figured was always going to be there. What an inspiration, what an incredible career from where he started out as kind of a clown character to being this incredible, sought-after guitarist, to becoming an inventor, innovator, and back to being this amazing musician and entertainer. Thank you for doing this tribute to Les. It's very sweet and I'm glad I could join you to talk about him.

In 2009, Les Paul and Michael Cochran wrote and assembled a highly acclaimed 368-page coffee table biography. Collector copies are still available online.

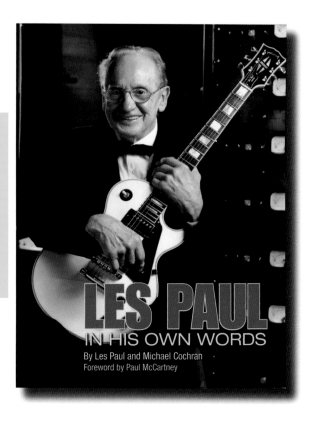

Michael Cochran

Steve: Les told us many years ago he was working on a book that would be his autobiography. He said it would have incredible pictures and stories you hadn't heard before. He was excited about this book.

Johnnie: That stunning book is entitled *Les Paul: In His Own Words*. The co-author of the book is Michael Cochran. Mike, thanks for joining us.

Michael: Oh, I'm happy to be with y'all tonight.

Johnnie: Your book came out in summer of 2005, right?

Michael: Yes, it took three years to write and it was published in '05.

Johnnie: Tell the story of how you came to write it. It happened after writing the Chet Atkins book that you met Les, right?

Michael: You're right. I'd written the Chet Atkins biography, *Chet Atkins: Me and My Guitars,* and my brother, Russ, who is a publisher, published it. It was very well received. I suppose most people who know anything about Les Paul and/or Chet Atkins, they know the two were good friends. They related to each other a lot over the years. In fact, Les Paul was one of Chet's primary heroes. He was a major influence on Chet, and so Chet had some very nice things to say about Les in his book. When it was published, we sent Les a copy of it as a gesture of respect. My brother and I didn't know Les at that point. We had seen him perform a couple of times, but we'd never met the man. He was impressed with the Chet Atkins book and called my brother Russ to tell him so, and the conversation led from one thing to another, and the next thing you know we'd made an agreement with Les to do a similar book for him. The result is the beautiful coffee table book you have.

Steve: One of the first things I was struck by when I first

opened the book was the extraordinary photography. A lot of pictures were taken at Les's home in New Jersey. The first time you went to his house, were you kind of overwhelmed (*laughter*) not only with Les, but with all the things?

Michael: Oh sure. I don't think we were overwhelmed, but certainly our feelers were up for a number of different reasons. For one thing, when word got around we were going to do a book about Les Paul with Les Paul, a number of people suggested he could be difficult. My brother and I were regular attendees at the Chet Atkins Appreciation Society gathering every year in Nashville. It was a five-day event with guitarists from all over the world. We introduced our Chet Atkins book, and naturally, it was a big hit there. Well, when some of those same people heard we were going to do a book about Les Paul, they took us aside and said, "Boy, you guys are in for a tough time." Because, as you guys know, you've known him a long time, he was a great person, but he had a reputation for being a little hard to get along with sometimes, especially if someone crossed him. So we didn't know what to expect that day in June in 2002 when we knocked on his door at his home in Mahwah. We were there to meet him for the first time. He met us himself at the door, he welcomed us in, and we got along famously from the very beginning.

Whatever concerns we might've had that he was going to be difficult, or condescending, or whatever, didn't turn out to be true at all. In fact, one of the first things that happened that day when we met him, we settled down in his living room, and the conversation you would expect took place. At some point, he said, "Now where are you boys from?" My brother, Russ, said, "I live in West Plains, Missouri," and I said, "I live a hundred miles away in Springfield, Missouri." As soon as he heard Springfield his eyes lit up. He started asking me questions about Springfield. He said, "Springfield, Missouri. Is KWTO still on the air there? Is KBEX still there?" I said, "They sure are. As a matter of fact, I've worked for both of them." Well, it turned out he had lived in Springfield and had worked on staff at radio station KWTO the day it went on the air, Christmas Day, 1933. He was still Rhubarb Red then, and he was working with Sonny Joe Wolverton as a duo known as the "Ozark Apple-Knockers."

Johnnie: Again, you're talking about 70 years later. The recall was remarkable. His memory was right there.

Michael: It was instantaneous. He said, "Is KWTO still on the air? I put that station on the air!" We were off and running. Right then and there, we knew we were going to be able to write his book. We immediately had a rapport thanks to having something to talk about that we had in common.

Steve: He certainly was an amazing storyteller. He remembered details and sometimes he might embellish a story a little, but he could recall the specifics like you were reading it from a book. I always liked to play some of his music that would surprise him. I got ahold of a CD that you'd have to find in the Nat King Cole section. It was one of the Jazz at the Philharmonic concert CDs that Les was on. In fact, I think it was the first Jazz at the Philharmonic.

Michael: Yes, it was.

Steve: There's this wonderful jam session between Nat King Cole and Les. We had Les on and I played some of that live session, and I said, "Les, this was in the mid-'40s, right?" Without missing a beat, he said, "It was in 1947, it was a Sunday night," and he went on to describe the weather that night!

Johnnie: And he had no idea Steve was going to blindside him with that piece of music, but, without hesitation, he was able to go right back to that day and call up the details like it was yesterday. I loved the punchline to the story. He said, "I'll never forget, you know, men wore hats back then and they were so moved by our performance that they took off their hats and tossed them in the air. I'll never forget looking out into the audience at a sea of hats going up in the air."

Michael: Nat King Cole's usual guitar player, Oscar Moore, had run off with a woman. That's how Les got the opportunity to play with the gig with Nat. Oscar Moore was a tremendous guitarist and always played with Nat and wasn't available that night because according to Les he was "shacked up." (*laughter*)

Johnnie: He no doubt loved that part of the story.

Michael: Oh yeah! He liked to say they slipped a pizza under the door and left Oscar alone. You know, that was a remarkable performance for a number of reasons. One thing was black and white musicians playing together, in the '40s. That did not happen. It was the first time jazz had been played in the prestigious Philharmonic Hall, and it was a real good thing for Les. He got on that stage and he held his own with some of the greatest players of the day. He made a lot of new fans that night.

Steve: It's one of those records that, even today, the electricity jumps out at you. A lot of people think of Nat King Cole and they think of this soft ballad singer, but Nat King Cole knew his way around a keyboard, and the two of them going at each other, back and forth, trading fours, that's exciting music.

Michael: And the neat thing about it is Les said they didn't even know the performance was being recorded. You appreciate that fact, because if you have a microphone and you know a recording is being made, it can have an effect on how you perform, how you behave, what you play, and what you do with the thought that it may live on forever. Those guys didn't know they were being recorded, so the spontaneity is 100 percent pure. That was recorded on a transcription machine with a single microphone. Someone drug one of those great big disc cutters back there and set up one microphone and aimed it at the stage.

Johnnie: Thank goodness that stuff is still around today in a good quality CD format. A couple of years ago, a CD came out of Fred Waring and the Pennsylvanians with Les performing with them. These were radio shows and the incredible thing was the difference between the broadcasts for the West Coast

compared to what was aired for the Midwest and East Coast.

Steve: It was different, because at this point Les was going back and forth between an electric and an acoustic guitar. One of the fascinating things to me is to listen to those acoustic shows and you hear the Django Reinhardt influences all over Les's playing.

Michael: Oh yeah, he had Django's licks down. He could just about out-Django Django. There's a picture in the book of Les on the Waring show playing acoustic guitar. It shows how he sat on a high stool to get his acoustic guitar up closer to the microphone. They went back and forth for a while, but it wasn't too long before the consensus for the electric guitar was so strong that he went exclusively with the electric guitar.

Johnnie: That's one of the gems in this stunning book that Les endorsed 100 percent. Mike, I wonder if you, while writing the book, experienced what we experienced talking to him over the years. He would name drop and I would get so tickled. He might casually mention Judy Garland and I would say "The Judy Garland?" And he would say, "Yes," and he was off on a Judy Garland tangent. But there one celebrity he talked about that he always spoke of differently. That was Bing Crosby.

Steve: He went to a different place when he talked about Bing.

Johnnie: There was a sadness in his voice. It was like he still missed his dear friend all these years later, and you could tell that out of all the famous people he came to know, Bing was right up there at the top.

Steve: There was a level of respect he had for Bing Crosby that came through in his voice, and you really never heard that when Les talked about anybody else.

Michael: You know, that's true. Bing and Django were at the top. People today know something about Bing, but sadly, he's kind of faded into the woodwork now. Younger folks probably know him from his movies, but don't know about his greatness as a performer. At the time Les recorded "It's Been A Long, Long Time" with Bing, Bing was the biggest star in America. He had not only hit movies, but hit songs, sold-out concerts, a radio show, and product endorsements. He was as big as it gets when that record was made. Bing did Les a tremendous favor by having him play on that song. It was a huge #1 hit at the end of World War II. Everybody was coming home from Europe and the Pacific, and here's this song that says, "Kiss me once, kiss me twice, kiss me once again. It's been a long, long time." Bing recorded that just with Les on guitar and a fellow on bass. It's a very sparse recording. Even though Les had received a lot of attention on the Fred Waring coast-to-coast radio show, that song with Bing made his stock go up like a rocket. The association with Bing Crosby and the fact that their first record together was a huge hit record brought a great deal of attention to Les.

Johnnie: Then, as the story goes, Bing bought Les the first Ampex tape recorder.

Michael: Yes, yes he did. It was a gift to Les from Bing.

Johnnie: That's important, too, in the whole history of recording techniques and multi-track recording that we know today. If it hadn't been for Bing doing that, Lord knows where we'd be today.

Michael: Yes, but we mustn't forget that Les had already made some remarkable recordings using just disc cutting machines in the garage studio behind his house in Hollywood. "Lover," his ground-breaking first recording, featured, well, you wouldn't technically call it multi-tracking, but he stacked tracks. He would lay down a track on an acetate disc and then, on another machine, lay down another acetate disc, play another instrument line with the first disc and combine them so he kept stacking them up like that. So he was already doing his multi-instrumental layering of tracks in his recordings before he got the tape recorder from Bing.

Steve: And as a result of what he'd been doing up until the point he got the Ampex from Bing, it was getting him a lot of attention for the quality of the recordings he was doing.

Michael: That's very true. For those who may not know, Les and his first wife, Virginia, lived in a little bungalow in Hollywood with a one-car garage out back. He and some of his friends turned it into a little recording studio, and using these disc cutters, Les would say, "We cut those records with a nail." They actually got a sound out of that little studio that none of the big studios, Capitol, Decca, none of them could get. Of course, Decca was huge — they were Crosby's label. Think of that: These big-time studios could not match the sound Les was getting out of his garage.

Les and Michael at Les's home in Mahwah, New Jersey

Steve: Speaking of that studio, were you able to verify the legend of W.C. Fields recording at Les's studio and Fields never paying Les for that session.

Michael: Yes, it's true. Les told me that. In fact, another one of the warnings we got from people before writing the book with Les was, "He's full of hot air. You can't believe most of the stories he'll tell you." Well, I've got to tell you folks, I did the research. That's one of the reasons the book took three years to write. We made every effort to verify facts and get facts to make sure what we were saying was true. So many of the things Les told me that I might have questioned and said, "Gee, I don't know Les, I'm going to have to check this out." Well, he would be right! He would be on the money over and over and over again. The very few times he did have his facts wrong, if I presented that to him, if I showed him the proof, if I showed him, for example, the article in Photoplay magazine with a different date, he'd say "I guess that's right." Yes, sure he embellished things, but who doesn't?

Johnnie: He was a great storyteller.

Michael: Like Dizzy Dean once said, "It ain't braggin' if you done it." (*laughter*)

Steve: Absolutely right!

Johnnie: Mike Cochran, thank you for doing such a beautiful job of telling Les's story in your book, *Les Paul: In His Own Words.*

Tommy Emmanuel

Tommy Emmanuel

(Music playing out of a commercial break)

Steve: As we continue our celebration of the life of Les Paul, we had to bring in the man you just heard playing with Les. We're so glad that Tommy Emmanuel could join us tonight.

Johnnie: Tommy, thank you for joining us.

Tommy: I never heard the tune you played with me and Les.

Steve: That's "Blue Moon" from the *Chasing Sound* soundtrack. It's great! I'm surprised you'd never heard it.

Tommy: I remember well the night we played it together. You know, that song points up the way Les thought. He thought like a horn section. I'm playing the tune, keeping the melody, and he does all these little things around me which is a bit like a horn section. That was one of the traits of his playing. He didn't think like other people. *(laughter)* In fact, he did nothing like other people. He was an amazing guy.

Steve: Do you think that had to do with the time in which he grew up and the work he did with big bands? He would throw in big band riffs. In fact, if you listen to "How High the Moon," that's a good example of the big band influences.

Tommy: Yes, and he multi-tracked himself so he would become the whole section. It's brilliant. That's one of the things, one of the many things, I stole from him. When I play a tune I try to put in little riffs, think like a horn section or orchestra, and never think like a guitar player and put myself in that box. Always live outside the box. That's a very Les Paul way of doing things.

Steve: If I'm not mistaken, the first time you really got a chance to talk to Les, you were in our studio and he called in.

Tommy: That's right.

Steve: Then you went to New York. What was it like the first time you stepped on stage with him and played with Les?

Tommy: I remember that vividly. I was so honored to be there and was thrilled to be in his presence, as I always was. Les said something I'll never forget. He said, "If there's a heaven on earth, it must be standing up here playing this guitar." Every time I went to visit him, I'd sit back in that tiny dressing room off to the side of the stage, and me and Frank Vignola would play tunes for him while Les ate his dinner. He was just in heaven. I have photos in my bedroom of Les and I. Ha! He would kiss me on the lips and call me "boy." He was just a real daddy to me, and I allowed him to be. I loved on him and I let him love on me the same way. We always had that relationship. It was the same way with Chet Atkins. I loved him for how he was as a man, and I never wanted anything from him. I just wanted to see him have a great time — to feel the love in that moment.

Johnnie: Tommy, you don't know this, but every night you showed up at the club and performed with Les, we knew he would call us afterward. He was so energized after he would perform with you.

Tommy: Really? (*laughter*)

Johnnie: Absolutely! You probably don't know that every single night you stopped in to perform with him he would say to us, "Tommy Emmanuel makes me a better guitarist. I have to work hard to keep up with that kid." We put him on the spot a number of times and asked him, "Who's the best guitarist out there today?" Every time, he answered without hesitation, "Hands down, Tommy Emmanuel."

Tommy: Maybe he didn't have his hearing aid on! (*laughter*)

Johnnie: He also loved your sense of humor, and I know you enjoyed his.

Tommy: We were like a couple of kids. We'd pick on each other and the audience. Then he'd get that New York comedienne up there who had a potty mouth. But he was hilarious. Les always drew the best from people around him.

Steve: He was all about putting on a show. For all the hits, million-sellers, Grammys, I honestly think he was most at home at a place like the Club Iridium — a small club with a bunch of people, and

jamming with good musicians. **That really was heaven to him.**

Tommy: It certainly was. Another thing you've got to know about him is he rehearsed. He wanted to play and play his best. His sound check could go on for two hours. Most of us get it done in half an hour. He would play and jam just because he wanted to play. When it was my time to check my sound I'd do it in a few minutes, because the crew, the sound guys, were so good. Well, Les would walk out to the front of the club to listen to what I was doing and even comment. He might say, "You could use a little more bass," or whatever. He was dedicated. That's just a great way for a person to be at his age, or any age.

Steve: Tommy, one of the things that always fascinated me was he knew what sound he wanted, and yet a lot of people don't know he had not one, but two hearing aids. In fact, he told us he had been working with a company on the development of a new hearing aid. You think of people with hearing aids and you assume they don't, or can't, appreciate sound. But he knew when the sound was right.

Tommy: Absolutely.

Johnnie: And he demanded it.

Tommy: Yes. I picked up his guitar once and sat where he sat, and I played it. The sound was beautiful. So inspiring to just hold and play his guitar. That's another one of the many things I learned from him: Get your sound right. One of my strongest memories of working with Les was the night we did the Carnegie Hall concert for his 90th birthday. Toward the end of the show, when we were all out on stage singing "Let the Good Times Roll," I jumped up on the drum riser. I was playing and dancing around. The lights made silhouettes of everybody in front of me. I could see Les's silhouette in his bent-over position as he would attack the guitar, committed to every note, while he laughed his head off. He was so happy. It was such a beautiful scene, I took a photo in my mind, and that's where I went today when I heard he had passed. I closed my eyes and I was right back there behind him in Carnegie Hall.

Steve: A lot of people don't know the lengths he went to continue playing. He had crippling arthritis and an elbow that wouldn't move.

Johnnie: And he lived in New Jersey and the club was in New York. When we talk about the lengths he would go to to work, I'm reminded of one of my favorite stories. In recent years there had been horrible rains that resulted in flooding in New Jersey. People's houses were washing away in the floods. Well, come Monday Les said, "All right everybody, we're going to work." They all balked at that because they were sure the roads weren't passable. He told us his car was loaded, so he hopped in and drove himself to New York. He told us, "I had to; I had a show to do!" I asked, "You actually drove yourself?" He said, "Sure, I'd ridden there enough times, I knew how to get there." (*laughter*)

Steve: Have you ever ridden with him, Tommy?

Tommy: No.

Steve: I guess it could be a hair-raising experience.

Tommy: I had quite an experience with his buddy Chet Atkins. Chet was driving long after he should have been, but he wasn't about to give it up. One day he parked the car badly in front of a pancake parlor we were going to. He got out of the car, tripped, and fell. I said, "Chief, you're really scaring me. Why don't you let me drive?" He said, "No, no, no!" We went on to breakfast with Steve Cropper, Vince Gill and a few other guys. When we got outside, I still couldn't convince him to let me drive. We drove a few miles, and he said he needed to stop for gas. He drove into the station and hit a pump! He got out and laughed like crazy. I said, "You going to quit now?" He said, "Oh, all right." (*laughter*)

Steve: Bad driving must be a commonality among extraordinary guitar players. We've heard first hand of the experience — and emphasis on experience — of riding with Les. His house is on a hill, pretty high up with a winding road. He would get in his Lincoln and take that winding road down doing about 80.

Tommy: You're kidding!

Steve: No, really, we've talked to those that survived.

Johnnie: I guess if you screamed he realized he had an audience.

Steve: That was his sense of humor. Tommy, would you agree his sense of humor came out in his music?

Tommy: No question. One note, one riff, and you knew this was the personality of a person who ate up life, who challenged life. I saw him as somebody who took the words carpe diem and put them in neon lights to live by. I would hope that's how I approach life. I would strive to be that way and just suck as much marrow out of life as I can.

Johnnie: And savor it. It was always obvious to us when he would call in on Tuesday mornings after doing two shows, that he wanted to decompress and savor what he had just experienced. Tommy, we couldn't talk about Les and his love for life without talking to you. Thank you for joining us.

Tommy: I know that Les is probably hanging out with Django and Chet now. We know he's in a wonderful place. I actually envy him for that. But for now, we have his music and our memories, and for that, we are thankful.

Holli Brown, Madame Brown Photography

Doyle Dykes

Steve: Doyle, talk about the first time you got up on stage at the Iridium and played with Les.

Doyle: I was playing the guitar I had purchased that afternoon in hopes of getting Les to autograph it. It had little bitty strings on it, but I didn't have time to change them, and honestly didn't think I would be playing anyway. Well, Les found out I was in the audience and asked me on stage, and I think that guitar sounded like Grandpa Jones would have said was "baling wire on a 2x4!" I was so nervous — anytime you're in the presence of a legend it does something to you on the inside. You just can't explain it. It's fun, it's cool, it's scary, it's overwhelming. I was feeling all of those things, and I relied on my fingers to do the best they could. I had so much fun each time I played on stage with Les, but that first night I felt like he treated me like the rock stars that would stop in to visit. Like Keith Richards, or Paul McCartney.

Steve: But Doyle, you were one of those guitarists that when you stepped on stage with Les, you knew he could get into a musical jam with you. He didn't have to play down to you, he played up to you.

Johnnie: He enjoyed every time you stopped in, and he would call us and tell us so.

Doyle: Well, he was certainly the kind of guy you could never get anything over. For one thing, Les was so quick and quick-witted, not only with his guitar but talking. The way he moved the show along with his sense of timing was like old-school vaudeville. Like Grandpa Jones at the Opry — very few people have that skill, and Les certainly did. He was, in my opinion, an entertainer's entertainer.

The second time I went to play with him, I brought my guitar and I played a tune he and Chet Atkins had recorded on the *Chester & Lester* album. I played "Meditation," one of my favorites from the album. Well, he looked right at me and said, "I never did know that song." I said, "Well, you sounded great when you recorded it AND you won a Grammy!" Next I went into "Avalon" and he was all over it. It was "Katie, bar the door!" and it was so much fun. When you'd hit on a song he really liked, it just made history for me. Les was such an influence on my dad, and thus, he was on me as well. He will be greatly missed. He was a wonderful man. A lot of things go into making a legend, and I have to say they aren't always the character that Les Paul was. To me that was the main ingredient in him.

Authors' note: Along with hosting our own radio tribute to Les, other media outlets who knew of our friendship with him and Les's regular appearances on our show asked if we would add our comments to their tributes. Before we went on the air that night, Dana Kozlov from Chicago's CBS station, WBBM-TV, brought a crew out to our house to record a segment, and when we finished our own show early the next morning, we appeared on ABC's WLS-TV with Tracy Butler, pictured above.

Understandably, these were very bittersweet appearances as recounting the joy of our time with Les was tempered with the sad reality of his loss.

2014 Gibson Les Paul Studio Deluxe II with a 1960s neck © Tom Grubbe

The Club 400
in Waukesha
hosted the
beginnings of
Les Paul and
Mary Ford's
remarkable
career and life
together.

CLUB 400

Opened in August 1894, the Northwestern Hotel provided year-round services to travelers and train crews. The building became a boarding house, cigar store, soft drink shop and then a tavern.

On January 6, 1948, George and Ralph Polfuss (Les Paul's father and brother) opened the Club 400 after major renovations changing it to a nightclub. It was named after the Chicago Northwestern train "400" that stopped across the street at the depot. Les Paul and Mary Ford played their guitars together for the first time at the grand opening.

George Polfuss owned a grocery store in 1903 three doors west of the Club 400. The Club 400 has been on the National Register of Historical Places since 1995.

Funded by 400 Club
Waukesha County Historical Museum - 2007

Les Paul Foundation

31

Celebrating the End Where it Began

Friday, August 21, 2009

We'll never forget the way the clouds looked the day we drove from Chicago up to Waukesha for Les's gravesite funeral service. You may think that we're being overly dramatic, but, trust us, we had never seen a sky like that before, nor have we seen one like it since. And we're more than familiar with dramatic skies from our time spent on Florida's Gulf Coast. Rain was in the forecast, and we occasionally drove through a small downpour, but even though no serious storms materialized, the cloud formations and coloring were breathtaking — not in an ominous way, rather in a "you'll always remember this" way.

We always will.

Many people had the opportunity to pay their respects to Les at events in New York and at Milwaukee's Discovery World. The service we were driving to was a private, family funeral and we were honored when Les's son, Russ, said that he and Les considered us family and invited us to attend. Although we'd been to Waukesha, we'd never been to the part of town where Prairie Home Cemetery is located. Even if we hadn't been using our car's navigation system, we would have known we were in the right area because we started seeing people standing on the sidewalks, holding signs with sayings like "Thank you, Les" or "Rest in peace, Wizard of Waukesha." Some were just holding a guitar. The closer we got to the cemetery, the more people we saw. As we drove through the cemetery entrance, we were stopped by security to verify that our names were on the list.

Fans scattered throughout the cemetery were kept at a respectful distance from the tent where the service was being held, until the ceremony finished and the family had departed. As we entered the tent, the first people we saw were Russ Paul, Chris Lentz, Michael Braunstein, Sue Baker and Muriel Anderson. There is a saying that goes something like, "There is the family you're born into, and there is the family you choose." As we looked around, we saw familiar faces of the people Les had chosen, not only to associate with, but to be his family. We both felt very touched to have been included among those gathered under that tent.

As the fullness of this singularly extraordinary life was recounted, the understandably sad mood was frequently punctuated with laughter as stories of Les's wicked sense of humor, which had always been such a large part of his personality, were shared. We could all feel Les laughing along. Those lighter moments did a lot to soothe the sense of grief we were all feeling.

Steve Palec

| *With our longtime friend and fellow lover of Les, Muriel Anderson* | *Russ Paul, seated, and his son Gary, with a video of Les playing in the background* |

Members of the military stood at attention during the funeral. Milwaukee radio personality Steve Palec, who we had last seen when we shared the stage at Les's Waukesha homecoming concert, served as the emcee for the service. As the service concluded, he said, "I can't imagine a world without music, and I can't imagine music without Les Paul. We love you, Les."

Following a 21-gun salute, a distant trumpet played "Taps" as the American flag that was draped over Les's casket was folded and handed to Russ.

When the service was over, we all departed the cemetery and headed for the place where we knew Les would have wanted us to wind up — the place where it really all began for him: Club 400. This unimposing corner tavern was the laboratory that saw the early beginnings of the transformation that ultimately morphed Lester Polsfuss and Colleen Summers into Les Paul and Mary Ford.

The club's walls were filled with photos, paintings and posters of Les at various stages of his career. TV screens played constant videos of Les in performance. It didn't take a lot of time to walk the length of the club and up to the area where Les and Mary spent many nights honing their craft. Soaking up this small club's ambience, it was easy to see how it had shaped Les's desire to return to live performing, initially at Fat Tuesday's and ultimately at the Iridium — both small clubs that allowed the kind of intimate performer/audience feedback that Les loved.

As the photos and videos were being shown, a constant flow of Les Paul stories were being traded among longtime friends who, like Muriel Anderson, put recording projects and other commitments on hold to travel to Waukesha for the service. Some of Les's family members we hadn't previously met, such as his daughter, Colleen, and Russ's son, Gary, were at the Club 400 gathering, as was Larry Nelson, then mayor of Waukesha, who spoke at the funeral service. Although most of the conversation centered around stories from Les's past, his manager, Michael Braunstein, Sue Baker and Chris Lentz told us what little they knew at that moment about The Les Paul Foundation's plans for a future permanent gravesite memorial that would celebrate Les's life and accomplishments.

Russ enjoyed, as we all did, the fact that instead of typical tavern fare, the Club 400 menu that day consisted of Les's favorite foods: grilled cheese, lemon tarts and, of course, beer.

For several hours, the Club 400 was once again home to Les's music and his family and friends. And yes, it did seem as if we could feel his presence. We are absolutely certain that Les would have happily approved of this intimate, informal celebration of his life.

We said our goodbyes, and as we left Waukesha, we pulled over at the Waukesha County Historical Museum where the marquee, shown at right, was a perfect punctuation to a day of emotional highs and lows.

An oversized, brightly-painted Les Paul guitar greets visitors to the
Les Paul exhibit at the Waukesha County Museum.

The Museum and the Monument

We operate under the "big purse theory" — the bigger the purse, the more stuff you'll find to carry around in that purse. It's been proven time and again that a smaller purse = less stuff and, surprise, you can survive!

We have to believe the "big purse theory" applied to Les's house. It started out as a one-story, seven-room house in 1952. When he and Mary had children, adding to his two children from a previous marriage, the house had to grow to accommodate the family.

Les and Mary originally moved to New Jersey so they could record their television show for Listerine right there in the house. The house eventually had to be expanded to accommodate sets and props that needed to be stored. As time went on, the house, built on the side of a granite hill, had a floor plan that grew by a sitting room here, a recording studio over there.

At last count, Les told us he had 37, or was it 38, rooms in his Mahwah, New Jersey house. You have to believe, like the "big purse theory," the more room that was available, the more stuff needed to be saved. As he said, "Like my mother, I save everything." Television show props and sets, along with guitars from Gibson, filled the rooms. At one time, Les said Gibson was sending him nine or 10 guitars a month until he said, "Enough!" He firmly drew the line when they called to ask when he wanted the "Les Paul Piano" delivered. He passed on that.

Les often envisioned his early inventions, tape recorders,

guitars and memorabilia being displayed in a museum, and there have been several exhibits. The Smithsonian featured various treasures on loan from Les for display. Les is represented at The Rock and Roll Hall of Fame in Cleveland in its inductees' exhibit as well as an exhibit in the *Architects of Rock and Roll*. Les is one of three featured "architects." There is a Les Paul in Mahwah exhibit in the Mahwah Museum where, by appointment, you can go in and actually play one of Les's guitars. And, as we related in an earlier chapter, he was proud to be at the opening of the Les Paul's House of Sound exhibit in Milwaukee and was a bit overwhelmed by the display of his life's work. Even with all of these venues featuring Les and showcasing his treasures, he still longed for a display in his hometown of Waukesha, Wisconsin.

The Waukesha County Museum proposed the idea of a permanent Les Paul exhibit in the 1980s. It wasn't until 2002 that Les gave them the go-ahead to start planning. In 2004, Les told the Associated Press that he thought an exhibit in Waukesha would be more personal than the other exhibits. He said he wanted people to know everything he had started when he was a child right there in that town.

As a result of personnel changes, financial concerns and decisions on just how the exhibit would present Les, it wasn't until June 9, 2013, on what would have been Les's 98th birthday, that the *Les Paul: The Wizard of Waukesha* exhibit opened to the public. It is the landmark museum's first permanent display, touted as the largest Les Paul exhibit in the country to date. Knowing that this permanent exhibit in Waukesha was a dream that Les had for a long time, we were excited to be invited to the red-carpet, by-invitation-only, "rock and roll black tie" preview event on Saturday night, June 8.

When we arrived at the stately museum at 101 West Main Street, the Gibson bus was parked out front. Some people were entering on the red carpet, but most, like us, stopped to have a picture with the oversized, brightly painted Les Paul guitar out front.

An amazingly life-like cardboard cutout of Les greets visitors to the exhibit.

Once inside the museum, it was elbow to elbow with people, many making their way to the other floors where food and drink as well as live music had been set up. After we got a sense of what was where, we made our way to the Wizard of Waukesha exhibit. On our way to the beginning of the display, we stopped at a life-sized Les stand up (which was of him sitting down) and had our pictures taken.

When we entered the exhibit, it immediately became evident that this display was going to chronicle Les's life from his birth right there in Waukesha. There was his "living room laboratory," featuring household objects that Les had torn apart and reworked in his early invention days. There were examples of his industry-changing inventions through the years, as well as his performing career as a "local boy who had done good," to his successful professional career with Mary Ford. The museum also gave special attention to the most important person in Les's life, his mother. Included in that part of the display was the Miller Beer can trophy Les had made as a gift for his mother on her 100th birthday.

Around every corner there were inventions, like the harmonica holder he had made out of his brother's wire coat hanger in his very early entertaining days right there in Waukesha. There were strummable guitars, and awards like the medal he was given upon induction into the National Inventors Hall of Fame. If you didn't know anything about Les Paul, this museum exhibit did a great job of telling his story, and if you thought you knew Les, there were still some surprises.

His spirit was felt throughout the display, thanks not only to the artifacts shown, but also to the Les Paul quotes that covered the walls. It was fun walking through the exhibit and hearing people reading the quotes aloud. Les's sense of humor and wisdom was evident in so many.

After taking in the marvelous exhibit and shooting more pictures and some video (which you can see on our YouTube page: *www.youtube.com/user/SteveAndJohnnieShow*), we gathered in a room to hear speakers talk about the excitement of, at last, seeing Les's dream become a reality. We met up with Les's manager Michael Braunstein, Les's close friend and photographer, Chris Lentz, and Sue Baker from the Les Paul Foundation. As we talked, there was unanimous agreement that Les would have been pleased and he would not, as he had feared, be forgotten thanks to this exhibit in his hometown.

LEFT: *The Les Paul memorial at Prairie Home Cemetery in Waukesha*

Over the live music, we made plans to meet the next afternoon on what would have been Les's 98th birthday. It was agreed that we would all pay Les a visit. A time was set to gather at his gravesite.

It was one of those perfect June Sunday afternoons at the Prairie Home Cemetery in Waukesha. Because of our travels, we had only seen pictures of the monument from the dedication ceremony on September 11, 2011. The pictures did not do it justice. No picture can impart the impressive, regal look of the circle of walls that seemed to beckon once you were inside the front gates.

As we walked up to the gravesite, one of the first things to grab our attention was a slightly larger granite wall with a 3-D Les Paul guitar and his signature etched in the stone.

The low slab walls are beautifully done. Les's biography and a list of significant awards and achievements are etched in granite, and there are stone benches — one of Les's design ideas to offer a place for his friends and family to "sit a spell" and visit, reflect or even play guitar. We and our friends Gary and Sue Schroeder were joined by Michael, Chris, and Sue Baker and her husband Carl. Over the next few hours, we did just what Les wanted: We sat a spell, visiting, enjoying each other's company and reflecting on our friendships with Les and each other.

A number of people, some of whom were guitar players,

LEFT TO RIGHT: *Carl Baker, Steve, Chris Lentz, Michael Braunstein, Sue Baker*

Guitar picks left on the granite monument as tributes to Les

stopped by to pay their respects and noted, as if he were a family member or close friend, that it was Les's birthday. A few times, we heard someone comment on the grave next to Les's. Some people said, "That must be Mary Ford buried next to Les, and that must be her maiden name." When it seemed appropriate, one of us would quietly explain to the curious that Evelyn Stutz Polsfuss, the person buried next to Les, was his mother. In planning his burial, one of Les's requests was to have his mother's grave moved next to his.

Michael Braunstein and Sue Baker gave us a lovely explanation of how the monument design came about, and the decisions that they, through the Les Paul Foundation, had made on the

Les and perhaps the greatest influence in his life, his mother Evelyn, are buried side by side.

quotes that were used and etched in granite.

The "Les stories" started, and we shared a few laughs. Michael, Chris and Sue were unaware of some of our Les stories, like the time we surprised Les on the air with a visit from his hero, Paul Harvey.

A touching aspect of the Les Paul monument design is the 3-D Les Paul guitar that is a part of the larger headstone in the monument. The neck of that guitar has become the place where guitarists, in paying tribute, will leave a pick. Dozens of colorful picks lay along the neck of the guitar, a perfect gesture of respect to Les.

As the afternoon drew to a close, we all agreed the time we spent at the gravesite was a perfect way to celebrate Les's life and legacy. The fact it would have been his 98th birthday and his friends had gathered to laugh, talk, share Les stories and reflect on our times spent with him seemed like we were doing exactly what he had hoped we would do in remembering him.

*Left to right: **Steve and Johnnie, Sue Baker, Michael Braunstein, and Chris Lentz***

Afterword

Writing this book absolutely has been a labor of love. Going through our respective memories and archives was, at times, like having another conversation with Les. Coming across a forgotten "treasure," like the foam cheesehead hat he signed to us, we could almost hear him laughing.

Those times we needed to "phone a friend" to clarify a point or verify a memory usually led to a longer conversation than was originally intended as we found ourselves sharing more Les stories that would lead to still more Les stories. One of the constants from our Les Paul archeological digs was that they wound up putting smiles on the faces of everyone involved in the conversations.

Les would have liked that.

The transcribed conversations we included, unless otherwise notated, are the conversations we had with Les, and the stories are left intact, just the way he told them. One of our goals with this book was to give you "A Little More Les" and, in doing so, do our best not only to give you a peek into the friendship we were fortunate enough to have with him, but also to help you get to know this amazing, multi-faceted man's personality the way we did.

"Nice guys play Les Paul's" (sic) was the graffiti we saw one day on the sidewalk outside our favorite guitar store, Guitar Works, in Evanston, Illinois. The merit of that statement is for guitarists to debate, but when we stopped to snap a picture, we

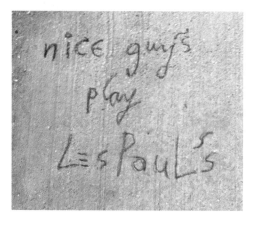

both said, "and Les Paul was himself one of the nice guys."

After revisiting our almost two-decade friendship with Les, we think it's also fair to say that, as is the case with most wizards, he was a wonderfully complex man who, along with loving guitars,

–absolutely loved life;

–was an inquisitive thinker who chased sound and other imponderables to the end;

–was passionate about many things, including his friends;

–was naturally funny (OK — sometimes a rascal!);

–constantly reinvented his extraordinary talents to deal with whatever slings and arrows life sent his way;

–was justifiably deemed an entertainer's entertainer by entertainers;

–was a people lover (all ages and genders);

–had the kind of "smarts" that can't be taught;

–was and will continue to be an inspiration;

and was someone we hope you feel you now know a little better as a result of reading this book.

Thank you for picking it up. We sincerely hope you enjoyed getting to know *A Little More Les.*

Steve and *Johnnie*

To Steven Johnnie
Love you! Rhubarb Red.

And ... a little more

*I*n case the previous pages have whetted your appetite for "a little more," we've put together a list of selected goodies that will taste very good to your ears and eyes.

Albums*

(*We call them albums because some are available on vinyl!)

The Complete Decca Trios-Plus (1936-47)

Never heard Les as "Rhubarb Red," or "It's Been a Long, Long Time," the recording Les made with "the most important person I ever worked with ... in my life" Bing Crosby? You'll find them here, along with many other rare treasures.

Jazz at the Philharmonic: "Body and Soul," featuring Nat King Cole & Les Paul

This is a genuinely historic live recording. Although most of the album will leave you shaking your head in amazement, it's worth the price of admission just to hear the instrumental duel Les and Nat get into on "Blues-Part 1" and "Blues-Part 2."

Les Paul – The Legendary Fred Waring Broadcasts

Thank goodness Fred Waring saved these live radio performances. You'll hear the Les Paul Trio (with Chet Atkins' brother, Jimmy, on vocals and rhythm guitar) as they were featured on Waring's broadcasts to the East and West coasts. Fortunately for us, due to technical limitations at that time, each broadcast was done separately. This gives us the luxury of hearing Les playing the same song with both electric and unamplified guitar. On the unamplified versions, it's easy to hear the influence Django Reinhardt had on Les. It also makes you wonder what we would hear if the technology had been in place to record Les and Django jamming backstage in New York.

Les Paul – V-Disc Recordings

During a recording ban in the '40s, the only recording the musicians' union allowed was for a special series of "V-Discs" that were sent to the troops during the second world war. (The V stood for victory.) It's particularly interesting to hear Les and his trio perform a jazzy, pre-Mary Ford or multiple tracks, version of "How High The Moon."

The Best of the Capitol Masters: 90th Birthday Edition

Speaking of Mary, taken from the now hard to find the "Legend and the Legacy" box set, this collection has the hits and an episode of Les's radio show.

Chester & Lester

If this Grammy-winning album is not in your collection, put this book down and go get it NOW! It's got Les Paul and Chet Atkins playing together, for heaven's sake! It just doesn't get better.

Les Paul & Friends: American Made, World Played

Les told us he wanted to make a rock and roll album by his 90th birthday and boy, did he ever! This Grammy-winning album salute to both Les Paul, the man, and Les Paul, the guitar, finds Les trading licks with Eric Clapton, Steve Miller, Sting, Keith Richards and more. Of particular note is the Sam Cooke vocal, "Good News," which finds Les and Jeff Beck playing along with the isolated vocal from Sam Cook's older recording. It's a wonderful example of the kind of technology and playing that Les loved. Also, check out Les's version of "Caravan," which won him another Grammy for this individual performance.

DVDs

Chasing Sound and *Les Paul Live in New York*

Both of these DVDs were lovingly produced by John Paulson. *Chasing Sound* is an overview of Les's career with great footage of some of his New York shows, his homes and travels. *Les Paul Live in New York* is a terrific commemorative edition containing some of Les's final performances. Wherever you are, if the energy in the room doesn't go up while you watch Les and Tommy Emmanuel trading licks on "Blue Moon," something is drastically wrong.

Abbott & Costello In Their First TV Comedy Series, Vol. 4 With Les Paul & Mary Ford (Colgate Comedy Hour)

On this TV show, originally aired in 1954, you'll see Les and Mary do a live version of "There's No Place Like Home." This performance shows another example of Les's amazing good luck. During the song, Mary is playing the same guitar licks as Les does. Les, supposedly frustrated at Mary's ability to play as well as he does, plays harder and harder licks, which actually resulted in his breaking a string. Fortunately, the song was over and their next number was a lip-synced version of "Tiger Rag," so Les didn't have to worry about how his guitar would have sounded.

Books

Les Paul: In His Own Words by Les Paul and Michael Cochran

If you've read all of our book, you know we talked extensively with Michael Cochran about this book in a previous chapter. It's a great book that resides in our collection and belongs in yours, too. Yes, it's available in the trade edition.

The Early Years of the Les Paul Legacy 1915-1963 by Robb Lawrence and *The Modern Era of the Les Paul Legacy 1968-2009* by Robb Lawrence.

Although these excellent companion books are geared more to the guitar collector, they also give a good overview of Les's life right up to his last days. Like Michael Cochran, Robb spent a great deal of time with Les to get the story and the guitar's history right. In fact, we first met Robb while he was doing some research at *Muriel Anderson's All Star Guitar Night* tribute to Les.

Chris Lentz

Acknowledgments

*M*ost of us have "someday lists." Writing this book was right at the top of ours, but without the help of the people listed below, all the bells, whistles and love we've tried to put between its covers might not have happened.

So thank you, Thank You, THANK YOU!

- To The Les Paul Foundation, and specifically Russ (Rusty) Paul, Michael Braunstein, Sue Baker, Chris Lentz and Jeff Salmon, thank you all for helping us keep the facts straight, adding some very important pictures to our words, always extending your friendship to us and, more importantly, always being REAL friends to Les.
- Along with our thanks, warm hugs to Duane and Deed Eddy, Charlie Daniels, Doyle Dykes, Frank Vignola, Muriel Anderson and Tommy Emmanuel. We are honored to call them friends, and when they heard what we were up to, they immediately agreed to be a part of our bringing you *A Little More Les*. Thank you for taking the time to share your thoughts and feelings and for expressing your enthusiastic support for this book. And a special thank you to Paula Szeigis for directing Charlie from the plane to the computer.
- On the night we lost Les, friends quickly gathered via telephone. Lou Pallo, Nicki Parrott, Ron Sturm, Tommy Shaw, Michael Cochran and others were nice enough to join us in the wee hours of a long and difficult day to pay tribute to Les. They brought comforting words to those of us mourning Les's passing. And a special thank you to Jim Corboy for finding Tommy in the studio.
- To all the WGN Radio management types who, over the years, gave us the freedom to juggle commercials and "stretch" the "format" to accommodate Les. You GOT it! We appreciated it then and even more now. So thank you, in particular, to Mary June Rose, Tom Langmyer and, most recently, Jimmy de Castro and Todd Manley, for saying,

"Yes! What can we do to help?" the moment you first heard about this book.

- We can never forget our wonderful gang of producers who always MADE our shows: Paula Cooper, Dan Sugrue, Denise Rybicki, Bob Kessler, Steve Buchman, Catie Stiehl.
- To Orion and Gloria Samuelson, a HUGE thanks for planting the Bantry Bay seed ... and for the wonderful dinner.
- Aubrey Mumpower, thank you for realizing the importance of having backup copies. Many times you said, "They might come in handy." Boy, were you right!
- Joel Brennan and Paul Krajniak, thank you for sharing your stories on WGN, making Bing Crosby's dream for Les a reality and for welcoming us into The Les Paul House of Sound and the very special Pabst Theater concert.
- Steve Palec, thank you for unselfishly sharing the stage, your memories and your photos.

And, speaking of photos, a heartfelt THANK YOU to the photographers whose pictures were used to enhance our words.

- To Chris Lentz, the archivist for The Les Paul Foundation, one of Les's best friends and "go-to" photographer, not only do we appreciate the use of your pictures and the time you spent unearthing the best quality photos, but we really appreciate your vote of confidence and belief that Les would have liked this book.
- To Edward Butkovich, aka "Popcorn Eddie," a dear friend to us and to our show. You attended and documented musical events we couldn't get to because of our schedule, and the music plays through your photos.
- Joel Paterson, one of the busiest, hardest-working musicians in Chicago, opened his rare photo archives. Joel got to play with Les on stage at the Iridium and shows his appreciation for Les in his CD, *Handful of Strings*.
- John Kruzan, our brother-in-law, thank you for having your camera ready to capture "the moment" backstage at the Iridium.
- Holli Brown: Traveling around the world with her father, Doyle Dykes, she learned the importance of using her fingers to make music AND pictures.

- Joe Cooper, the brother of producer/newswoman Paula Cooper, is a bit of a packrat (as was Les), and shared pictures, memories and memorabilia.
- To John Paulson, the man behind the wonderful *Chasing Sound* documentary who allowed us to use stills from the film, thank you!
- Jim Joiner is a Les Paul fan and longtime member of our "extended WGN family" of listeners. Like all good photographers, Jim was in the right place at the right time.
- Joann O'Hare, Kevin Harnack and the *Waukesha Freeman*: Thank you for documenting the Wizard's return to Waukesha and allowing us to share your photographs.
- And a special thank you to Will Crockett, our "official" photographer, for always making us want to look as good as the pictures he takes of us.

And finally … Diane Montiel and Steve Alexander, your passion for the written word combined with your warmth, your patience and your creativity are invaluable gifts to all the authors who have worked with you and will be fortunate enough to work with you in the future. Thank you for letting us join their ranks … and for accepting our "Friend" requests.

And finally, finally … a special thank you to John Putman for being the supportive father and father-in-law that you've been for this project and every other thing we've attempted … including our marriage.

May 29, 2015
WGN Walk of Fame
induction ceremony

Will Crockett